Operational Risk
with Excel and VBA

John Wiley & Sons

Founded in 1807, John Wiley & Sons is the oldest independent publishing company in the United States. With offices in North America, Europe, Australia, and Asia, Wiley is globally committed to developing and marketing print and electronic products and services for our customers' professional and personal knowledge and understanding.

The Wiley Finance series contains books written specifically for finance and investment professionals as well as sophisticated individual investors and their financial advisors.

Book topics range from portfolio management to e-commerce, risk management, financial engineering, valuation and financial instrument analysis, as well as much more.

For a list of available titles, visit our Web site at www.WileyFinance.com.

Operational Risk
with Excel and VBA

Applied Statistical Methods
for Risk Management

NIGEL DA COSTA LEWIS

WILEY

John Wiley & Sons, Inc.

Published by John Wiley & Sons, Inc., Hoboken, New Jersey.
Published simultaneously in Canada.

For general information on our other products and services, or technical support, please
contact our Customer Care Department within the United States at 800-762-2974,
outside the United States at 317-572-3993 or fax 317-572-4002.

Wiley also publishes its books in a variety of electronic formats. Some content that
appears in print may not be available in electronic books.

For more information about Wiley products, visit our web site at www.wiley.com.

Library of Congress Cataloging-in-Publication Data
Lewis, Nigel Da Costa.
    Operational risk with Excel and VBA : applied statistical methods for
risk management / Nigel Da Costa Lewis.
        p.   cm.
"Published simultaneously in Canada."
Includes index.
    ISBN 0-471-47887-3
    1. Risk management—Statistical methods.   2. Risk
management—Mathematical models.   I. Title.
HD61 .L49 2004
658.15′5′0285554—dc22

                                                    2003023869

Printed in the United States of America.

10 9 8 7 6 5 4 3 2 1

In loving memory of my mother-in-law,
Lydora.
Her devotion and wisdom nurtured my wife
into becoming the encouraging source
of strength that she is today.
These qualities have inspired
and enabled me to complete this work.

Contents

Preface

Until a few year ago most banks and other financial institutions paid little attention to measuring or quantifying operational risk. In recent years this has changed. Understanding and managing operational risk are essential to a company's future survival and prosperity. With the regulatory spotlight on operational risk management, there has been ever-increasing attention devoted to the quantification of operational risks. As a result we have seen the emergence of a wide array of statistical methods for measuring, modeling, and monitoring operational risk. Working out how all these new statistical tools relate to one another and which to use and when is a not a straightforward issue.

Although a handful of books explain and explore the concept of operational risk per se, it is often quite difficult for a practicing risk manager to turn up a quickly digestible introduction to the statistical methods that can be used to model, monitor, and assess operational risk. This book provides such an introduction, using Microsoft Excel and Visual Basic For Applications (VBA) to illustrate many of the examples. It is designed to be used "on the go," with minimal quantitative background. Familiarity with Excel or VBA is a bonus, but not essential. Chapter sections are generally short—ideal material for the metro commute into and from work, read over lunch, or dipped into while enjoying a freshly brewed cup of coffee. To improve your understanding of the methods discussed, case studies, examples, interactive illustrations, review questions, and suggestions for further reading are included in many chapters.

In writing this text I have sought to bring together a wide variety of statistical methods and models that can be used to model, monitor, and assess operational risks. The intention is to give you, the reader, a concise and applied introduction to statistical modeling for operational risk management by providing explanation, relevant information, examples, and interactive illustrations together with a guide to further reading. In common with its sister book *Applied Statistical Methods for Market Risk Management* (Risk Books, March 2003), this book has been written to provide the time-starved reader, who may not be quantitatively trained, with rapid and succinct introduction to useful statistical methods that must otherwise be gleaned from scattered, obscure, or mathematically obtuse sources. In this sense, it is not a book about the theory of operational risk management or mathematical statistics per se, but a book about the application of statistical methods to operational risk management.

Successful modeling of operational risks is both art and science. I hope the numerous illustrations, Excel examples, case studies, and VBA code listings will serve both as an ideas bank and technical reference. Naturally, any such compilation must omit some models and methods. In choosing the material, I have been guided both by the pragmatic "can do" requirement inherent in operational risk management, and by my own practical experience gained over many years working as a statistician and quantitative analyst in the City of London, on Wall Street, at the quantitative research boutique StatMetrics, and in academia. Thus, this is a practitioners' guide book. Topics that are of theoretical interest but of little practical relevance or methods that I have found offer at best a marginal improvement over the most parsimonious alternative are ignored. As always with my books on applied statistical methods, lucidity of style and simplicity of expression have been my twin objectives.

Acknowledgments

M any people have helped considerably during the process of researching and writing this text. I particularly would like to thank StatMetrics for providing me with the time and financial resources to complete this project. I would also like to express my sincere appreciation to Angela Lewis for her wonderful cooperation, understanding, and support throughout the period of this research. The inspiration for this text came from a discussion I had with an organization keen to set up an operational risk department. It became clear by the end of my discussion that their analysts and senior management lacked even a basic understanding of what can and cannot be achieved using statistical methods.

Following this conversation I decided to "act out" various roles to gather information about the approach, tools, and techniques of operational risk. The most enjoyable role was as a job seeker, in which my resume would be forwarded to potential employers who were seeking a analyst to model their operational risk. Almost inevitably, I would be offered an interview and would then play the role of a badly informed candidate or a super knowledgeable expert. Through this process it became clear that there is little consensus on how operational risk should be modeled and very little understanding of the role statistical methods can play in informing decision makers. I particularly wish to thank and at the same time apologize to those anonymous individuals who interviewed me as a real candidate for a position in their operational risk departments. I am deeply indebted to them all.

Operational Risk
with Excel and VBA

CHAPTER 1

Introduction to Operational Risk Management and Modeling

Operational risk (OR) is everywhere in the business environment. It is the oldest risk facing banks and other financial institutions. Any financial institution will face operational risk long before it decides on its first market trade or credit transaction. Of all the different types of risk facing financial institutions, OR can be among the most devastating and the most difficult to anticipate. Its appearance can result in sudden and dramatic reductions in the value of a firm. The spectacular collapse of Barings in 1995, the terrorist attack on the World Trade Center in September 2001, the $691 million in losses due to fraud reported by Allied Irish Bank in 2002, and the widespread electrical failure experienced by over 50 million people in the northeastern United States and Canada in August 2003 are all concrete but very different illustrations of operational risk. The rapid pace of technological change, removal of traditional trade barriers, expanding customer base through globalization and e-commerce, and mergers and consolidations have led to the perception that OR is increasing. Indeed, although many functions can be outsourced, OR cannot. Increasingly, banks and other financial institutions are establishing OR management functions at the senior executive level in an effort to better manage this class of risk. In this chapter we discuss the definition of OR, outline the regulatory background, and describe the role of statistical methods in measuring, monitoring, and assessing operational risk.

WHAT IS OPERATIONAL RISK?

There is no generally accepted definition of OR in the financial community. This lack of consensus relates to the fundamental nature of operational risk itself. Its scope is vast and includes a wide range of issues and problems that fall outside of market and credit risk. A useful starting point is to acknowledge that OR encompasses risk inherent in business activities across an

1

organization. This notion of OR is a broader concept than "operations" or back and middle office risk and affords differing definitions. For example, Jameson (1998) defines OR as "Every risk source that lies outside the areas covered by market risk and credit risk."

Typically, this will include transaction-processing errors, systems failure, theft and fraud, "fat finger"[1] trades, lawsuits, and loss or damage to assets. Jameson's definition is considered by many as too broad in the sense that it includes not only operational risk but business, strategy, and liquidity risks as well. An alternative provided by the British Bankers' Association (1997) states, "The risks associated with human error, inadequate procedures and control, fraudulent and criminal activities; the risk caused by technological shortcomings, system breakdowns; all risks which are not 'banking' and arising from business decisions as competitive action, pricing, etc.; legal risk and risk to business relationships, failure to meet regulatory requirements or an adverse impact on the bank's reputation; 'external factors' include: natural disasters, terrorist attacks and fraudulent activity, etc."

Another frequently quoted definition of OR is that proposed by the Basel Committee on Banking Supervision (2001b): "The risk of loss resulting from inadequate or failed internal processes, people systems or from external events." In this categorization OR includes transaction risk (associated with execution, booking, and settlement errors and operational control), process risk (policies, compliance, client and product, mistakes in modeling methodology, and other risks such as mark-to-market error), systems risk (risks associated with the failure of computer and telecommuni-

---

OTHER SOURCES OF RISK

There are three broad classifications of the risk facing financial institutions: operational risk, market risk, and credit risk. Market risk is the risk to a financial institution's financial condition resulting from adverse movements in the level or volatility of interest rates, equities, commodities, and currencies. It is usually measured using value at risk (VaR). VaR is the potential gain or loss in the institution's portfolio that is associated with a price movement of a given confidence level over a specified time horizon. For example, a bank with a 10-day VaR of $100 million at a 95 percent confidence level will suffer a loss in excess of $100 million in approximately one two-week period out of 20, and then only if it is unable to take any action to mitigate its loss. Credit risk is the risk that a counterparty will default on its obligation.

cation systems and programming errors), and people risk (internal fraud and unauthorized actions).

However we choose to define OR, our definition should allow it to be prudently and rigorously managed by capturing the business disruption, failure of controls, errors, omissions, and external events that are the consequence of operational risk events.

THE REGULATORY ENVIRONMENT

Traditionally, financial institutions have focused largely on market and credit risk management, with few if any resources devoted to the management of operational risks. The perception that operational risk has increased markedly over recent years, combined with the realization that quantitative approaches to credit and market risk management ignore operational risks, has prompted many banks to take a closer look at operational risk management. Indeed, the fact that the risk of extreme loss from operational failures was being neither adequately managed nor measured has prompted many regulators to issue guidelines to their members. In the United States, as early as 1997 the Federal Reserve Bank issued a document entitled "The Framework for Risk-focused Supervision of Large, Complex Institutions." In June 1999 the Basel Committee (1999) signaled their intention to drive forward improvements in operational risk management by calling for capital charges for OR and thereby creating incentives for Banks to measure and monitor OR: "From a regulatory perspective, the growing importance of this risk category has led the committee to conclude that such risks are too important not to be treated separately within the capital framework."

The New Capital Adequacy Framework (also referred to as the New Capital Accord) proposed by the Basel Committee exposed the lack of preparedness of the banking sector for operational risk events. Indeed, in a consultative document issued in January 2001, the Basel Committee reflected (2001a): "At present, it appears that few banks could avail themselves of an internal methodology for regulatory capital allocation [for OR]. However, given the anticipated progress and high degree of senior management commitment on this issue, the period until implementation of the New Basel Capital Accord may allow a number of banks to develop viable internal approaches."

By the early 2000s regulators were beginning to "get tough" on failures in operational risk management. Severe financial penalties for failing to monitor and control operational procedures are now a reality. Two examples from the first quarter of 2003 illustrate the new regulatory environment.

BASEL COMMITTEE ON BANKING SUPERVISION

The Basel Committee on Banking Supervision represents the central banks of Belgium, Canada, France, Germany, Italy, Japan, Luxembourg, the Netherlands, Spain, Sweden, Switzerland, the United Kingdom, and the United States. It was established at the end of 1974 and meets four times a year to develop supervisory standards and guidelines of best practice for national banking systems. Although the committee does not possess any formal supranational supervisory authority, its recommendations shape the international banking system. In 1988, the committee introduced a capital measurement system (commonly referred to as the Basel Capital Accord, or Basel I) that provided for the implementation of a risk measurement framework with a minimum capital charge. In June 1999, the committee issued a proposal for a New Capital Adequacy Framework (known as Basel II) to succeed Basel I. Basel II began the process of institutionalizing operational risk as a category for regulatory attention. Operational risk was required to be managed alongside other risks. Indeed, the proposed capital framework required banks to set aside capital for operational risk.

Mis-selling: In April 2003, Lincoln Assurance Limited was fined £485,000 by the United Kingdom's Financial Services Authority (FSA) for the mis-selling of 10-year savings plans by its appointed representative, City Financial Partners Limited, between September 1, 1998, and August 31, 2000. The operational risk event of mis-selling occurred because Lincoln Assurance Limited failed to adequately monitor City Financial Partners Limited and so failed to ensure that City Financial Partners Limited only recommended 10-year savings plans where they were appropriate for customers' needs.

Systems failure: In February 2003 the Financial Services Authority fined the Bank of Scotland (BoS) £750,000 for the failure of one of its investment departments to administer customers' funds appropriately. Between November 1999 and August 2001 problems with BoS systems used to administer personal equity plans (PEPs) and individual savings accounts (ISAs) implied that the bank could not be sure how much money it was holding on behalf of individual customers.

The above examples underscore the fact that as a prerequisite to good operational risk management, firms must have good processes and procedures in place. Systemic failings in internal procedures such as staff training and information systems management and control put investors at risk and increase the risk of fraud going undetected and the possibility of catastrophic operational losses. In today's regulatory environment systemic failure also results in heavy regulatory fines. Good operational risk management makes sound commercial sense.

WHY A STATISTICAL APPROACH TO OPERATIONAL RISK MANAGEMENT?

The effectiveness of operational risk management depends crucially on the soundness of the methods used to assess, monitor, and control it. Commercial banks, investment banks, insurance companies, and pension funds, recognizing the central role of statistical techniques in market and credit risk management, are increasingly turning to such methods to quantify the operational risks facing their institutions. This is because modern statistical methods provide a quantitative technology for empirical science; they offer the operational risk manager the logic and methodology for the measurement of risk and for an examination of the consequences of that risk on the day-to-day activity of the business. Their use can improve senior management's awareness of the operational risk facing their institution by highlighting the expected losses due to operational failures, identifying unexpected losses, and emphasizing the risk associated with starving key business units of their institution of resources. In the language of senior management, statistical methods offer a mechanism for the assessment of risk, capital, and return. Given this, the continued search for value by customers and shareholders, and regulators seeking to force banks to set aside large amounts of capital to cover operational risks, a sound understanding of applied statistical methods for measuring, monitoring, and assessing operational risk is more than an optional extra, it is now a competitive imperative.

DISTINGUISHING BETWEEN DIFFERENT SOURCES OF RISK

Consider a bank that holds bonds in XYZ Corp. The value of the bonds will change over time. If the value fell due to a change in the market price of the bond, this would be market risk. If the value fell as a result of the bankruptcy of XYZ Corp, this would be credit risk. If the value fell because of a delivery failure, this would be operational risk. In each of the three cases the effect is a write-down in the bonds' value, but the specific cause is a consequence of different risks.

SUMMARY

Operational risk has been described as the oldest of risks, yet the application of statistical methods to operational risk management is a new and rapidly evolving field. This is because regulators have now elevated operational risk management to the forefront of risk management initiatives for banks and other financial institutions. The outcome is likely to be tighter internal controls and a drive toward better measurement, monitoring, and modeling of operational losses. Virtually all financial institutions are now paying attention to the application of statistical methods to their OR. In the remaining chapters of this book we focus attention on *what* statistical method to use and *how* these methods can improve a firm's overall management of OR events. As we shall see, there are significant benefits to be gained from the use of statistical methods. Of course, the careful use of statistical methods in itself is not an assurance of success, but it is a means of calculating in advance the probability and possible consequences of an unknown future OR event, allowing managers to make better-informed decisions.

REVIEW QUESTIONS

1. What do you consider to be the weaknesses of the definitions of OR discussed in this chapter? What alternative definitions would you consider more appropriate?
2. Despite being the oldest risk facing financial institutions, OR is the least monitored. Why?
3. What are the potential benefits to the firm, customers, and shareholder of monitoring OR? In your opinion, do these benefits outweigh the costs?
4. In what way could VaR be used in an OR context?
5. Why should statistical methods play a central role in the analysis of OR?

FURTHER READING

Further discussion surrounding the definition of operational risk can be found in British Bankers' Association (1997) and Jameson (1998). Details on the changing regulatory environment for risk management are documented in Basel Committee on Banking Supervision (1999, 2001a, 2001b, 2001c, 2003) and Alexander (2003).

CHAPTER 2

Random Variables, Risk Indicators, and Probability

Operational risks are endogeneous in the sense that they are based on an institution's internal operational environment. As such, they will vary significantly from organization to organization. Although market and credit risk can be managed to some degree through the capital markets, OR is fundamentally different because it can only be managed by changes in process, people, technology, and culture. Given this and the continual reshaping of the business landscape through mergers, restructuring, and rapid technological and regulatory change, how can we capture the complex uncertainty surrounding future OR events? The notion of random variables, OR indicators, and probability described in this chapter provides us with some of the tools we require. Probability offers a formal structure for describing the uncertainty in the business environment. Through its use, despite the reality that OR does not lend itself to measurement in the same way as market or credit risk, we can gain valuable insights into the nature of the uncertainty surrounding future OR events. In this chapter we outline the basic concepts of applied probability and demonstrate how they can be useful in an OR setting.

RANDOM VARIABLES AND OPERATIONAL RISK INDICATORS

Underlying all statistical methods are the concepts of a random experiment, or experiment of chance, and a random variable. A random variable is a variable that can take on a given set of values. A random experiment is the process by which a specific value of a random variable arises.

EXAMPLE 2.1 NUMBER OF TRADES THAT FAIL TO SETTLE WHEN EXPECTED AS A RANDOM VARIABLE

The number of trades that fail to settle when expected varies from one day to the next. In the language of statistics, the number of failed trades on any specific business day is a random variable, the settlement process is an experiment, the passage of time from one day to the next is a trial, and the number of failed trades at the end of the day is the outcome. At the start of business on a particular day, the experiment begins. At this stage the outcome of the experiment is unknown. Will the number of failed trades be 0, 1, 5, or 200? At the end of the business day the outcome of the experiment, the observed number of failed trades, is known.

The costs incurred through mistakes made in carrying out transactions, such as settlement failures, and the loss of business continuity when operations are interrupted for reasons such as electrical failure or the failure to meet regulatory requirements, are all examples of random variables. The key point to note is that a random variable is actually a function that associates a unique numerical value to every outcome of a random experiment. In writing, we denote a random variable by X and the value it takes by x. When a random variable X is observed on N occasions, we obtain a succession of values denoted by $\{x_1, x_2, x_3, \ldots, x_N\}$, each of which provides us with a realization of X at specific points in time. We may have observed the number of failures on the five days, for example, from August 19 to August 23 as $\{5, 0, 0, 1, 0\}$. We also may write this sequence as $\{x_1 = 5, x_2 = 0, x_3 = 0, x_4 = 1, x_5 = 0\}$.

TYPES OF RANDOM VARIABLE

There are two fundamental types of random variable, discrete and continuous. A discrete random variable may take on a countable number of distinct values. These are usually measurements or counts and take on integer values such as 0, 1, 2, 3, and 4. In Example 2.1 the number of trades that fail to settle when expected is a discrete random variable because it can only take on the values 0, 1, 2, 3, and so on. A continuous random variable is one that can take on any real value, that is, a variable that can take any real number in a given interval. An example of a continuous random variable of interest to OR managers is the value of trades that fail to settle when expected. In this example, we observed that the discrete random variable (the number of trades that failed to settle) on the five days from August 19 to August 23 as $\{5, 0, 0, 1, 0\}$; the value of these trades was $\{\$250,000, 0, 0, \$500,000, 0\}$.

Since the number of trades that fail to settle when expected and the value of trades that fail to settle when expected are random variables that can be used to provide information on a OR event, they are called *operational risk indicators*.

OPERATIONAL RISK INDICATORS

Operational risk indicators are random variables that are used to provide insight into future OR events. For example, a rising number of trades that fail to settle may be indicative of failing settlement or back office procedures. There are numerous risk indicators that firms can monitor to assess future OR events. Losses due to the failure of a vendor to perform outsourced processing activities correctly and unauthorized transfers of money by employees into their personal bank accounts are examples of OR events for which we seek to find suitable OR indicators. Some risk indicators may generally be applicable to all businesses, while others will be specific to a particular business. The key objective of risk indicators is to provide insight into future problems at their earliest stages so that preventive action can be undertaken to avert or minimize a serious OR event.

PROBABILITY

We use probability to help characterize risk indicators, the number of OR events, and the size of OR losses. Intuitively, a probability should lie between 0 and 1. An outcome or event that cannot occur should have a probability of 0, and an event that is certain to occur will have a probability of 1. What is the probability that the number of trades that fail to settle when expected today will be the same as yesterday, equal to yesterday, or more than yesterday? Since one of these outcomes is certain to occur, the probability is 1. Probability values indicate the likelihood of an event occurring. The closer the probability is to 1, the more likely the event is to occur. For example, suppose completion, within the next three days, of projects A and B is uncertain, but we know the probability of completion of project A is 0.6 (60 percent) and the probability of completion of project B is 0.25 (25 percent). These probability values provide a numerical scale for measuring our uncertainty in the sense that they inform us that project A is more likely to be completed within the next three days' time than project B. More formally, we say that probability provides a numerical scale for measuring uncertainty.

If E is an event of interest (for example a high settlement loss), we denote Prob(E) to be the probability of E. We also write Prob($\neg$E) as the probability of the complementary event of E not occurring. For simplicity, we shall assume the events E and ¬E are mutually exclusive (that is, if E occurs, ¬E cannot occur, and vice versa). Probability satisfies two basic properties:

1. *Convexity property:* $0 \leq \text{Prob}(E) \leq 1$
2. *Complement property:* $\text{Prob}(E) + \text{Prob}(\neg E) = 1$

Convexity tells us that the probability of an event always lies between 0 and 1. The complement property tells us that the sum of the probabilities of the event E and ¬E must sum to 1. For example, if the probability of completion of project A is 0.6 (60 percent), then the probability of not completing project A must be 0.4 (40 percent).

EXAMPLE 2.2 COMPLEMENT PROPERTY AND THE NUMBER OF TRADES THAT FAILED TO SETTLE

To illustrate the complement property, let:

- A represent the event that the number of trades that failed to settle when expected today is equal to number of trades that failed to settle yesterday.
- B represent the event that the number of trades that failed to settle when expected today is greater than the number of trades that failed to settle yesterday.
- C represent the event that number of trades that failed to settle when expected today is less than the number of trades that failed to settle yesterday.

We would expect $\text{Prob}(A) + \text{Prob}(B) + \text{Prob}(C) = 1$. This is because either A, B, or C is certain to occur. Furthermore, given $\text{Prob}(A)$ and $\text{Prob}(B)$, we can find $\text{Prob}(C)$, which is equal to $1 - [\text{Prob}(A) + \text{Prob}(B)]$. Now suppose $\text{Prob}(A) = 0.3$ and $\text{Prob}(B) = 0.2$; then $\text{Prob}(C) = 1 - (0.3 + 0.2) = 0.5$.

Mutually Exclusive Events

Given two events A and B that cannot both occur together, the probability that either A or B occurs is equal to the sum of their separate probabilities, or $\text{Prob}(A \text{ or } B) = \text{Prob}(A) + \text{Prob}(B)$. We have already seen in Example 2.2 that either the number of trades that failed to settle when expected today is equal to (event A), greater than (event B), or less than (event C) the number of trades that failed to settle yesterday. Therefore, using the rule of mutually exclusive events, we can write $\text{Prob}(A \text{ or } B \text{ or } C) = \text{Prob}(A) + \text{Prob}(B) + \text{Prob}(C)$, which in this case equals 1.

FREQUENCY AND SUBJECTIVE PROBABILITY

We can distinguish two basic approaches for calculating probability: the frequency approach and the subjective approach. The frequency approach gives an objective status to the notion of probability by rendering it a property of real-world phenomena. It asserts that probability should be interpreted as stemming from the observable stability of empirical frequencies. For example, suppose an operational risk manger is interested in settlement loss, given product complexity and staff experience. Using the frequency approach, he or she might conclude that the probability of a very large loss is 0.5 percent because the empirical frequency of a repeated series of a large number of settlements with a given level of staff experience and product complexity is approximately 0.5 percent.

Subjective probability renders the notion of probability subjective by regarding it as "degrees of belief" on behalf of individuals assessing the uncertainty of a particular situation. It depends on personal viewpoints and prior experience. For example, an operational risk manager might conclude the probability of a very large settlement loss is 0.25 percent. Another operational risk manager with similar experience might conclude it is only 0.01 percent. Given the potential differences that can arise between experts' subjective probabilities, why should we use them? Where empirical data does not exist, numerical measures of probability can only be obtained via subjective probability. In other words, if we have not empirically measured the relevant risk factors, we can only rely on expert opinion in the form of subjective probabilities.

Conditional Probability

The conditional probability of an event A given another event B is the probability that A will occur given that B has occurred. We write it as Prob(A | B). We can calculate the conditional probability using the rule

$$\text{Prob(A | B)} = \frac{\text{Prob(A and B)}}{\text{Prob(B)}}$$

EXAMPLE 2.3 CONDITIONAL PROBABILITY OF A SERIOUS TRANSACTION ERROR GIVEN A COMPUTER FAILURE

To illustrate this rule, let us suppose B represents the event that the "computer system fails," which occurs with probability 0.2, and A to be the event "serious transaction error." If events A and B occur jointly with probability 0.05, then

$$\text{Prob(A | B)} = \frac{\text{Prob(A and B)}}{\text{Prob(B)}} = \frac{0.05}{0.2} = 0.25$$

So the probability that we observe a serious transaction error given we have already observed a computer system failure is 0.25.

We can rearrange the formula for conditional probability so that

$$\text{Prob}(A \text{ and } B) = \text{Prob}(B)P(A \mid B)$$

Using the above example, we calculate the joint probability Prob(A and B) = Prob(B)Prob(A | B) = 0.2 × 0.25 = 0.05, which is as expected. If Prob(A | B) = Prob(A), then the events A and B are said to be *statistically independent*. This means the occurrence of B does not alter the probability that A will occur.

STATISTICAL INDEPENDENCE

What is the value of statistical independence? To gain an insight into its value, consider two potential risk indicators X and Y. Suppose the OR manager is interested in using one of these indicators to provide information about the OR event Z. Let us suppose he finds that for the potential risk indicator X

$$\text{Prob}(Z \mid X) = \text{Prob}(Z)$$

and for potential risk indicator Y

$$\text{Prob}(Z \mid Y) \neq \text{Prob}(Z)$$

Since Z and X *are* statistically independent, he or she concludes that X is not a useful risk indicator for the OR event Z. However, since Y and Z *are not* statistically independent, he or she also concludes that Y may be a useful risk indicator of Z.

The formula for conditional probability allows the measurement of uncertainty given prior information. On occasion, we will have information on A (for example, a serious transaction failure) and may wish to make a probabilistic statement about B (computer system failure); to do this, we can use Bayes' theorem, which states that

$$P(B \mid A) = \frac{P(A \mid B)P(B)}{P(A)}$$

The key value of Bayes' theorem and the law of conditional probability is that they allow us to reason from uncertain evidence to arrive at a verdict using frequency or subjective probabilities.

EXAMPLE 2.4 USING BAYES' THEOREM TO REASON ABOUT A COMPUTER SYSTEM FAILURE

In Example 2.3, we denoted the event "computer system fails" by B and the event "serious transaction error" by A. Furthermore, we saw that Prob(B) = 0.2 and Prob(A | B) = 0.25. Suppose Prob(A) = 0.15, and we observe that a serious transaction error has occurred. What is the likelihood that the computer system has failed? In this situation we have evidence about event A and we wish to use this information to update our knowledge of event B. We can use Bayes' theorem, in which case we calculate

$$\text{Prob (B | A)} = \frac{0.25 \times 0.2}{0.15} = 0.3$$

PROBABILITY FUNCTIONS

Probability functions give a complete representation of the possible outcomes of a random variable. They inform us what outcomes are possible and how likely they are. This is important because once we have knowledge of the possible outcomes and their probability of occurrence, we can begin to quantify the operational risks we face.

Probability Mass Function and Probability Density Function

Every discrete random variable has a probability mass function that tells us the probability with which the discrete random variable takes any particular value. For example, if we are interested in the discrete random variable $X =$ "Citywide electrical failure," which takes the value 1 if the event occurs and 0 otherwise, the probability mass function $p(x)$ takes the numerical values

$$\text{Prob}(X = 0) = p(0) = \frac{999}{1,000}$$

$$\text{Prob}(X = 1) = p(1) = \frac{1}{1,000}$$

In this case $p(0)$ and $p(1)$ make up the probability distribution for the random variable. The low value of $p(1)$ informs us that this OR event occurs with low probability and is in this sense unlikely. Figure 2.1 illustrates the probability distribution of a discrete random variable that can take discrete values between 1 and 9. From it we see that $p(X = 1) = 0.3$ and $p(X = 9) = 0.045$.

Associated with every continuous random variable is a corresponding continuous probability density function that we denote by $f(x)$. Figure 2.2

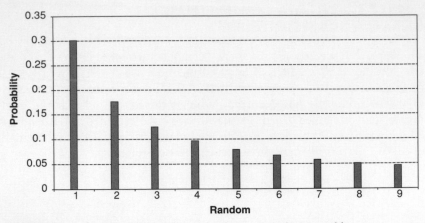

FIGURE 2.1   Probability distribution of a discrete random variable.

illustrates a probability distribution for a continuous random variable. Since $f(x)$ is a continuous function, the area between any two points x_1 and x_2 represents the probability that the random variable will lie between these two values. We write this as

$$\text{Prob}(x_1 < X \leq x_2) = \int_{x_1}^{x_2} f(x) \ dx$$

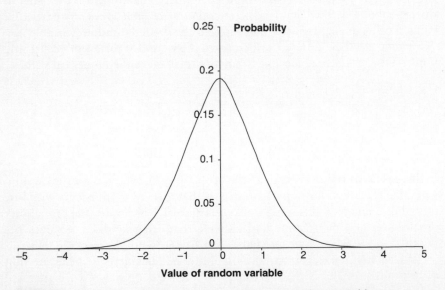

FIGURE 2.2   Probability distribution of a continuous random variable.

Since probabilities cannot be negative, the probability mass function and the probability density function satisfy $p(x) \geq 0$ and $f(x) \geq 0$. In addition, we have already seen that the sum over all possible outcomes is equal to 1 so that $\sum_x p(x) = 1$ and $\int_{-\infty}^{\infty} f(x)\,dx = 1$.

Cumulative Distribution Function and Percentile Function

For any random variable X, the cumulative probability is measured by the cumulative distribution function. It is defined as

$$F(x) = \text{Prob}(X \leq x) = \begin{cases} \sum_{x \leq k} p(x) & \text{if } X \text{ is discrete} \\ \int_{-\infty}^{x} f(u)\,du & \text{if } X \text{ is continuous} \end{cases}$$

If X is a discrete random variable, then the cumulative distribution function $F(x)$ is a step function, as illustrated in Figure 2.3. If X is a continuous random variable, then $F(x)$ is a continuous function, as illustrated in Figure 2.4. In this case, given a probability density function $F(x)$, then

$$F(x) = \int_{-\infty}^{x} f(u)\,du$$

The αth percentile $(0 \leq \alpha \leq 1)$ is that value of a random variable X, say x_α, which indicates the percentage of a probability distribution that is equal

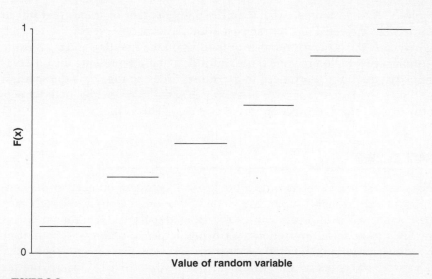

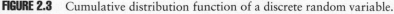

FIGURE 2.3 Cumulative distribution function of a discrete random variable.

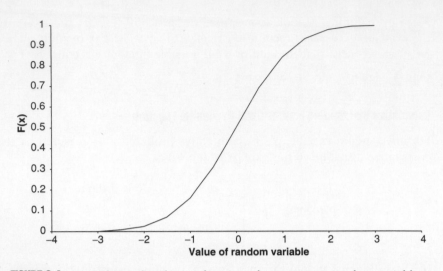

FIGURE 2.4   Cumulative distribution function of a continuous random variable.

to or below x_α. Given the distribution function, $F(x)$ the percentile function is $F^{-1}(1 - \alpha)$.

EXAMPLE 2.5 PERCENTILES OF THE NUMBER OF TRADES THAT FAIL TO SETTLE WHEN EXPECTED

Suppose X is a random variable of the daily number of trades that fail to settle when expected. If over the past 1000 days we observe $\{x_1, \ldots, x_{1000}\}$, where x_1 is the observed number of failures on the first day and x_{1000} is the number observed on the one thousandth day, and p represents the observations $\{x_1, \ldots, x_{1000}\}$ arranged in ascending order, so that p_1 is the smallest and p_{1000} the largest, the 99th percentile is equal to or greater than 99 percent of the values recorded in $\{p_1, \ldots, p_{1000}\}$. This is p_{990}.

CASE STUDIES

For the first few chapters of this book, we illustrate a number of the concepts raised through simple case studies. Working carefully through each case study will reinforce many of the ideas discussed. Operational risk is intrinsic to financial institutions, yet being harder to quantify, it cannot be so easily categorized and modeled as is the case with market and credit risks. The basic objectives of an operational risk manager are (1) identifying the operational risks the financial institution is exposed to, (2) assessing their

> ## OPERATIONAL VALUE AT RISK
>
> The aim of setting aside capital for operational risk events is to ensure the availability of sufficient economic capital to allow continued operation in an adverse environment or when internal operational failures have generated large unexpected losses. Operational value at risk (OPVaR) is one way to calculate operational risk capital provision. It is defined as the operational risk capital sufficient, in most instances, to cover operational risk losses over a fixed time period at a given confidence level. OPVaR can be calculated provided we know $F^{-1}(1 - \alpha)$. A 99 percent OPVaR implies $\alpha = 1$ percent, which in this case is the 99th percentile, and thus $\text{OPVaR}_{0.99} = F^{-1}(1 - 0.99) = F^{-1}(0.01)$.

extent, (3) setting aside capital for potential losses, and (4) mitigating the potential of OR events to cause business losses. In the following case studies we illustrate how we can begin to use the ideas presented in this chapter to achieve some of these objectives.

CASE STUDY 2.1: DOWNTOWN INVESTMENT BANK

Downtown Investment Bank has just begun to develop its operational risk activities. At this early stage, it has employed an MBA graduate named Richard to enhance its OR operation. The head of operational risk, Mr. Bellyfan, has asked Richard to investigate the relationship between system downtime and serious transaction errors. In particular, Mr. Bellyfan insists that serious transaction errors are more likely when the system fails and asks Richard to confirm his assertion. After initial difficulty finding any data, which is not unusual in OR management, Richard eventually obtains the data presented in Table 2.1. The table shows whether there was a system failure, transaction failure, or both during each month from May 1999 to April 2004. Richard, fresh out of business school, recalls his teaching on empirical statistics and decides to use all of the data because of the small sample size.

Table 2.2 presents the recoded data used by Richard. In this table Richard codes a failure with the value 1, and 0 otherwise. The third column in this table takes a value 1 if both a system failure and a serious transaction error occur. Hence in May 2003, a serious transaction error occurred jointly with a system failure and so all elements in this row take the value 1.

How can Richard investigate the relationship between the two failures? Recalling a lecture he attended on conditional probability, he decides to calculate the probability of a serious transaction error given a system failure. In order to calculate this probability, he requires information on the

TABLE 2.1 Data on Serious Transaction Errors and System Downtime

Month	System Failure	Serious Transaction Error	Month	System Failure	Serious Transaction Error
31-May-99	No	No	30-Nov-01	Yes	No
30-Jun-99	No	Yes	31-Dec-01	No	No
31-Jul-99	No	No	31-Jan-02	Yes	Yes
31-Aug-99	No	Yes	28-Feb-02	No	Yes
30-Sep-99	No	Yes	31-Mar-02	Yes	No
31-Oct-99	Yes	No	30-Apr-02	No	No
30-Nov-99	No	No	31-May-02	No	Yes
31-Dec-99	No	Yes	30-Jun-02	Yes	Yes
31-Jan-00	Yes	No	31-Jul-02	Yes	No
29-Feb-00	No	Yes	31-Aug-02	Yes	Yes
31-Mar-00	Yes	Yes	30-Sep-02	No	No
30-Apr-00	Yes	No	31-Oct-02	Yes	No
31-May-00	Yes	Yes	30-Nov-02	No	No
30-Jun-00	No	No	31-Dec-02	Yes	Yes
31-Jul-00	No	Yes	31-Jan-03	Yes	No
31-Aug-00	No	No	28-Feb-03	Yes	Yes
30-Sep-00	No	No	31-Mar-03	Yes	No
31-Oct-00	No	Yes	30-Apr-03	Yes	No
30-Nov-00	Yes	No	31-May-03	Yes	Yes
31-Dec-00	Yes	Yes	30-Jun-03	Yes	No
31-Jan-01	No	Yes	31-Jul-03	No	No
28-Feb-01	Yes	Yes	31-Aug-03	No	Yes
31-Mar-01	Yes	No	30-Sep-03	No	Yes
30-Apr-01	No	Yes	31-Oct-03	Yes	Yes
31-May-01	Yes	Yes	30-Nov-03	No	Yes
30-Jun-01	Yes	Yes	31-Dec-03	Yes	Yes
31-Jul-01	No	No	31-Jan-04	No	No
31-Aug-01	Yes	Yes	29-Feb-04	Yes	No
30-Sep-01	Yes	Yes	31-Mar-04	No	Yes
31-Oct-01	No	Yes	30-Apr-04	No	No

joint probability of a system failure and serious transaction error and the probability of a system failure. He obtains these probabilities by counting the number of 1's in each column of Table 2.2 and dividing by the number of rows, which in this case is 60. Using this method he calculates the approximate probabilities as follows:

- Probability of serious transaction error = 32/60 ≈ 0.53
- Probability of system failure = 30/60 = 0.50
- Probability of system failure and serious transaction error = 16/60 ≈ 0.27

TABLE 2.2 Recoded Data on Serious Transaction Errors and System Downtime

Month	Both Fail	System Failure	Serious Transaction Error
31-May-99	0	0	0
30-Jun-99	0	0	1
31-Jul-99	0	0	0
31-Aug-99	0	0	1
30-Sep-99	0	0	1
31-Oct-99	0	1	0
30-Nov-99	0	0	0
31-Dec-99	0	0	1
31-Jan-00	0	1	0
29-Feb-00	0	0	1
31-Mar-00	1	1	1
30-Apr-00	0	1	0
31-May-00	1	1	1
30-Jun-00	0	0	0
31-Jul-00	0	0	1
31-Aug-00	0	0	0
30-Sep-00	0	0	0
31-Oct-00	0	0	1
30-Nov-00	0	1	0
31-Dec-00	1	1	1
31-Jan-01	0	0	1
28-Feb-01	1	1	1
31-Mar-01	0	1	0
30-Apr-01	0	0	1
31-May-01	1	1	1
30-Jun-01	1	1	1
31-Jul-01	0	0	0
31-Aug-01	1	1	1
30-Sep-01	1	1	1
31-Oct-01	0	0	1
30-Nov-01	0	1	0
31-Dec-01	0	0	0
31-Jan-02	1	1	1
28-Feb-02	0	0	1
31-Mar-02	0	1	0
30-Apr-02	0	0	0
31-May-02	0	0	1
30-Jun-02	1	1	1
31-Jul-02	0	1	0
31-Aug-02	1	1	1
30-Sep-02	0	0	0
31-Oct-02	0	1	0
30-Nov-02	0	0	0

TABLE 2.2   *(Continued)*

Month	Both Fail	System Failure	Serious Transaction Error
31-Dec-02	1	1	1
31-Jan-03	0	1	0
28-Feb-03	1	1	1
31-Mar-03	0	1	0
30-Apr-03	0	1	0
31-May-03	1	1	1
30-Jun-03	0	1	0
31-Jul-03	0	0	0
31-Aug-03	0	0	1
30-Sep-03	0	0	1
31-Oct-03	1	1	1
30-Nov-03	0	0	1
31-Dec-03	1	1	1
31-Jan-04	0	0	0
29-Feb-04	0	1	0
31-Mar-04	0	0	1
30-Apr-04	0	0	0

Therefore Probability (Serious transaction error | System failure) = 0.27/ 0.50 ≈ 0.53. Since this is approximately equal to the probability of a serious transaction error, Richard concludes that system failure and serious transaction error are independent. But how does he tell Mr. Bellyfan?

CASE STUDY 2.2: MR. MONDEY'S OPVaR

In early 2004 Andrew Mondey, vice president of OR at a middle-size national bank, was faced with the problem of estimating the 95 percent 1-month OPVaR for his organization. He had been diligently collecting data on the value of OR losses over the past few years and now had a database going back 100 months. The full set of data is shown in Table 2.3. Recalling that OPVaR is a percentile, he reorganizes the data into Table 2.4, in which the OR losses are ranked by size. From this table Mr. Mondey picks the 95th observation and therefore concludes that the 95 percent 1-day OPVaR = $88,875.

CASE STUDY 2.3: RISK IN SOFTWARE DEVELOPMENT

The software development unit of a small investment firm is considering the possibility of replacing some of its highly experienced but costly programmers with more junior staff. Stephen, an operational risk analyst, has been asked to assess the likely impact on the number of serious software defects introduced into a new and critical product if the proposal takes place. After a degree of discreet digging around for empirical data, Stephen produces the information shown in Table 2.5. It shows the number of software modules developed by two different types of programmer. Type A programmers are

TABLE 2.3 Operational Risk Losses of a Middle-size National Bank

Month	Loss ($)	Month	Loss ($)	Month	Loss ($)
1	0	35	0	69	52,000
2	0	36	0	70	0
3	66,178	37	0	71	0
4	0	38	23,863	72	11,982
5	0	39	53,158	73	0
6	43,711	40	46,490	74	1,060
7	0	41	51,641	75	0
8	0	42	36,182	76	74,339
9	16,442	43	0	77	0
10	0	44	0	78	0
11	0	45	0	79	85,512
12	0	46	0	80	0
13	0	47	0	81	60,034
14	0	48	76,578	82	0
15	0	49	72,873	83	0
16	0	50	0	84	42,512
17	45,442	51	0	85	0
18	0	52	0	86	0
19	0	53	0	87	0
20	0	54	0	88	20,998
21	0	55	0	89	0
22	85,803	56	49,709	90	0
23	87,363	57	0	91	41,402
24	0	58	0	92	0
25	0	59	0	93	95,153
26	89,028	60	0	94	0
27	0	61	10,488	95	88,875
28	0	62	0	96	0
29	0	63	0	97	0
30	0	64	0	98	91,067
31	55,567	65	0	99	89,797
32	0	66	34,194	100	0
33	0	67	0		
34	97,916	68	0		

TABLE 2.4   Operational Risk Losses Ranked by Size of a Middle-size National Bank

Rank	Loss ($)	Rank	Loss ($)	Rank	Loss ($)
1	0	35	0	69	1,060
2	0	36	0	70	10,488
3	0	37	0	71	11,982
4	0	38	0	72	16,442
5	0	39	0	73	20,998
6	0	40	0	74	23,863
7	0	41	0	75	34,194
8	0	42	0	76	36,182
9	0	43	0	77	41,402
10	0	44	0	78	42,512
11	0	45	0	79	43,711
12	0	46	0	80	45,442
13	0	47	0	81	46,490
14	0	48	0	82	49,709
15	0	49	0	83	51,641
16	0	50	0	84	52,000
17	0	51	0	85	53,158
18	0	52	0	86	55,567
19	0	53	0	87	60,034
20	0	54	0	88	66,178
21	0	55	0	89	72,873
22	0	56	0	90	74,339
23	0	57	0	91	76,578
24	0	58	0	92	85,512
25	0	59	0	93	85,803
26	0	60	0	94	87,363
27	0	61	0	95	88,875
28	0	62	0	96	89,028
29	0	63	0	97	89,797
30	0	64	0	98	91,067
31	0	65	0	99	95,153
32	0	66	0	100	97,916
33	0	67	0		
34	0	68	0		

more experienced than type B. Steven decides to use this information to calculate the probability that the next module to be developed (of similar size and complexity to those considered in Table 2.5) will have fewer serious defects than the industry average if

1. It was developed by a type A programmer.
2. It was developed by a type B programmer.

TABLE 2.5 Number of Modules Developed by Two Types of Programmer

Programmer A		Programmer B		Total	Developed
Modules developed	<Industry average	Modules developed	<Industry average	All	<Average
1,910	875	2,887	925	4,797	1,800

In order to achieve this, Steven uses the following notation:

1. P_A denotes the event that the module is developed by a type A programmer.
2. P_B denotes the event that the module is developed by a type B programmer.
3. Z denotes the event that the module has fewer serious defects than the industry average.

Using the law of conditional probability Steven notes that:

$$\text{Prob}(Z \mid P_A) = \frac{\text{Prob}(P_A \text{ and } Z)}{\text{Prob}(P_A)}$$

and

$$\text{Prob}(Z \mid P_B) = \frac{\text{Prob}(P_B \text{ and } Z)}{\text{Prob}(P_B)}$$

Using the frequency definition of probability and the data from Table 2.5, Stephen calculates

$$\text{Prob}(P_A) = \frac{1,910}{4,797} = 0.398\,(39.8 \text{ percent})$$

$$\text{Prob}(P_B) = \frac{2,887}{4,797} = 0.602\,(60.2 \text{ percent})$$

$$\text{Prob}(P_A \text{ and } Z) = \frac{875}{4,797} = 0.182\,(18.2 \text{ percent})$$

$$\text{Prob}(P_B \text{ and } Z) = \frac{925}{4,797} = 0.193\,(19.3 \text{ percent})$$

Therefore:

$$\text{Prob}(Z \mid P_A) = \frac{\text{Prob}(P_A \text{ and } Z)}{\text{Prob}(P_A)} = \frac{0.182}{0.398} = 0.457\,(45.7 \text{ percent})$$

$$\text{Prob}(Z \mid P_B) = \frac{\text{Prob}(P_B \text{ and } Z)}{\text{Prob}(P_B)} = \frac{0.193}{0.602} = 0.321\,(32.1 \text{ percent})$$

These results indicate that if a programmer of type A develops the module, there will be a higher probability that it will have less serious defects than if a programmer of type B develops the module. This is as we might expect, as programmers of type A are more experienced than programmers of type B. However, the advantage of using probability is that it gives us a scale on which to assess this difference.

USEFUL EXCEL FUNCTIONS

Excel has many probability and related functions of value in OR management. One of the most useful is the Percentile() function, which returns the percentile of a given data set. It is illustrated in the workbook Operational Risk 02.xls worksheet Case study 2.2 and also discussed further in review question 6 below. Other valuable functions include the Normsinv(), which calculates the percentile function for a standard normally distributed random variable, and Normsdist(), which calculates the probability distribution of a standard normally distributed random variable. Other useful functions for continuous probability distributions include Betadist() for the cumulative beta probability density function, Chidist() for the chi-squared distribution, Expondist() for the exponential distribution, Fdist() for the F distribution, Gammadist() for the gamma distribution, Lognormdist() for the lognormal distribution, Tdist() for the Student's t distribution, and Weibull() for the Weibull distribution. Excels coverage of discrete probability distributions is not quite as extensive as the continuous case; however, it does provide functions for some of the important discrete distributions including Negbinomdist() for the negative binomial distribution, Binomdist() for the binomial distribution probability, Hypgeomdist() for the hypergeometric distribution, and Poisson() for the Poisson distribution. A number of percentile functions (also known as inverse functions) for specific distributions are also available, including Betainv() for the beta distribution, Chiinv() for the chi-squared distribution, Finv() for the F probability distribution, Gammainv() for the gamma cumulative distribution, Loginv() for the lognormal distribution, and Tinv() for the Student's t distribution. We shall see many of these and other functions in action in later chapters.

SUMMARY

Random variables, operational risk indicators, and probability provide us with some of the tools we require to gain insights into the nature of the uncertainty surrounding future OR events. We can capture such uncertainty using a probability function and a cumulative probability function. The percentile function is also useful because it offers us a mechanism for calculating OPVaR. The concept of probability and probability functions can assist OR managers in their efforts to control losses, keep their organization competitive, and protect shareholder value regardless of how they define OR. However, probability is not the only tool we need. As we see in the next chapter, knowledge of a random variable average value is also important for effective OR management.

REVIEW QUESTIONS

1. List four examples of random experiments alongside their associated random variables. From your list identify the continuous and discrete random variables.
2. Identify four potential OR events. What do you think are potential risk indicators for these OR events and why?
3. Can you explain why probability is useful for describing OR events?
4. Suppose the probability of the event "a serious transaction error" is 0.2 and the probability of the event "computer system failure and a serious transaction error" is 0.1. What is the probability of a computer system failure given that you have observed a serious transaction error?
   - How does this probability change if the probability of a serious transaction error is 0.5?
   - What would you expect if the two OR events were statistically independent or dependent?
5. Describe each of the following and explain why they may be important tools for characterizing OR events and OR indicators:
   - Probability mass function
   - Probability density function
   - Cumulative distribution function
   - Percentile function
6. Open the workbook Operational Risk 02.xls and use worksheets Case study 2.1 and Case study 2.1(a) to investigate the impact of a change in the number of system failures and serious transaction errors on the conditional probability of a transaction error given a system failure. Do you agree with Richard's conclusion of statistical independence?
7. In the same workbook the worksheet Case study 2.2 gives the data collected by Mr. Mondey and the formula he used to calculate OPVaR. Cell C11 contains the Excel function Percentile(), which can also be used to calculate OPVaR for this data.
   - Investigate the impact of changing the value of the percentile used (cell C9) on the value returned by Mr. Mondey's approach and Excel's Percentile() function.

- How would you explain these differences?
- Type the value 0.69 into cell C9 and compare the different OPVaR values. Which is preferable and why?

8. Is there a role for subjective probabilities in OR practice? How should we deal with situations in which data is nonexistent?

FURTHER READING

Operational value at risk is based on value at risk, which is frequently reported in market risk management. Lewis (2003) provides an excellent, accessible introduction to the use of VaR and other statistical methods in market risk management. More advanced reading on VaR is provided by Butler (1999), Duffie and Pan (1997), Bahar et al. (1997), and Holton (1997).

CHAPTER 3

Expectation, Covariance, Variance, and Correlation

We have seen that risk indicators and OR events are the outcome of a random experiment whose realized values are determined by an underlying probability function. At the start of business on a particular day the random experiment begins. At this stage the outcome of the experiment is unknown, and the OR manager will be interested in the typical or average value of his or her risk indicators, how they vary from one day, week, or month to the next, and the interrelationship between OR indicators, in addition to their relationship with OR events. The typical value of an OR event or risk indicator is measured by its *expected value*, its variability by *variance*, and the interrelationship between risk indicators and OR events by *correlation*. In this chapter we introduce these measures and discuss their relevance to OR modeling. We begin with the concept of expected value of a risk indicator or OR event and end by measuring the association between risk indicators, using covariance and correlation.

EXPECTED VALUE OF A RANDOM VARIABLE

The expected value of a random variable, denoted by $E[X]$, is a measure of the mean or average value. The expected value of a discrete random variable X is calculated as

$$E[X] = \sum_x x p(x)$$

EXAMPLE 3.1 SYSTEM FAILURE RISK AND THE EXPECTED NUMBER OF SYSTEM SUPPORT STAFF AVAILABLE

To illustrate the calculation of expected value, consider the number of system support staff available on particular day. The operational risk manager may be concerned about the risk of a system failure which he or she believes is related to the staffing level in the system support department on a particular day. In this case the OR event of interest is "system failure" and the OR indicator is "number of system support staff available." We denote the risk indicator by X, and note that it is a discrete random variable. The manager knows that on any day there is always at least one individual available and at most nine. Therefore, X can take on values between 1 and 9.

The probability of each specific value is given in the second column of Table 3.1, from which we see that the probability that $X = 1$ is 0.301. The third column of this table gives the values of $X \times P(x)$. For example, for the first row $X = 1$ and $P(1) = 0.301$, $X \times P(1) = 1 \times 0.301 = 0.301$. Taking the sum of all of the values in the third column, we find $E[X] = 3.44$. This informs us that the average or center of mass of the distribution lies between 3 and 4. Since X can only take on the value 3 or 4 (and not values in between), the expected value will never be observed. However, we might feel comfortable saying that we expect the number of system support staff available on a particular day will be around 3. The operational risk manager can use this figure to assist in his or her assessment of whether to hire agency staff.

Working through Example 3.1, you will see that the expected value is a probability weighted average of the possible values of the random variable. If X is continuous, this probability weighted average is given by

$$E[X] = \int_{-\infty}^{\infty} x f(x)\, dx$$

TABLE 3.1 Calculation of Expected Value of a Discrete Random Variable

X	Probability	$X \times P(x)$
1	0.301	0.301
2	0.176	0.352
3	0.125	0.375
4	0.097	0.388
5	0.079	0.396
6	0.067	0.402
7	0.058	0.406
8	0.051	0.409
9	0.046	0.412

Furthermore, if Y is some function of X, denoted by $Y = G(X)$, then $E[Y] = \sum_x G(x)p(x)$ if X is discrete, and $E[Y] = \int_{-\infty}^{\infty} G(x)f(x)\,dx$ if X is continuous.

UNDERSTANDING EXPECTED VALUE

There is not too much to remember about expected values. Provided you keep in mind the following two points, you will remain on the right track:

1. In Chapter 2 we saw that the value of a random variable is the result of an experiment of chance. The expected value is the long-run probability weighted average of a large number of experiments of chance; that is, if you perform the random experiment on many occasions and take the probability weighted average, this will be the expected value. Since it is an average, its value may never actually be observed.
2. A common mistake is to assume that the expected value of a random variable will be the value you would observe if the random experiment were performed once. This is not the case. The expected value is the long-run average value of a random variable.

EXAMPLE 3.2 EXPECTED OPERATIONAL LOSS AND THE INTERNAL MEASUREMENT APPROACH TO REGULATORY CAPITAL CHARGE

An internal measurement approach is one way for a bank to calculate its operational risk capital charge. In this method commercial activities are categorized into a number of business lines. For each business line the following are calculated:

1. An exposure indicator (EI) that measures the size of the risk exposure of the specific business line.
2. An expected frequency of OR loss events calculated from a probability distribution of loss events (PE).
3. An expected severity of OR loss given an OR loss event calculated from a severity of loss probability distribution (LGE).

The expected operational loss for a specific business line is then calculated as

$$E[\text{OR loss}] = \text{EI} \times \text{PE} \times \text{LGE}$$

The regulatory capital charge (RCC) for the specific business line is then calculated as

$$RCC = E[\text{OR loss}] \times \gamma$$

where γ is a factor determined by the regulator. The total capital charge is the sum across all the bank's business lines.

NEW BASEL CAPITAL ACCORD METHODS OF CALCULATING OPERATIONAL RISK CHARGE

The New Basel Capital Accord outlines three methods for calculating the OR capital charge. The first is the basic indicator approach, in which the required capital is determined by multiplying a financial indicator such as gross income by a fixed percentage. The second is the standardized approach, in which a bank divides its function into a number of business lines. For each business line, the required operational risk capital is calculated by multiplying an indicator, typically the gross income or asset size of the business line, by a fixed percentage. The total operational risk capital charge is the sum of the required capital across all the business lines. The third method is a type of internal measurement approach based on a bank's internal risk management system. In this approach, OR is categorized based on business lines and event types determined by the regulators. The total capital charge is the sum of the required capital across each business line and each event-type combination.

Rules of Expectation

There are a number of rules of expectation that are useful:

Rule 1: The expectation of a constant C is the constant:

$$E[C] = C$$

Rule 2: If X is a random variable and C is a constant, then

$$E[XC] = CE[X]$$

and

$$E[X + C] = C + E[X]$$

Rule 3: The expected value of the sum of two random variables X and Y is the sum of their expected values:

$$E[X + Y] = E[X] + E[Y]$$

Rule 4: Given two random variables X and Y, the conditional expectation of X given Y is denoted by $E[X \mid Y]$. If X is continuous, it is defined by

$$F[X \mid Y] = \int_{-\infty}^{\infty} x f(x \mid y) \, dx$$

If X is discrete, it is defined by

$$E[X \mid Y] = \sum_{x} x \, p(x \mid y)$$

EXAMPLE 3.3 EXPECTED SHORTFALL AS A CONDITIONAL EXPECTATION

Operational value at risk measures the distribution percentile, disregarding losses beyond α. In effect, it tells us what is the most we can expect to lose if αth percentile occurs. How much can we expect to lose if an OR event beyond OPVaR occurs? The BIS Committee on the Global Financial System (2000) identifies this problem as tail risk. Tail risk can be modeled using expected shortfall (ES):

$$ES_{1-\alpha} = E[X \mid X > OPVaR_{1-\alpha}]$$

Expected shortfall is the conditional expectation of loss given that the loss is beyond the OPVaR level α. By definition, expected shortfall considers losses in the more extreme tail of a probability distribution than OPVaR.

VARIANCE AND STANDARD DEVIATION

The variance of a random variable is a measure of spread or dispersion of the probability density or mass function. If X is a discrete random variable with mean μ_X, variance is defined by

$$\text{Variance } (X) = \sum_{x} (x - \mu_X)^2 p(x)$$

If X is a continuous random variable, it is defined by

$$\text{Variance } (X) = \int_{-\infty}^{\infty} (x - \mu_x)^2 f(x) dx$$

Variance is non-negative and measured in squared units of X. The further the values of X tend to fall from their expected value, the larger will be the variance. The standard deviation (which we frequently shorten to Stdev) of a random variable X is the square root of variance. It is also a measure of dispersion, but measured in the same units as X.

COVARIANCE AND CORRELATION

Given two random variables X and Y with mean and standard deviation μ_X, σ_X, and μ_Y, σ_Y, respectively, their covariance is given by

$$\text{Covariance}(X, Y) = E[(X - \mu_X)(Y - \mu_Y)]$$

Covariance measures the linear relationship between X and Y, and it will be positive if X and Y tend to have the same sign with high probability and negative if they tend to have opposite signs with high probability. Unfortunately, the actual value of covariance has little meaning because it depends on the variability of X and Y. However, we can rescale covariance to lie between −1 and +1 by dividing it by the product of the standard deviation of X and the standard deviation of Y; this measure is known as the *correlation coefficient* between X and Y:

$$\text{Correlation}(X, Y) = \frac{\text{Covariance}(X, Y)}{\sigma_X \sigma_Y}$$

The correlation coefficient is a unitless measure of the linear relationship between X and Y. Figure 3.1 plots the relationship between two random

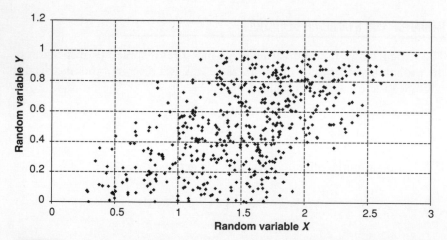

FIGURE 3.1   Positive correlation of 0.6 between two random variables.

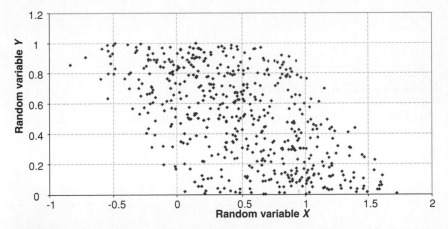

FiGURE 3.2 Negative correlation of −0.6 between two random variables.

variables that have a positive correlation of 0.6, and Figure 3.2 plots the relationship between two random variables that have a negative correlation of −0.6. A perfectly positive linear relationship between X and Y occurs when Correlation $(X, Y) = 1$, and a perfectly linear negative relationship occurs when Correlation $(X, Y) = -1$. These relationships are illustrated in Figures 3.3 and 3.4, respectively. In this sense, the correlation coefficient is a better measure of linear relationship than the covariance.

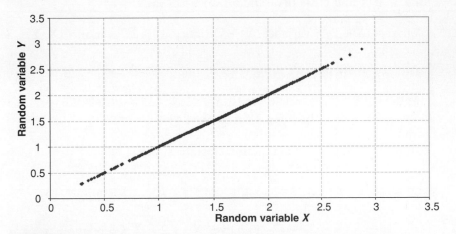

FiGURE 3.3 Perfect positive correlation between two random variables.

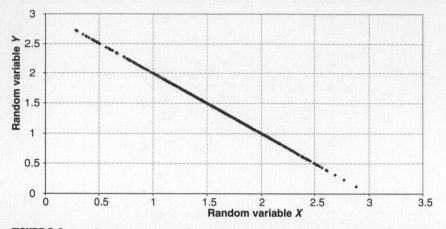

FIGURE 3.4 **FIGURE 3.4** Perfect negative correlation between two random variables.

SOME RULES FOR CORRELATION, VARIANCE, AND COVARIANCE

Rule 1: If X is a random variable and α is constant, then

$$\text{Variance}(X + \alpha) = \text{Variance}(X)$$

Rule 2: If X is a random variable and α is a constant, then

$$\text{Variance}(X \times \alpha) = \alpha^2 \text{Variance}(X)$$

Rule 3: If X and Y are two random variables then

$$\text{Variance}(X + Y) = \text{Variance}(X) + \text{Variance}(Y) + 2\text{Covariance}(X, Y)$$

We can also write this rule using correlation, in which case we have

$$\text{Variance}(X + Y) = \text{Variance}(X) + \text{Variance}(Y) + 2\text{Correlation}(X, Y) \\ \times \text{Stdev}(X) \times \text{Stdev}(Y)$$

Rule 4: If $X^1, \ldots, X^N$ are random variables, then

$$\text{Variance}(X^1 + \cdots + X^N) = \sum_{i=1}^{N} \text{Variance}(X^i) + 2\sum_{j=1}^{N}\sum_{k=1}^{N} \text{Covariance}(X^j, X^k)$$

$$= \sum_{i=1}^{N} \text{Variance}(X^i) + 2\sum_{j=1}^{N}\sum_{k=1}^{N} \text{Correlation}(X^j, X^k) \\ \times \text{Stdev}(X^j) \times \text{Stdev}(X^k)$$

Rule 5: If X and Y are independent, then

$$\text{Correlation}(X, Y) = 0$$

Rule 6: If $X^1, \ldots, X^N$ are independent identically distributed (that is, independent and from the same probability distribution), then

$$\text{Correlation}(X^i, Y^j) = 0 \quad \text{for all } i \neq j$$

Rule 7: If $X^1, \ldots, X^N$ are independent identically distributed random variables, then

$$\text{Variance}(X^1 + \cdots + X^N) = \sum_{j=1}^{N} \text{Variance}(X^j)$$

CASE STUDIES

Case study 3.1 and case study 3.2 explore some of the ideas presented in this chapter. They also develop the idea that even though we may not have any empirical observations, we can still obtain expected values. This is so provided we are able to use subjective probabilities elicited from relevant experts such as business managers or senior management.

CASE STUDY 3.1: EXPECTED TIME TO COMPLETE A COMPLEX TRANSACTION

Mr. Breedon, an OR manager at a small financial institution, has taken on a university student, Bernard, as a summer intern. Mr. Breedon is concerned about the time it takes to process certain complex transactions. His feeling is that the operational procedures of the back office need revamping because it seems to be taking the back office "too long" to process these transactions. Since he is very busy and not sure if his intuition is correct, he asks Bernard to investigate.

Bernard speaks with the head of processing operations and finds out that they classify their transaction times for these particular trades into three groups: Those that take approximately 3 minutes to complete, those that take around 6 minutes, and those that take approximately 12 minutes to complete. Bernard asks the head of operations to give him data for each of these classifications so that he can calculate approximate probabilities. Unfortunately, no such data is collected. Rather than return to Mr. Breedon empty-handed, and mindful of the possibility of a full-time permanent position when he completes his degree, Bernard asks each of the four staff members who process these transactions for their subjective probabilities

TABLE 3.2   Individual Subjective Probabilities of the Time
Taken to Complete a Complex Transaction

	Average Time		
	3 minutes	6 minutes	12 minutes
Person 1	0.82	0.17	0.01
Person 2	0.79	0.18	0.03
Person 3	0.78	0.19	0.03
Person 4	0.85	0.14	0.01

for each classification. These values are reported in Table 3.2. Bernard is pleasantly surprised by the close agreement between the subjective probabilities. Encouraged by this finding, he decides to use the average of the subjective probabilities, as shown in Table 3.3.

Bernard then calculates the expected time to complete a transaction as:

$$E(\text{time to complete transaction}) = (0.81 \times 3 \text{ minutes})$$
$$+ (0.17 \times 6 \text{ minutes})$$
$$+ (0.02 \times 12 \text{ minutes}) = 3.69 \text{ minutes}$$

Using the rule that Variance $(X) = E(X^2) - E(X)^2$, Bernard calculates that

$$E(X^2) = (0.81 \times 9) + (0.17 \times 36) + (0.02 \times 144) = 16.29$$

and therefore

$$\text{Variance (time to complete a transaction)} = 16.29 - E(X)^2$$
$$= 16.29 - (3.69)^2 = 2.67$$

and the corresponding standard deviation is equal to 1.64 minutes. Bernard's calculations are also contained in the Excel workbook Operational Risk 03.xls worksheet Case study 3.1.

TABLE 3.3   Average Time to Complete a Complex Transaction
Based on Subjective Probabilities

	3 minutes	6 minutes	12 minutes
Average	0.81	0.17	0.02

CASE STUDY 3.2: OPERATIONAL COST OF SYSTEM DOWNTIME

The IT (information technology) systems department of a trading and brokerage arm of a large multinational institution has requested that the IT system be shut down for between 10 and a maximum of 14 minutes every Monday during trading hours for essential maintenance. Dr. Young, the OR manager, would prefer this maintenance to be carried out during the evenings or on weekends. Unfortunately, deep budgetary cuts in the IT department have made senior management unresponsive to this idea. Dr. Young decides to calculate the dollar impact to the firm of the IT systems department request. He assumes a fixed cost of $12,000 and an additional cost of $1,125 for every minute the system is down. So his model for the total cost is simply

$$\text{Total cost} = \$12,000 + (\$1,125 \times X)$$

where X is the number of minutes the system is down.

Dr. Young then asks the IT systems manager to provide subjective probabilities of the time it should take to carry out the maintenance. These values are shown in Table 3.4. From this data, Dr. Young calculates the expected cost as

$$\text{Expected cost} = \$12,000 + (\$1,125 \times E[X])$$

where

$$E[X] = (0.1 \times 10) + (0.3 \times 11) + (0.3 \times 12) + (0.2 \times 13)$$
$$+ (0.1 \times 14) = 11.9 \text{ minutes}$$

Therefore, Dr. Young concludes that the expected cost is $25,387.50.

Excel and VBA Functions for Correlation, Covariance, and Variance

The correlation between two variables can be calculated in Excel using the Correl() function. Covariance can be calculated using the Covar() function. Given a sample of risk indicators or OR events, the variance and standard deviation are best calculated using the Var() and Stdev() functions, respectively. An alternative, if we have the entire population, is to use the

TABLE 3.4 Subjective Probabilities of System Downtime Provided by IT Manager

Minutes	10	11	12	13	14
Probability	0.1	0.3	0.3	0.2	0.1

Varp( ) function. We discuss the calculation of these measures of dispersion using sample data in more detail in the next chapter. Excel does not have a function for calculating the variance of the sum of two or more random variables. However, it is straightforward to write a simple function to calculate the variance between two random variables. We do this in the function Var_2( ). The code for this function is

```
Function Var_2(x As Range, y As Range)
        ' pass the data cells to the function
mean_x = Application.WorksheetFunction.Average(x)
        'calculate mean of x
mean_y = Application.WorksheetFunction.Average(y)
var_x = Application.WorksheetFunction.Var(x)
        ' calculate variance of x
var_y = Application.WorksheetFunction.Var(y)
cov = Application.WorksheetFunction.Covar(x, y)
var_2 = var_x + var_y + (2 * cov)
        ' return the value for the variance of x + y
End Function
```

Once entered into Excel, the function can be called by entering Var_2 (datarange1, datarange2). We illustrate its use in more detail in Case Study 4.1 and in the Excel workbook Operational Risk 04.xls.

SUMMARY

This chapter has presented an overview of approaches to measure the average value and variance of discrete and continuous random variables. We have also introduced the concepts of covariance and correlation. In the following two chapters we discuss the empirical version of these notions, and show how, given data, they can be easily calculated for OR indicators and used effectively in OR management.

REVIEW QUESTIONS

1. Explain why an OR manager would be interested in the

   - Expected value of an OR event
   - Correlation between OR indicators
   - Variance of an OR indicator

2. Suppose you were asked to investigate the time to complete a transaction in two distinct business units. Both business units process similar transactions and have a similar staffing level.

- Suppose business unit A had a higher processing time standard deviation than unit B. What, if any, conclusions might you draw?
- If you were told that business unit A had a lower expected processing time than business unit B, how would your conclusions alter?
- If you were told that business unit A also had a higher expected processing time than business unit B, how would your conclusions alter?

3. Can you explain why the

- Expected value of a constant is equal to the constant itself?
- Variance of a constant is zero?
- Expected value of a random variable is simply a probability weighted average?

4. Identify an operational risk event and three operational risk indicators.

- What do you expect the correlation between these risk indicators and the OR event to be (high, medium, low) and why?
- What do you expect the correlation between the risk indicators to be and why?

5. Take another look at Case Study 3.1. In your opinion, is the approach taken by Bernard acceptable? Why or why not?
6. Senior management has asked you to identify and justify possible risk indicators for computer system failure.

- What indicators do you feel are appropriate?
- How would you use the methods discussed in this and the previous chapter to justify your assertion?

7. Extend the function Var_2 so that it can calculate the sum of n random variables.

FURTHER READING

Expected shortfall is an important concept in market risk management. It will become increasingly important in OR as well. Lewis (2003) gives a number of examples of tail risk estimation and its practical use in risk management. Artzner et al. (1997, 1999) and BIS Committee on the Global Financial System (2000) are useful references if you are interested in the detailed arguments for the use of tail risk estimates.

CHAPTER 4

Modeling Central Tendency and Variability of Operational Risk Indicators

In the previous two chapters we outlined some of the ideas behind random variables and probability. In practice we will collect a sample of measurements on risk indicators and use the underlying theory of probability to help us in our decision making. Once we have measurements on our key risk indicators, we will need to summarize their essential characteristics. In this chapter we discuss how to do this using the empirical equivalent of expected value and variance.

EMPIRICAL MEASURES OF CENTRAL TENDENCY

Suppose we are interested in describing the typical value of a risk indicator X. Our first step would be to collect a sample of observations say $\{x_1, \ldots, x_N\}$. We denote the ith observation on the operational risk indicator by x_i, where i goes from 1 to N. From this sample of observations we could calculate a measure of central tendency, such as the arithmetic mean. The arithmetic mean (which we denote by $\bar{x}$) is the sum of the set of observations in a sample divided by the number of observations:

$$\bar{x} = \frac{x_1 + x_2 + \cdots + x_N}{N}$$

The formula for calculating $\bar{x}$ is known as an *estimator*, and the actual value $\bar{x}$ takes is known as an *estimate*. Notice the similarity *and* difference between the arithmetic mean and the expected value. The expected value is a measure of the center of a probability distribution, and the arithmetic mean is a measure of the center or typical value of a sample of risk factors. However, whereas expected value is a probability weighted metric, the arithmetic mean is an equally weighted metric because the divisor for all observations is N.

TABLE 4.1   Number of System Failures between January and May

January	February	March	April	May
23	35	25	27	50

EXAMPLE 4.1   AVERAGE NUMBER OF SYSTEM FAILURES BETWEEN JANUARY AND MAY

Suppose we observe system failures over five months, as shown in Table 4.1. The average number of failures is

$$\bar{x} = \frac{23 + 35 + 25 + 27 + 50}{5} = 32$$

There are alternative estimators for measuring the typical value of a sample. A popular alternative to the mean is the median. It is the value that is greater than or equal to half the values in the sample. For a continuous random variable with probability density function $f(x)$ it is actually the value such that

$$\int_{-\infty_1}^{x_{median}} f(x)\, dx = \int_{x_{median}}^{\infty} f(x)\, dx = \frac{1}{2}$$

From this definition we see that half the observations lie above the median, and half lie below the median. We can calculate the median by arranging the N observations of a sample in increasing order. The median is the $[(N + 1)/2]$th observation when N is odd and the average of the $(N/2)$th and the $[(N + 2)/2]$th observation when N is even.

EXAMPLE 4.2   MEDIAN NUMBER OF SYSTEM FAILURES BETWEEN JANUARY AND MAY

For illustration we return to Example 4.1. The ranked data is shown in Table 4.2. Since $N = 5$, the median is equal to the $(5 + 1)/2 = 3$rd observation. In this case median number of failures is equal to 27, which is slightly lower than the arithmetic mean of 32 calculated in Example 4.1.

TABLE 4.2   Ranked Number of System Failures between January and May

January	March	April	February	May
23	25	27	35	50

WHY USE THE MEDIAN?

Consider the following observations on system downtime over four days (Monday = 1 minute, Tuesday = 1 minute, Wednesday = 2 minutes, and Thursday = 40 minutes). The value 40 experienced on Thursday is 20 times higher than the next largest value and appears to be an outlier, or rogue value. If we use the arithmetic mean as our measure of central tendency, its value is $(1 + 1 + 2 + 40)/4 = 11$. Is this a good measure of the center of the observations? Not really, because most of the values lie between 1 and 2. In this case, since N is even, the median is the average of the $(N/2)$th = $4/2$ = 2nd observation and the $[(4 + 2)/2]$ = 3rd observation. Therefore, the median = $(1 + 2)/2 = 1.5$. This is a much better measure of the center of the sample than the mean. In fact the median is known as a *robust estimator* because it is less sensitive to extreme observations than the mean. It should be your first choice estimator of central tendency when your sample contains outlier observations.

MEASURES OF VARIABILITY

Operational risk indicators vary over time, with some time periods more volatile than others. For example, the installation of a new back office system may temporarily increase the number of settlement errors or amount of time taken to process trades as staff members familiarize themselves with the system. Measures of variability such as the variance and standard deviation attempt to capture this. The sample variance and standard deviation provide a measure of how tightly individual values are clustered around the arithmetic mean of a sample.

We encountered these measures when discussing random variables in the previous chapter. The empirical formulas are based on the idea of averaging the distance of each observation from the mean. For an individual observation x_i on a risk indicator X, the distance from the mean is measured by $x_i - \bar{x}$. For N observations in our sample, we therefore have N such distances, one for each x_i. Since $\sum_{i=1}^{N}(x_i - \bar{x}) = 0$, we use the squared distances, as $\sum_{i=1}^{N}(x_i - \bar{x})^2 \geq 0$. The estimator of the sample variance (S^2) is the average of these:

$$S^2 = \frac{\sum_{i=1}^{N}(x_i - \bar{x})}{N - 1}$$

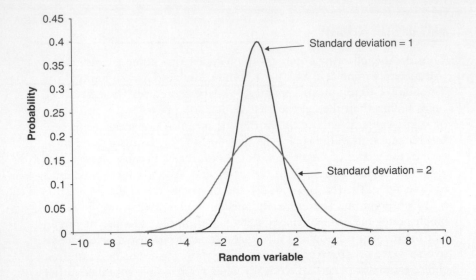

FIGURE 4.1   Impact changing the standard deviation of a probability distribution.

The sample variance is measured in squared units of the sample. The sample standard deviation S is the square root of S^2. When the observations cluster close together around the arithmetic mean, the sample variance and sample standard deviation will be small. The more spread out the observations are around the mean, the larger are the sample variance and sample standard deviation. This is illustrated in Figure 4.1, which shows two random variables with expected value equal to 0 and standard deviations equal to 1 and 2. Since variance is not in the same units as the observations, most risk managers prefer to quote the sample standard deviation, which is measured in the same units as the data.

CASE STUDIES

Many operational and business risks are correlated. This is particularly the case if we adopt a broad definition of operational risk to include business risks associated with the state of the economy or with political change. In Case Study 4.1 we investigate how one might approximate business risk using the measures introduced in this chapter.

CASE STUDY 4.1: APPROXIMATING BUSINESS RISK

Dr. Agbaje has recently transferred from the market risk department to the OR department of a internationally focused investment house. He was brought in because of his special expertise in statistical and mathematical methods. His first task is to calculate the business risk of the global operation. Business risk is defined as risk arising from changes in the market environment. Since he cannot measure this risk directly, he decides to use fee earnings as a proxy. His rationale is that increased competition or a sluggish economy can have a direct impact on fee earnings, which in turn reflect changes in the market environment and hence business risk.

Unfortunately, Dr. Agbaje is unable to find direct information on fee income for his company. Given time, he believes he could obtain this data, but he only has a matter of days before he needs to present his results to the CEO. Fortunately, he is able to obtain from an external agency the information presented in Table 4.3. This table gives the average of fees in the sector and annual economic growth over the period 1992–2004.

Dr. Agbaje, now slightly desperate because his meeting with the CEO is drawing nearer, decides to formulate a simple model. His model takes the form: Fee income = F(competitor fees, economic growth), where $F(.)$ is some function. Since time is short, Dr. Agbaje assumes a linear function: Fee income = competitor fees + economic growth. For now, this linear model will have to do; he will get better-quality data and build a more complex model later. Since Dr. Agbaje's background is in market risk, he decides to use the standard deviation or volatility of fee income as his actual measure of business risk. He calculates the variance of economic growth as 0.02 percent and the variance of average competitor fees as 0.23 percent. In addition he finds the covariance between these two variables is 0.00037185.

TABLE 4.3 Average Fees of the Sector and Economic Growth

Year	Average Competitor Fees (%)	Economic Growth (%)
1992	1.50	−1.0
1993	0.50	0.0
1994	2.50	1.5
1995	5.00	2.0
1996	7.50	1.3
1997	7.60	1.5
1998	8.90	5.0
1999	15.20	2.8
2000	12.50	2.5
2001	13.40	2.0
2002	1.40	1.5
2003	9.00	3.5
2004	5.00	3.8

Using the rule that Variance $(X + Y)$ = Variance (X) + Variance (Y) + 2 × Covariance (X, Y), Dr. Agbaje calculates:

Variance (fee income) = Variance (competitor fees)
        + Variance (economic growth) + 2
        × Covariance (competitor fees, economic growth)

and

Variance (fee income) = 0.2323% + 0.0247% + (2 × 0.00037185) = 0.3313%

Hence the standard deviation of fee income is $\sqrt{0.3313}$ percent ≈ 5.76 percent. Dr. Agbaje's only concern now is whether this figure is acceptable to his CEO. What do you think?

POPULATIONS AND SAMPLES

The population of a particular risk indicator consists of the entire set of past and future values. In practice we will only observe a subset or sample of these values. Our initial goal is to use the limited information provided by this sample to draw general conclusions about the population. As long as our sample is representative of the population from which it comes, we can use the sample estimator of the mean and standard deviation discussed in this chapter. If we had all of the observations from a population, could we use the same estimators? For the mean, the answer is yes. However, for the variance, we would need to use the population variance estimator:

$$\sigma^2 = \frac{\sum_{i=1}^{N} (x_i - \bar{x})^2}{N}$$

with σ being the population standard deviation. This estimator is very similar to the sample estimator of variance *except* that it is divided by N, whereas the sample variance estimator is divided by $N - 1$. It turns out that dividing by $N - 1$ ensures the sample variance estimator provides an *unbiased* estimate of the population variance. Bias refers to how far the sample estimate lies from the population characteristic we are trying to estimate. An unbiased estimator will yield the correct estimate of the population characteristic as the sample size increases.

Further details of Dr. Agbaje's calculations are given in the workbook Operational Risk 04.xls. Take a look at the worksheet Case Study 4.1. It gives the data and details of how the calculations can be carried out in Excel. The variance of a random variable is calculated using the function Var(). For example in cell E27 the function Var(E11:E23) calculates the variance of the competitor fees and returns a value of 0.23 percent. The only other built-in Excel function used in this worksheet is the function Covar() in cell E29, which calculates the covariance between competitor fees and economic growth. We could also use the function Var_2(), which calculates the variance of the sum of two random variables, introduced in the previous chapter. Its use in this example is shown in cell E35. The worksheet Case Study 4.1 simulation illustrates the calculation of business risk in differing economic and competitor fee environments. The simulation can be activated by pressing <F9>. It makes use of Excel's Randbetween() function and requires the activation of the analysis tool pack Addin which comes as standard with Excel.

EXCEL FUNCTIONS

The mean, median, variance, and standard deviation of a sample can be calculated using the Excel functions average(), median(), var(), and stdev(), respectively. In the situation in which we require the variance of the sum of two random variables, the user-defined function Var_2() is useful. This function can be extended easily to the situation in which we are interested in the variance of the sum of n random variables (see Question 7 from Chapter 3).

SUMMARY

Measures of central tendency, such as the mean and median, and measures of dispersion, such as the variance and standard deviation, are descriptive measures that can be used to summarize important features of our OR data. The advantage of using these metrics to summarize the center and dispersion of a risk indicator or OR event is that they are frequently reported in other areas of risk management and finance. In addition, they are widely understood summary statistics. However, reporting the mean and standard deviation of a risk factor or OR event is often not enough to adequately characterize the features of the underlying probability distribution. To gain further insight, we also require information on the shape, via metrics such as skew and kurtosis. We discuss these measures in the next chapter.

REVIEW QUESTIONS

1. Why take equal weights in calculating the arithmetic mean? Is it always suitable to treat all observations equally?
2. Suppose new observations contain more information about an OR indicator than older observations. How would you adjust the formula for the arithmetic mean to take this into account?
3. Given a sample on a risk factor that can take positive or negative values, which would you expect to be larger (mean or median) if:

   ■ The observations are symmetric?
   ■ The observations are asymmetric with more large positive values than large negative values (positively skewed)?
   ■ The observations are asymmetric with less large positive values than large negative values (positively skewed)?

4. Suppose you observe the following observations on system downtime:

Day 1	Day 2	Day 3	Day 4	Day 5	Day 6	Day 7	Day 8
2 mins	3 mins	0 min	0 min	1 min	1 min	4 mins	12 mins

   ■ Calculate the arithmetic mean and median. Which is the better measure and why?
   ■ Recalculate the arithmetic mean and median ignoring day 8. What do you conclude?
   ■ Calculate the standard deviation using all observations.

5. Can you explain the difference between sample and population? Which are we most likely to use as OR managers and why?
6. Use the following data to calculate business risk using the approach of Dr. Agbaje (Case Study 4.1):

Year	Average Competitor Fees (%)	Economic Growth (%)	Year	Average Competitor Fees(%)	Economic Growth (%)
1992	2.0	−1.0	1999	7.2	12.4
1993	1.0	0.0	2000	12.0	12.5
1994	4.0	1.5	2001	9.4	7.0
1995	3.0	2.0	2002	7.3	7.5
1996	6.0	3.0	2003	6.0	2.5
1997	8.0	4.0	2004	5.2	2.8
1998	8.0	9.0			

In your opinion, is the approach taken by Dr. Agbaje appropriate? What are the other feasible alternatives?

FURTHER READING

Further details on the use of measures of central tendency in risk management, and alternatives to those measures presented in this chapter, can be found in Lewis (2003).

CHAPTER 5

Measuring Skew and Fat Tails of Operational Risk Indicators

So far we have used measures of central tendency and dispersion to summarize a sample of operational risk indicators. Although these two measures allow us to reduce our sample to two numbers—the mean and variance—valuable additional insight into the shape of the probability distribution can be achieved by considering their degree of skew and "fat-tailedness," known as *kurtosis*. In this chapter we discuss these two metrics, and show how they can be calculated using traditional and robust statistical methods.

MEASURING SKEW

Consider the histograms of the three discrete operational risk indicators shown in Figure 5.1. The histogram on the top depicts the situation in which the risk indicator values are symmetrically distributed about their mean. The middle diagram depicts the situation in which the risk indicator is positively skewed, and the bottom diagram depicts the situation in which the risk indicator is negatively skewed. In this example, the main difference in shape between the three risk indicators is their degree of symmetry. The distributions in the middle and bottom diagrams of Figure 5.1 have one tail longer than the other.

The degree of skew is important in the practical modeling and measuring of risk indicators and OR events because it provides information about the likelihood of extreme events. Given a sample of size N on a continuous risk indicator with sample mean $\bar{x}$ and sample standard deviation S, we can calculate the degree of skew using the formula

$$\delta = \frac{\sum_{i=1}^{N} (x_i - \bar{x})^3 / N}{S^3}$$

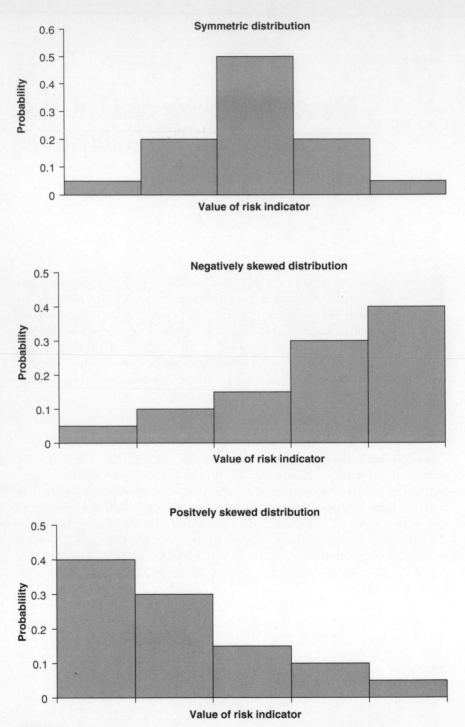

FIGURE 5.1 Symmetric, negatively and positively skewed risk indicators.

The important part of the formula is the numerator. We divide by S^3 to ensure that the estimator of skew is independent of the units of measurement. A symmetric distribution has skew equal to zero and large values are about as likely as small values. Negative skew indicates that large negative values are more likely than large positive values. Positive skew indicates that large positive values are more likely than large negative values.

EXAMPLE 5.1 CALCULATING SKEW FOR THREE SMALL SAMPLES

As an illustration, consider three separate samples of a random variable as shown in Table 5.1. Each sample has a mean of approximately 0 and a standard deviation of approximately 1. However, in this case the mean and standard deviation do not provide enough information to adequately summarize the data. On close inspection you will observe that sample 1 is symmetric around 0, sample 2 negatively skewed, and sample 3 positively skewed. Using the above formula, we estimate the skew for sample 1 = 0, the skew for sample 2 = −0.7 and the skew for sample 3 = 0.7.

Since for a skewed distribution the median is not equal to the mean, another popular measure of skew is

$$\delta_m = \frac{3\,(\text{mean} - \text{median})}{S}$$

If (mean − median) > 0, then the sample is positively skewed. If (mean − median) < 0, then the data is negatively skewed. If mean = median, the data is symmetric. A Visual Basic for Applications (VBA) function to calculate this measure is

```
Function Skew_m(x As Range)
mean = Application.WorksheetFunction.Average(x)
s = Application.WorksheetFunction.StDev(x)
Median = Application.WorksheetFunction.Median(x)
Skew_m = (3 * (mean - Median)) / s
End Function
```

Using this function with the data of Table 5.1, we calculate skew as 0 for sample 1, −1.8 for sample 2, and 1.8 for sample 3, indicating symmetric, negative, and positive skew, respectively. Excel also has a built-in function Skew( ) for calculating skew. The formula it uses is

$$\delta_{\text{Excel}} = \frac{N}{(N-1)(N-2)} \frac{\displaystyle\sum_{i=1}^{N} (x_i - \overline{x})^3}{S^3}$$

TABLE 5.1 Three Small Samples

Observation	Sample 1	Sample 2	Sample 3
1	−1.26	−1.64	1.64
2	−0.63	−0.29	0.29
3	0.00	0.60	−0.60
4	0.63	0.69	−0.69
5	1.26	0.63	−0.63
Average	0.00	0.00	0.00
Standard Deviation	1.00	1.00	1.00

Using this function with the data of Table 5.1, we estimate the skew for sample 1 = 0, the skew for sample 2 = −1.5, and the skew for sample 3 = 1.5.

Despite the fact that δ, δ_m, and δ_{Excel} are different estimators and will therefore differ in their numerical value, for the data in Table 5.1 they all convey the same information: that sample 1 is symmetric, sample 2 is negatively skewed, and sample 3 is positively skewed. Indeed, a very useful rule of thumb for assessing the degree of skew is

1. If the estimated skew is greater than 1 in absolute value, the distribution is highly skewed.
2. If the estimated skew lies between 0.5 to 1, the distribution is moderately skewed.
3. If the estimated skew is less than 0.5, the distribution is fairly symmetrical.

MEASURING FAT TAILS

Kurtosis is a measure of the weight in the tails of a probability distribution. If the sample has a large kurtosis, it will tend to have a distinct peak near the mean, decline quickly, and have heavy tails. If on the other hand the sample has a low kurtosis, it will tend to have a flat top around the mean. Kurtosis can be calculated using

$$\psi = \frac{\sum_{i=1}^{N} (x_i - \bar{x})^4 / N}{S^4}$$

where S is the sample standard deviation. Kurtosis is usually measured relative to the normal distribution, which has a kurtosis of 3 (we discuss the normal probability distribution in detail in Chapter 7). Relative kurtosis is calculated as

$$\kappa = \psi - 3$$

As illustrated in Figure 5.2, distributions with positive relative kurtosis have large tails and are called *leptokurtic*. Distributions with negative relative kurtosis have short tails and are called *platykurtic*. When $\kappa = 0$, the distribution has the same degree of peakedness as the normal distribution; such distributions are called *mesokurtic*.

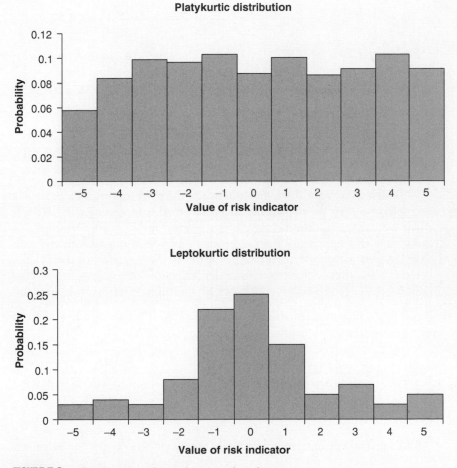

FIGURE 5.2 Platykurtic and Lepokurtic risk indicators.

EXAMPLE 5.2 MEASURING KURTOSIS
FOR THREE SMALL SAMPLES

In this example we return to Table 5.1 and calculate the kurtosis of each of the three samples. Since the mean for each sample is 0 and the variance is equal to 1, the kurtosis is simply

$$\psi = \frac{1}{5} \sum_{i=1}^{5} (x_i)^4$$

Therefore

For sample 1,

$$\psi_1 = \frac{(-1.26)^4 + (-0.63)^4 + (0.00)^4 + (0.63)^4 + (1.26)^4}{5} = 1.07$$

For sample 2,

$$\psi_2 = \frac{(-1.64)^4 + (-0.29)^4 + (0.60)^4 + (0.69)^4 + (0.63)^4}{5} = 1.55$$

For sample 3,

$$\psi_3 = \frac{(1.64)^4 + (0.29)^4 + (-0.60)^4 + (-0.69)^4 + (-0.63)^4}{5} = 1.55$$

Although we cannot distinguish between the three samples of Table 5.1 based solely on their mean and variance, we are able to distinguish between them if we use the additional measures of skew and kurtosis. Sample 1 is symmetric with a lighter tail than samples 2 and 3. Although samples 2 and 3 have the same degree of kurtosis, they differ in the direction of their skew.

Excel also offers a function for calculation of kurtosis, Kurt(). This function calculates the relative kurtosis of a sample. The formula used by Excel is

$$\psi_{Excel} = \left\{ \frac{N(N+1)}{(N-1)(N-2)(N-3)} \frac{\sum_{i=1}^{N} (x_i - \overline{x})^4}{S^4} \right\} - \frac{3(N-1)^2}{(N-2)(N-3)}$$

Since in the calculation of kurtosis the deviation $\left(\dfrac{x_i - \overline{x}}{S} \right)$ is raised

to the fourth power, it is very sensitive to values that lie a long way from the mean. Two robust alternatives are Groeneveld's (1998) relative kurtosis measure and Moors's (1988) kurtosis measure. Groeneveld's measure is given by

$$\psi_G = \frac{[P_{7/8} - 2\,P_{3/4} + P_{5/8}]}{[P_{7/8} - P_{5/8}]} - 0.144$$

where P_x is the xth percentile. A VBA function to calculate Groeneveld's measure is

```
Function Kurt_g(x As Range) ' pass the data cells to the function
p58 = Application.WorksheetFunction.Percentile(x, 5 / 8)
p78 = Application.WorksheetFunction.Percentile(x, 7 / 8)
p34 = Application.WorksheetFunction.Percentile(x, 3 / 4)
Kurt_g = ((p78 - (2 * p34) + p58) / (p78 - p58)) - 0.144
    ' main calculation
End Function
```

Moors's measure is given by

$$\psi_M = \frac{[P_{7/8} - P_{5/8}]}{[P_{3/4}]} - 1.2$$

A VBA function to calculate this measure is:

```
Function Kurt_m(x As Range)' pass the data cells to the function
p58 = Application.WorksheetFunction.Percentile(x, 5 / 8)
p78 = Application.WorksheetFunction.Percentile(x, 7 / 8)
p34 = Application.WorksheetFunction.Percentile(x, 3 / 4)
Kurt_m = ((p78 - p58) / p34) - 1.233 ' return the value
End Function
```

For Groeneveld's measure and Moors's measure a value greater than 0 indicates fatter tails than those of the normal distribution and a value less than 0 indicates thinner tails.

REVIEW OF EXCEL AND VBA FUNCTIONS FOR SKEW AND FAT TAILS

We can estimate the skew of a sample using the Excel-defined Skew( ) function or the user-defined Skew_m( ) function. Although these two functions will differ in their numerical value, they will generally convey the same information about the direction of skew. Kurtosis can be estimated using the Excel function Kurt( ). Alternative robust estimators can be obtained via Moors's measure, implemented in the function Kurt_m( ), or Groeneveld's measure, implemented in the function Kurt_g( ).

SUMMARY

Measures of central tendency and dispersion are not always sufficient to describe risk indicators or OR events. We frequently require additional information about the shape of the distribution generating risk indicators and OR events. Information about skew, kurtosis, mean and standard deviation will be required when we estimate frequency of loss and severity of loss probability models. In the next chapter we outline a formal procedure for testing the value of these and other metrics which may be of interest to the OR manager.

REVIEW QUESTIONS

1. Explain why the mean and variance alone are not necessarily adequate descriptors for a sample of a risk indicator or OR event.
2. Calculate the mean and median of the following data: 65 76 12 56 90 89 78 34. Calculate the degree of skew using all of the methods discussed in the chapter and comment on your findings.
3. Would you expect OR losses to be left or right skewed or symmetric? Why?
4. For the data of question 1, calculate the kurtosis using all the measures described in this chapter.

FURTHER READING

A detailed discussion of robust measures for calculating kurtosis can be found in Moors (1988) and Groeneveld (1998).

CHAPTER 6

Statistical Testing of Operational Risk Parameters

Many OR management decisions require the selection of a single alternative from a number of possible alternatives. The choice is generally made without knowing whether it is correct; that is, it is based on incomplete information. For example, a person either takes or does not take an umbrella to the office based upon both the weather report and possibly looking out the window to observe the current weather conditions. If it is not currently raining, this decision must be made with incomplete information.

Hypothesis testing provides a formal procedure for making rational decisions with incomplete information. The procedure is stated in such a fashion that another individual, using the same information, would make *exactly* the same decision. Setting up and testing hypotheses about estimates of OR events or risk indicators is an essential part of OR practice. In order to formulate a hypothesis test, usually some theory about a risk indicator, model parameter, or OR event is put forward, either because it is believed to be true or because it is to be used as a basis for argument, for example, claiming that a new model of OR events is better than the current model because it fits the data better or results in a smaller capital charge. In this chapter we introduce the modern approach to hypothesis testing and outline its relevance to OR practice.

OBJECTIVE AND LANGUAGE OF STATISTICAL HYPOTHESIS TESTING

In the previous two chapters we discussed estimators for the sample mean, standard deviation, kurtosis, and skew. We saw that such estimates provide useful descriptive information about the underlying probability distribution. We also know that a sample estimate is only an estimate of the underlying population characteristic and will vary from sample to sample.

In fact, only by chance will we obtain the exact same sample estimate for two different samples.

How can we have confidence that our sample estimate reflects the actual value of the population characteristic rather than some rogue value? Intuitively, the larger the sample, the more confidence we may have in the sample estimates. Unfortunately, in OR we frequently have to deal with small data sets. In this circumstance we can use hypothesis testing to support our decision making. Hypothesis testing is a formal statistical procedure for determining whether a sample is consistent with a particular hypothesis about an unknown characteristic of the population from which the sample came.

Table 6.1 lists summary statistics for a sample of daily operational losses over 260 days. The sample estimate of the average loss is $434,045, relative kurtosis of daily operational losses is approximately 2.26, and skew is 1.78. We know that if we were to take another sample over a different time period, say 300 or 500 days, the sample estimates will be different. A key question is: How can we be sure the sample estimates are not due to chance when in fact the real population estimates take on very different values? To illustrate this, consider the estimate of the relative kurtosis, that takes on a value of 2.26. How can we be confident that the true population value is not actually 0? The answer will need to provide us with evidence on whether 2.26 is in some sense significantly different from 0. The way this problem is approached through hypothesis testing is to calculate how often we would get a sample estimate as large or larger than 2.26 if the population relative kurtosis really was equal to 0 and therefore the sample estimate of 2.26 was due to chance. If a value as large or larger than 2.26 occurs by chance frequently, then chance is a feasible explanation of the observed value. However, if such a value only occurs by chance very rarely, then chance is probably not a feasible explanation. This is the essence of the scientific approach to research. The scientific approach to research operates by disproving unsatisfactory hypotheses and proposing improved hypotheses that are testable. Statistical hypothesis testing is based on a similar principle.

To carry out a hypothesis test, we are required to form two mutually exclusive hypothesis statements known as the *null hypothesis* (H_0) and the alternative hypothesis H_A. We start with a null hypothesis that we assume

TABLE 6.1   Summary Statistics for Operational Losses

Summary Statistic	Operational loss
Standard Deviation	$ 73,812
Average	$434,045
Kurtosis	2.26
Skew	1.78

is correct. Since our goal is to reject the null hypothesis, in favor of the alternative hypothesis, the null hypothesis is *always* chosen to be the hypothesis in which there is no or zero change

The *significance level* (often denoted by α) is the probability that you are prepared to accept in *incorrectly* rejecting the null hypothesis. Its value is the acceptable error threshold for rejecting the null hypothesis when the null hypothesis is in actual fact true. What value should we choose for the significance level? In general, we want it to be small, and in practice it is common to set it at 0.01, 0.05, or 0.1. The significance level is often reported as a percentage, that is, 1 percent, 5 percent, and 10 percent. Incorrectly rejecting the null hypothesis when it is true is know as a *type I error*. When using the 1 percent significance level, we make a type I error 1 percent of the time or less. A *type II error*, typically denoted by β, is the probability of failing to reject the null hypothesis when it is false. What value should we choose for a type II error? We would like to make our type II error as small as possible. The power of a statistical hypothesis test measures the test's ability to reject the null hypothesis when it is actually false. It is calculated as $1 - \beta$. The maximum power a test can have is 1, and the minimum is 0. It seems logical to require any hypothesis test to have as high a power as possible, which in turn requires a small type II error.

STEPS INVOLVED IN CONDUCTING A HYPOTHESIS TEST

The easiest way to become familiar with hypothesis testing is to work through an example. Given the sample estimate of relative kurtosis, which we denote by $\hat{\kappa}$, the first step is to specify a null and alternative hypothesis. Differentiating the null and alternative hypothesis can be easily achieved if you remember that the null hypothesis is the hypothesis that includes any of the equalities $=$, $\geq$, or $\leq$. We investigate the null hypothesis that the population kurtosis is equal to 0 against the alternative that it is greater than 0. We write this as

$$\text{Test } H_0: \kappa = 0 \text{ against } H_A: \kappa > 0$$

Since we are only interested in values greater than the null, this is known as a *one-sided test*. We note that if we specified our alternative hypothesis as $H_A: \kappa \neq 0$, our test would be a *two-sided test*.

The next step involves setting an appropriate significance level. We choose $\alpha = 5$ percent as the convention adopted in much of the scientific and research literature. We then need to calculate an appropriate *test statistic*. A test statistic, which we denote by $\hat{T}$, is a function of the sample data. Its estimated value is used to decide whether or not to reject the null hypothesis. For every parameter that we can estimate there is an appropriate test statistic.

In this section we focus on the test statistic for kurtosis. Other test statistics will be introduced throughout the remainder of the book.

Given a sample of size N, the test statistic for a relative kurtosis hypothesis test is

$$\hat{T} = \frac{\hat{\kappa}}{\sqrt{24/N}}$$

Suppose we calculate the value of this test statistic, as

$$\hat{T} = \frac{2.26}{\sqrt{24/260}} = 7.44$$

Since the estimate of $\hat{T}$ will vary from sample to sample, it is also a random variable. We know from previous discussions that random variables have an associated probability distribution. What is the probability distribution of $\hat{T}$? In this example, $\hat{T}$ is a standard normally distributed random variable. Figure 6.1 shows the probability distribution of $\hat{T}$. The mean of the distribution of $\hat{T}$ is zero because all test statistics are constructed on the assumption that the null hypothesis is valid and therefore the average difference between the sample estimate and population value should be 0. The probability distribution of the test statistic is usually referred to as the *sampling distribution of the test statistic,* or *sampling distribution* for short. The sampling distribution of the relative kurtosis test statistic is the

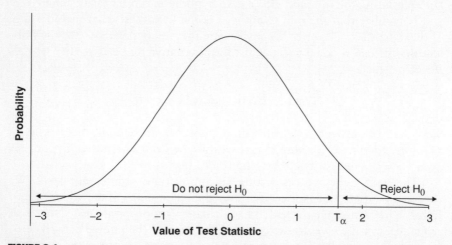

FIGURE 6.1 Sampling distribution for the kurtosis test statistic.

normal distribution. This is the most common sampling distribution. Other common sampling distributions include the Student's t distribution, F distribution, and chi-squared distribution. Tables for each of these distributions are given in Appendix 1.

The next stage of hypothesis testing involves calculating the critical value of the test statistic denoted T_α. This is the value beyond which the null hypothesis becomes untenable. The value of T_α can be obtained from the percentile function of the test statistic $F_{\hat{T}}^{-1}(1 - \alpha)$. Since we set $\alpha = 5$ percent and $\hat{T}$ is a standard normal random variable, we will wish to obtain the value of $T_{0.05}$. The critical values are tabulated in Table A.1. In this table we look up the closest value of $F(z)$ to $(1 - \alpha)$ and read across to find the value z that is the critical value T_α. In our example, $\alpha = 0.05$ so $(1 - \alpha)$ = 0.95. Looking in Table A1, we find $F(z) = 0.949497$ is the closest value to 0.95. Reading across, we see that this corresponds to a value of Z =1.64; therefore, the critical value $T_{0.05} = 1.64$. We can also obtain the critical value using the Normsinv function of Microsoft Excel. For this example we simply type Normsinv(0.95), and the function returns a value of 1.64. Thus, for a one-sided test we see that $T_{0.05} = 1.64$. This is the critical value for our hypothesis test.

Finally, we compare the value of the test statistic to the critical value and use this comparison to decide whether to reject the null hypothesis. For this example we reject the null hypothesis in favor of the alternative hypothesis if $\hat{T} > T_\alpha$. Since $\hat{T} = 7.44 > T_{0.05} = 1.64$, we reject the null hypothesis of no kurtosis. The rationale for rejection of the null if $\hat{T} > T_\alpha$ is illustrated in Figure 6.1. It shows the sampling distribution of the test statistic $\hat{T}$. From this diagram we can see that if the null hypothesis is true, then values of the test statistic $\hat{T}$ near 0 are much more likely than values far away from 0. Indeed, the null hypothesis is rejected *only* if the evidence against it is strong since the estimate of $\hat{T}$ could not easily have been produced by chance. This can be seen in Figure 6.1, in which values of $\hat{T}$ beyond T_α are assumed not to furnish us with sufficient evidence in terms of probability to accept H_0; therefore, for values beyond T_α we reject H_0. When the null hypothesis, is rejected in favor of the alternative hypothesis, the result is referred to as *statistically significant.*

Many statistical packages report the *p value* of the test statistic alongside the critical value and the estimate of the test statistic. The *p* value is the probability that the test statistic is greater than or equal to $\hat{T}$. The *p* value for the kurtosis test statistic is given by $1 - F(|\hat{T}|)$. It can be calculated in Microsoft EXCEL using the function normsdist($\hat{T}$). In this case normsdist(7.44) is approximately equal to 1, and therefore $1 - F(|\hat{T}|)$ lies close to 0. Since the value of $1 - F(|\hat{T}|)$ is less than the significance level 0.05, we reject the null hypothesis.

TWO-SIDED HYPOTHESIS TESTING

In the above example, we were only interested in values greater than the null since our test was

$$\text{Test } H_0: \kappa = 0 \text{ against } H_A: \kappa > 0$$
and we reject the null hypothesis if $\hat{T} > T_\alpha$.

This is known as a *one-sided* hypothesis test. A one-sided test is a test in which we are only interested in values greater (or less) than the null. Another one-sided hypothesis test is

$$\text{Test } H_0: \kappa = 0 \text{ against } H_A: \kappa < 0$$
and we reject the null hypothesis if $\hat{T} < T_\alpha$.

A *two-sided* hypothesis test is a test in which we are interested in values greater and smaller than the null hypothesis. We write this as

$$\text{Test } H_0: \kappa = 0 \text{ against } H_A: \kappa \neq 0$$
and we reject the null hypothesis if $|\hat{T}| > T_\alpha$

In the two-sided case we calculate the critical value using $\alpha/2$. For example if $\alpha = 5$ percent, the critical value of the test statistic is $T_{0.025}$. In Microsoft Excel we type `Normsinv(1-0.025)`, which returns a value of 1.96; therefore, $T_{0.025} = 1.96$. Since in the above example $\hat{T} = 7.44$ and $|7.44| > 1.96$, we reject the null hypothesis.

CONFIDENCE INTERVALS

In the previous section we considered setting up and testing a hypothesis for an unknown population parameter. For most OR problems statistical testing of this type will be inadequate. For example, suppose we reject the null hypothesis that the kurtosis is equal to 0. Faced with this result, the OR manager is likely to ask, "Since I have established that the kurtosis is not equal to 0, what else does this result tell me about the kurtosis for the population as a whole?" Questions of this kind require information beyond that provided in simple hypothesis testing. They require information on a range of plausible values in which the population parameter is likely to lie. Such information is provided by constructing a confidence interval around a sample estimate. A confidence interval is an interval constructed from a sample, which includes the parameter being estimated with a specified probability know as the confidence level.

EXAMPLE 6.1 CALCULATING A CONFIDENCE INTERVAL FOR AVERAGE OPERATIONAL LOSSES

To illustrate this idea, suppose the mean operational loss $\overline{X}$ = $434,045 and set α = 5 percent so that we have a $(1 - \alpha)$ = 95 percent confidence interval around the estimate of the mean. Such an interval can be calculated using

$$\overline{X} \pm z_\alpha \times \text{Stdev}(X)$$

Stdev(X), the standard deviation of X, is equal to $73,812, and z is the standard normal variable for α = 5 percent. Using the Normsinv( ) function, we see that Normsinv(0.95) = 1.64 (of course, we could also use Table A.1). Therefore, we set z = 1.64 and calculate the 95 percent confidence interval as $312,635 to $555,455. What does this tell us? It specifies a plausible range of values within which the unknown population mean may lie. In this case the OR manager may feel comfortable stating the average OR loss as $434,045, although we have 95 percent confidence that the actual (population) value will lie somewhere close to this value, say, between $312,635 and $555,455.

WIDTH OF A CONFIDENCE INTERVAL

If a risk indicator was sampled on many occasions, and the confidence interval calculated each time, then $(1 - \alpha)$ percent of such intervals would cover the true population parameter being estimated. Therefore, the width of the confidence interval measures how uncertain we are about the unknown population parameter. A very narrow interval indicates less uncertainty about the value of the population parameter than a very wide interval. Notice that since a confidence interval is a function of a sample, it is itself a random variable and will therefore vary from sample to sample.

CASE STUDY 6.1: STEPHAN'S MISTAKE

Stephan, a hot-shot MBA graduate from a leading North American university, is keen to prove himself on his first day in his new position as junior risk manager of GAI Investment Bank. He has been asked by his boss Dr. Richards to write a report on the impact of mispriced trades on daily reported profit and loss over the previous 12 months. Since the impact on profit and loss can be negative or positive and given that Stephan has no reason to believe the impact should be positive or negative, he assumes the process generating mispriced trades has a normal distribution with a 0 mean. He then decides to take a random sample of 20 mispriced trades ($N = 20$) and find $\bar{x}$ (the average value of mispriced trades) has a positive impact of \$52,325 on the reported profit and loss. After talking to a number of coworkers, he assumes the population standard deviation σ is equal to \$3,000 and decides to test formally whether the population mean is greater than \$52,325. Denoting μ the population mean, Stephan wants to test

$$H_0: \mu = \mu_0 = \$50,000 \text{ against } H_A: \mu > \$50,000$$

The decision rule is to reject H_0 in favor of H_A if $\hat{T} > T_\alpha$, where

$$\hat{T} = \frac{\bar{x} - \mu_0}{\sigma / \sqrt{N}} = \frac{52,325 - 50,000}{3000 / \sqrt{20}} = 3.47$$

For a 5 percent significance level he finds $T_{0.05} = 1.64$ (see Table A.1), since $3.47 > 1.64$ Stephan rejects the null hypothesis in favor of the alternative hypothesis.

Dr. Richards reads Stephan's report with great interest. Unfortunately for Stephan, Dr. Richards is extremely unhappy with Stephan's assumption about the population standard deviation. Throwing down Stephan's hastily prepared report, Dr. Richards barks, "How can we possibly know what this value is?" Stephan is dumbstruck, and he fears his first day in his new job is not going very well.

Why was Dr. Richards so angry? Well, in OR management we will rarely know the precise value of population parameters. The test statistic Stephan used assumed the population standard deviation was known. Stephan used the incorrect test statistic. He should have used the following test statistic:

$$\hat{T} = \frac{\bar{x} - \mu_0}{s / \sqrt{N}}$$

where s is the sample standard deviation.

In actual fact, this test statistic has a different sampling distribution than the statistic Stephan used. Stephan's test statistic is normally distributed, whereas the above test statistic has a Student's t distribution with $N - 1$ degrees of freedom. In many cases there is little difference between the two test statistics because the t distribution becomes approximately normally distributed as N becomes increasingly large. For the moment, let us suppose that $s = 3,000$; using the correct test statistic the value will be the same as before, that is, 3.47. From Table A.3, we see that $T_\alpha = 1.729$. Since 3.47 > 1.729, Stephan's rejection of the null hypothesis appears to be correct even through he used the wrong test statistic! Rather unfortunately for Stephan, Dr. Richards reworked Stephan's calculations and found the estimate of s was 7,878. Hence the value of the test statistic should have been 1.32, which is less than 1.729, and therefore he concludes that he cannot reject the null hypothesis.

EXCEL FUNCTIONS FOR HYPOTHESIS TESTING

The common sampling probability distributions of the normal, Student's t, chi-square, and F distributions can be accessed in Excel using the functions Normsdist( ), Tdist( ), Chidist( ), and Fdist( ) respectively. Inverse or percentile functions are also readily available. We have made some use of Normsinv( ) for the normal distribution. We can also use Tinv( ), Chiinv( ), and Finv( ) for the percentile functions of the Student's t, chi-square, and F distributions, respectively. The tables in Appendix 1 were all produced using Excel. Excel also provides a number of test procedures based on sampling distributions. Chitest( ), Ztest( ) and Ttest( ) based on the Chi squared, Normal, and Student's t sampling distributions, respectively.

SUMMARY

Setting up and testing hypotheses is full of pitfalls. The very first thing you should keep in mind is that hypotheses tests are designed to disprove hypotheses. The objective is to show that a null hypothesis is extremely unlikely because it's acceptance occurs with an unacceptably small probability. It is very important to realize that if the value of the test statistic results in the acceptance of the null hypothesis, *it does not follow* that we have grounds for believing this hypothesis to be true; rather, we have *no* grounds for believing it to be false. A null hypothesis is not accepted as true because it is not rejected.

Quantitative analysts often interpret the rejection of a hypothesis at the α percent level as implying that the probability that the null hypothesis is false is $1 - \alpha$. In fact, the α percent level of significance implies the observed test statistic result belongs to a class of results whose overall probability of occurrence *if* the null hypothesis is true is $1 - \alpha$. We encounter a number of hypothesis test statistics throughout the remainder of this book. The sampling distributions are always given and the values of the test statistic can be obtained from the tables at the end of this chapter or via the appropriate Excel function.

REVIEW QUESTIONS

1. Why is a test statistic a random variable?
2. Why is a confidence interval a random variable?
3. Which is more informative: a hypothesis test or a confidence interval? Why?
4. Explain the difference between a type I error and a type II error.
5. What do you feel is an acceptable significance level for your OR practice and why?
6. Calculate a 95 percent confidence interval around the estimate of the mean in Case Study 6.1.
   - Investigate what happens to the width of the interval for a 99 percent and 90 percent confidence interval, respectively.
   - Supposing $N = 10$ in Case Study 6.1, would Stephan's conclusion have been different?
   - What happens when $N = 1000$?

FURTHER READING

To gain a full appreciation of the pros and cons of classical hypothesis testing, you need to read Chatfield (1985), Clark (1963), Carver (1993), Levin (1993), and Wilcox (1998). Applications in other areas of risk management are given in Lewis (2003).

CHAPTER 7

Severity of Loss Probability Models

Fitting a probability distribution to data on the severity of loss arising from an OR event is an important task in any statistically based modeling of operational risk. The observed data to be modeled may consist of actual values recorded by a business line, or may be the result of a simulation. In fitting a probability model to empirical data, the general approach is first to select a general class of probability distributions and then find the values for the distributional parameters that best match the observed data. In this chapter we discuss the entire process of how to select, estimate, and assess suitable probability models for the severity of loss arising from an OR event.

NORMAL DISTRIBUTION

We begin our discussion of severity models with the normal distribution. A continuous random variable X is said to follow a normal distribution with mean μ and standard deviation σ if it has the probability density function given by

$$f(x) = \frac{1}{\sqrt{2\pi\sigma^2}} \exp\left(-\frac{1}{2\sigma^2}(x - \mu)^2\right) \quad -\infty < x < \infty$$

If $\mu = 0$ and $\sigma = 1$, the distribution is known as the *standard normal distribution*. The standard normal distribution is illustrated in Figure 7.1. The normal distribution is bell-shaped and symmetric around μ, the mean. This implies a normally distributed random variable has zero skew and the median and mode equal μ, the mean. The distribution has a kurtosis equal to 3.

The formula for the normal probability density function actually defines a family of distributions depending on the parameters μ and σ. The parameter μ is known as a *location parameter* because changing the mean shifts the curve along the x axis, as shown in Figure 7.2. The parameter σ

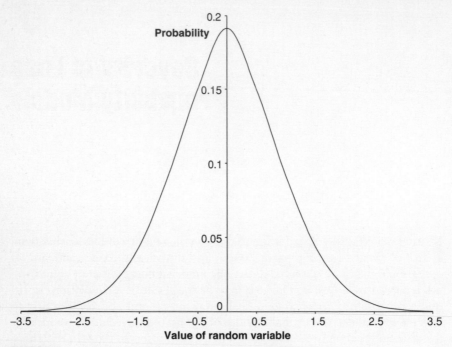

FIGURE 7.1   Standard normal probability distribution.

is known as a *scale parameter* because changing the standard deviation changes the spread of the curve, as illustrated in Figure 7.3.

Open the spreadsheet *Normal Distribution* in the workbook Operational Risk 07.xls. It provides an interactive example of this phenomenon. Experiment with differing values of the standard deviation (cell C8), and note how the distribution flattens as the value increases and becomes more peaked as the value decreases. Do the same thing with the mean (cell C7), and notice how the location of the distribution moves along the horizontal axis.

PARAMETERS OF PROBABILITY DISTRIBUTIONS

The most flexible probability distributions will have parameters for location, scale, and shape. The location parameter controls where on the horizontal axis the distribution is centered, the scale parameter controls the spread of probability around the center of the distribution, and the shape parameter controls the shape of the distribution. The normal distribution only has parameters for location and scale.

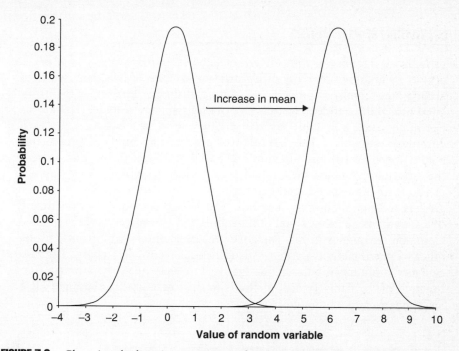

FIGURE 7.2 Changing the location parameter of a Normality distributed random variable.

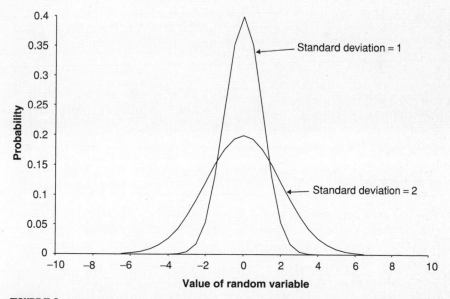

FIGURE 7.3 Changing the scale parameter of a Normality distributed random variable.

ESTIMATION OF PARAMETERS

Probability distributions are determined by their parameters. In order to obtain a suitable probability model for our severity of loss data, we need, among other things, to obtain an estimate of the parameters of the postulated probability model. How can we obtain such an estimate? The answer lies in choosing a suitable estimator. There are three basic categories of parameter estimation. The first involves plotting the empirical data against a cumulative probability function on special graphical paper. The value of the estimated parameters can then be read off the graphical plot. Graphical methods are often used because of their simplicity and speed. However, they are less accurate than other methods. The second category involves the use of a system of equations equal to the number of parameters to be estimated. Common techniques in this category are the method of moments, probability weighted methods, order statistics, and percentile matching. The third category is optimization methods that seek to maximize or minimize some function of the data. Typical methods in this category are the methods of least squares and maximum likelihood.

THE DIFFERENCE BETWEEN AN ESTIMATOR AND AN ESTIMATE

To illustrate the difference between an estimator and an estimate, consider the *estimator* for the arithmetic mean of a sample of N observations on a random variable X that follows the normal distribution

$$\overline{X} = \frac{1}{N} \sum_{i=1}^{N} x_i$$

If for a specific sample $\overline{X} = 2.3$, then 2.3 is our *estimate*.[1] In practice, the form of an estimator will depend on which probability distribution is selected as the most suitable for a given sample.

BETA DISTRIBUTION

The standard beta distribution is most useful when the severity of loss is expressed as a proportion. Given a continuous random variable x, such that $0 \le x \le 1$, the probability density function of the standard beta distribution is given by

$$f(x) = \frac{x^{\alpha-1}(1 - x)^{\beta-1}}{B(\alpha, \beta)}$$

where

$$B(\alpha, \beta) \ = \ \int\limits_0^1 u^{\alpha-1}(1-u)^{\beta-1}du, \ \alpha \ > \ 0, \ \beta \ > \ 0$$

The parameters α and β control the shape of the distribution. By their careful selection, as illustrated in Figures 7.4 and 7.5, it is possible to achieve a very wide variety of density shapes.

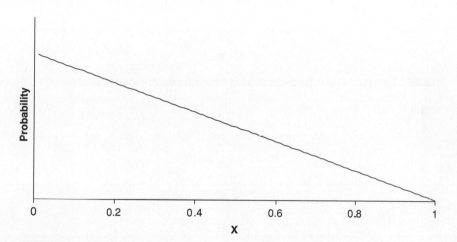

FIGURE 7.4a   Beta distribution of for various parameter values.

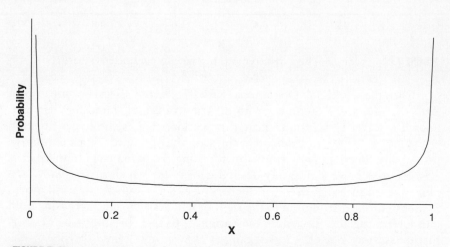

FIGURE 7.4b   Beta distribution of for various parameter values.

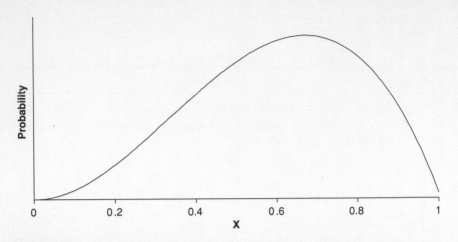

FIGURE 7.5a   Additional Beta distributions for various parameter values.

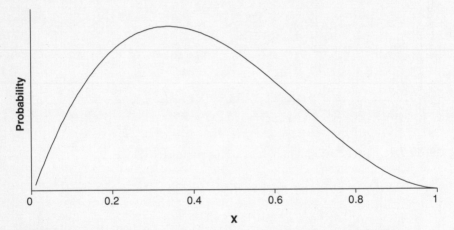

FIGURE 7.5b   Additional Beta distributions for various parameter values.

Open the workbook Operational Risk 07.xls, and select the spreadsheet *Beta Distribution*. Experiment with differing values of α and β What happens if $\alpha = \beta = 1$? Scrutinize how this worksheet uses the Excel function BETADIST(x, α, β) to calculate values of the standard beta cumulative probability function. Notice how by adjusting the parameters α and β, it is possible to achieve almost any desired density for which the random variable X lies in the range of 0 to 1. Increasing either parameter by itself moves the mean of the distribution to the right or left, respectively. Increasing both parameters together decreases the variance. In fact, by taking a transformation such as $Y = aX + b$, we can get almost any desired density on the interval $(b, a + b)$.

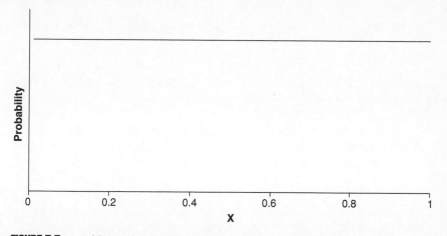

FIGURE 7.5c Additional Beta distributions for various parameter values.

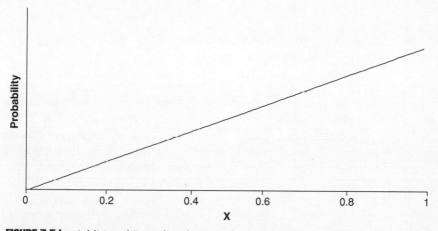

FIGURE 7.5d Additional Beta distributions for various parameter values.

The mean of the beta distribution is given by

$$\text{Mean} = \frac{\alpha}{(\alpha + \beta)}$$

and $\text{Standard deviation} = \sqrt{\dfrac{\alpha\beta}{(\alpha + \beta)^2\,(\alpha + \beta + 1)}}$

The parameters of this distribution can be easily estimated using the following (method of moments) equations:

$$\hat{\alpha} = \overline{X}\left[\left(\frac{\overline{X}(1 - \overline{X})}{S^2}\right) - 1\right] \qquad \hat{\beta} = (1 - \overline{X})\left[\left(\frac{\overline{X}(1 - \overline{X})}{S^2}\right) - 1\right]$$

The following VBA function can be used to obtain the parameter estimates of a beta distribution:

```
Function est_beta(data As Range, which As Boolean)
Dim mean As Double
Dim var As Double
Dim alpha As Double
Dim beta As Double
Dim temp As Double
Mean = Application.WorksheetFunction.Average(data)
var = Application.WorksheetFunction.var(data)
temp = ((mean * (1 - mean) / var) - 1)
If which = True Then est_beta = mean * temp
        ' return alpha
If which = False Then est_beta = (1 - mean) * temp
        ' return beta
End Function
```

The function will return an estimate of α if the which Boolean variable is set to True or β if it is set to False. For example est_beta(c1:c1000,True) will estimate α using data in cells C1 to C1000. To illustrate the application of this function, select the worksheet Beta Estimation in the workbook Operational Risk 07.xls. This worksheet uses the est_beta() function to estimate the parameters from simulated data from the standard beta distribution with known parameters. Enter values for the parameters α and β and press <F9> to run the simulation. Notice how the parameter estimates

---

GENERAL BETA DISTRIBUTION

In this section we have described the standard beta distribution. There is a more general beta distribution that can be used when the random variable x lies in the interval (a, b). The cumulative density function can be calculated in Excel using the function BETADIST(x,alpha, beta,a,b). The simulation in the worksheet Beta Estimation in the workbook Operational Risk 07.xls used the inverse beta function BETAINV(x,alpha,beta,a,b) with parameters BETAINV(RAND(),alpha, beta,0,1).

become closer to the actual values as the sample size increases. A sample of 1000 observations yields more accurate parameter estimates than a sample of only 10 observations. This raises the important point that when using estimators, increasing the number of observations used to obtain the estimate may substantially increase the accuracy of the estimate. As a rule of thumb, we should aim to collect at least 30 observations before attempting to estimate a severity of loss probability distribution.

ERLANG DISTRIBUTION

For continuous random variables where $0 \leq x \leq \infty$, the probability density function of the Erlang distribution is given by

$$f(x) = \frac{\left(\dfrac{x}{\alpha}\right)^{\beta-1} \exp\left(-\dfrac{x}{\alpha}\right)}{\alpha[(\beta - 1)!]}$$

with parameters $\alpha > 0$ and integer $\beta > 0$. The mean $= \alpha\beta$, and standard deviation $= \sqrt{\alpha^2\beta}$. Parameters of the distribution are estimated (method of moments) as

$$\hat{\alpha} = \frac{S^2}{\overline{X}} \text{ and } \hat{\beta} = \left(\frac{\overline{X}}{S}\right)^2$$

The Erlang distribution is closely related to the gamma distribution and we explore the impact of the parameters on the shape of the distribution in the section on the gamma distribution.

EXPONENTIAL DISTRIBUTION

For continuous random variables where $0 \leq x \leq \infty$, the probability density function of the exponential distribution is given by

$$f(x) = \frac{1}{\alpha} \exp\left(-\frac{x}{\alpha}\right)$$

where α is a scale parameter. The mean and standard deviation are equal to α, whereas the median is $\alpha \log 2$ and the mode is equal to 0. The distribution has a constant skew of 2 and kurtosis of 9. Since there is only one parameter, it can be easily estimated (maximum likelihood) by $\hat{\alpha} = \overline{X}^{-1}$ Figure 7.6 illustrates the exponential distribution with $\alpha = 1$. The worksheet Exponential Distribution in the workbook Operational Risk 07.xls allows you to explore how the distribution changes with differing values of α.

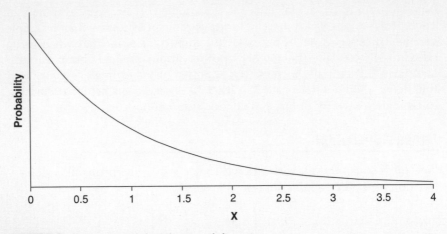

FIGURE 7.6 Exponential distribution alpha = 1.

GAMMA DISTRIBUTION

For continuous random variables where $0 \leq x \leq \infty$, the probability density function of the gamma distribution is given by

$$f(x) = \frac{\left(\dfrac{x}{\alpha}\right)^{\beta-1} \exp\left(-\dfrac{x}{\alpha}\right)}{\alpha \, \Gamma(\beta)}$$

where $\alpha > 0$ is a scale parameter and $\beta > 0$ is a shape parameter, and $\Gamma(\beta)$ is the gamma function given by $\Gamma(\beta) = \int_0^\infty \exp(-u)\, u^{\beta-1}\, du$. Thus, the gamma distribution is a generalization of the Erlang distribution where the parameter b is not restricted to be an integer. Figure 7.7 illustrates a gamma distribution with a = 5, and b = 0.5. You can explore the impact of changing the value of the parameters in the worksheet `Erlang & Gamma Distribution`.

The mean is equal to $\alpha\beta$ and the standard deviation, skew, and kurtosis are $\sqrt{\alpha^2\beta}$. Parameters can be estimated (method of moments) using the same estimator as for the gamma distribution:

$$\hat{\alpha} = \frac{s^2}{\overline{X}} \quad \text{and} \quad \hat{\beta} = \left(\frac{\overline{X}}{s}\right)^2, \text{ where } s \text{ is the sample standard deviation}$$

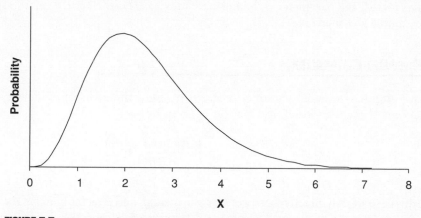

FIGURE 7.7 Gamma distribution alpha = 5, beta = 0.5.

The following VBA function can be used to obtain the parameter estimates:

```
Function est_gamma(data As Range, which As Boolean)
Dim mean As Double
Dim var As Double
Dim alpha As Double
Dim beta As Double
Dim temp As Double
mean = Application.WorksheetFunction.Average(data)
var = Application.WorksheetFunction.var(data)
If which = True Then est_gamma = var / mean
        ' return alpha
If which = False Then est_gamma = (mean / var ^ 0.5) ^ 2
        'return beta
End Function
```

The function will return an estimate of α if the which Boolean variable is set to True or β if it is set to False. For example est_gamma(c1:c1000,True) will estimate α using data in cells C1 to C1000. To illustrate the application of this function look at the worksheet Gamma Estimation in the workbook Operational Risk 07.xls. This worksheet uses the est_gamma function to estimate the parameters from simulated data from the gamma distribution with known parameters. Enter values for the parameters α and β and press <F9> to run the simulation.

As expected, the parameter estimates become closer to the actual values as the sample size increases.

LOGNORMAL DISTRIBUTION

For continuous random variables where $0 \le x \le \infty$, the probability density function of the lognormal distribution is given by

$$f(x) = \frac{1}{x\beta\sqrt{2\pi}} \; \exp\left(\frac{-[\log(x\,/\,\alpha)]^2}{2\beta^2}\right)$$

In this case we can directly interpret α as the median and β as the shape parameter. The mean is $\alpha\exp\left(\frac{1}{2}\beta^2\right)$ and the standard deviation is $\alpha\sqrt{(c^2 - c)}$ where $c = \exp\beta^2$. Parameters can be estimated (maximum likelihood) using

$$\hat{\alpha} = \exp\left(\frac{1}{n}\sum_{i=1}^{n}\log X_i\right) \text{ and } \hat{\beta} = \left[\frac{1}{(n-1)}\right]\sum_{i=1}^{n}\left(\log x_i - \log\hat{\alpha}\right)^2$$

Figure 7.8 illustrates the lognormal distribution with mean = 2 and standard deviation = 0.5. The worksheet `Lognormal Distribution` allows you to explore how the distribution changes with differing values of the parameters.

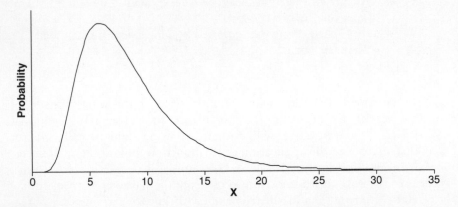

FIGURE 7.8 Lognormal distribution mean = 2, standard deviation = 0.5.

PARETO DISTRIBUTION

For continuous random variables where $1 \le x \le \infty$, the probability density function of the Pareto distribution is given by $f(x) = \alpha x^{-\alpha-1}$, where $\alpha < 0$ the is the shape parameter. The mean is $\dfrac{\alpha}{(\alpha - 1)}$, $\alpha > 1$, and the standard deviation is $\sqrt{\left(\dfrac{\alpha}{\alpha - 2}\right) - \left(\dfrac{\alpha}{\alpha - 1}\right)^2}$, $\alpha > 2$. Parameters can be estimated (maximum likelihood) using $\dfrac{1}{\hat{\alpha}} = \dfrac{1}{n} \sum_{i=1}^{n} \log x_i$.

WEIBULL DISTRIBUTION

The random variable X with probability density function

$$f(x) = \left(\frac{\beta x^{\beta - 1}}{\alpha^{\beta}}\right) \exp^{-(x / \alpha)^{\beta}}$$

for $x > 0$, has a Weibull distribution with scale parameter $\alpha > 0$ and shape parameter $\beta > 0$. Figure 7.9 illustrates the Weibull distribution with $\alpha = 10$ and $\beta = 5$. The worksheet Weibull Distribution allows you to explore how the distribution changes with differing values of the parameters.

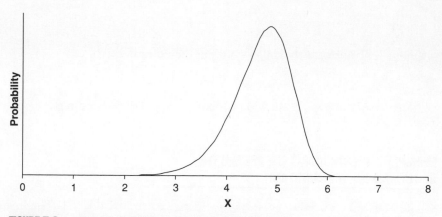

FIGURE 7.9 Weibull distribution alpha = 10, beta = 5.

For a sample of n observations $\{x_1, \ldots, x_n\}$, an estimate of α can be obtained as follows:

$$\hat{\alpha} = \exp\left(\tilde{Y} - \frac{\tilde{X}}{\hat{\beta}}\right)$$

where

$$\tilde{X} = \frac{1}{n} \sum_{i=1}^{n} \ln\left[\ln\frac{1}{\left(1 - \dfrac{i}{n+1}\right)}\right] \text{ and } \tilde{Y} = \frac{1}{n} \sum_{i=1}^{n} \ln x_i$$

To complete the calculation, we require an estimate of β. This can be achieved as follows:

Step 1: Calculate the mean rank P_i:

$$P_i = \frac{\text{rank}(x_i) - 0.3}{n - 0.4}$$

and

$$P_n = \frac{n}{n + \delta}$$

where δ is a small positive number that is 1E-15. The rank can be calculated using the Excel function Rank().

Step 2: Calculate the transformed rank T_i:

$$T_i = \ln\frac{1}{1 - P_i}$$

Step 3: Transform the data by taking the natural log:

$$y_i = \ln(x_i)$$

Step 4: Use the excel function Slope(Ti's,yi's) to obtain $\hat{\beta}$.

EXAMPLE 7.1 ESTIMATING THE PARAMETERS OF THE WEIBULL DISTRIBUTION

To illustrate this procedure, consider the data shown in Table 7.1. The first column shows the actual data. The second column shows the corresponding rank. The third column gives the values for P_i. For example,

TABLE 7.1 Calculation Required for Estimation of Weibull Parameters

Original Data	Rank	P_i	T_i	ln (x)
0.438	1	0.04795	−3.01323	−0.82554
2.413	2	0.11644	−2.08913	0.88087
3.073	3	0.18493	−1.58727	1.12265
3.079	4	0.25342	−1.23012	1.12460
3.137	5	0.32192	−0.94550	1.14327
3.198	6	0.39041	−0.70326	1.16253
3.918	7	0.45890	−0.48750	1.36558
4.287	8	0.52740	−0.28835	1.45559
4.508	9	0.59589	−0.09864	1.50585
4.981	10	0.66438	0.08782	1.60563
5.115	11	0.73288	0.27767	1.63218
5.592	12	0.80137	0.48015	1.72134
5.848	13	0.86986	0.71254	1.76610
5.958	14	0.93836	1.02474	1.78473
6.013	15	1.00000	3.60378	1.79392

$$P_1 = \frac{\text{rank}(x_1) - 0.3}{n - 0.4} = \frac{1 - 0.3}{n - 0.4} = 0.0$$

The forth column gives the values of the natural logarithm of the original data (first column). Table 7.2 shows the estimate of the parameter values, alongside the values of $\overline{X}$ *and* $\overline{Y}$

OTHER PROBABILITY DISTRIBUTIONS

There are a very wide variety of probability models that could be used for modeling the severity of loss. Examples include logistic, Cauchy, LogLogistic, Chi LogWeibull, Cobb-Douglas, Lorentz, Maxwell, and Fisk probability distributions. Since the severity of loss is bounded by 0, symmetric distributions such as the normal, Cauchy, and logistic distributions may not be suitable choices.[2] We have restricted our attention to those probability dis-

TABLE 7.2 Estimates of Weibull Parameters and Intermediate Values

$\hat{\beta}$	1.814
$\hat{\alpha}$	4.784
$\overline{X}$	−0.5128
$\overline{Y}$	1.2826

tributions that we have found to be flexible, accurate, and relatively easy to fit to simulated or empirical data.

WHAT DISTRIBUTION BEST FITS MY SEVERITY OF LOSS DATA?

In estimating the parameters of a number of potential probability distributions, we will eventually need to decide which, if any, best represent our observations. There are two basic approaches to answer this question. The first involves drawing a graph known as a *probability plot*. The second approach involves the use of formal statistical hypothesis testing.

Probability Plot

A probability plot is a graphical technique for determining if sample data comes from a specific probability distribution. It is a plot of the quartiles (or percentages) of points below a given value of the sample data set against the quartiles of the postulated probability distribution. A straight line (known as the *reference line*) is also plotted. If the sample comes from the postulated probability distribution, the plotted points will fall along this reference line. Departures from the reference line indicate departures from

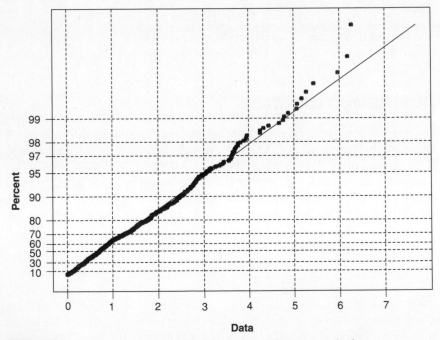

FIGURE 7.10 Exponential Probability Plot for well fitting sample data.

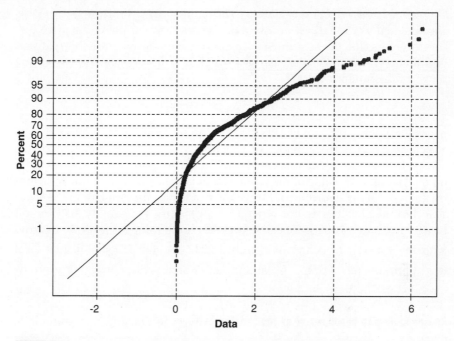

FIGURE 7.11 Exponential Probability plot for poorly fitting sample data.

the specified distribution. Figure 7.10 illustrates an exponential probability plot for a sample data set. In this case the data points lie close to the reference line and we conclude that an exponential probability distribution is an acceptable probability model for this data. Figure 7.11 illustrates an exponential probability plot for the situation in which the data does not appear to follow an exponential distribution. In this case the data points do not lie close to the reference line, and an alternative probability model will need to be selected.

Formal Test Statistics

There are numerous test statistics for assessing the fit of a postulated severity of loss probability model to empirical data. In this section we focus on two of the most general: the Kolmogorov-Smirnov goodness of fit test and the Anderson-Darling goodness of fit test. In discussing these two test statistics, we shall assume we have a sample of N observations on the severity of loss random variable X. Furthermore, we will be interested in testing H_0: Samples come from the postulated probability distribution, against H_1: Samples do not come from the postulated probability distribution.

Kolmogorov-Smirnov goodness of fit test: The Kolmogorov-Smirnov test statistic is calculated as the largest absolute deviation between the cumulative distribution function of the sample data and the cumulative probability distribution function of the postulated probability density function over the range of the random variable:

$$T = \max \left| S_N(x) - F(x) \right|$$

over all x, where the cumulative distribution function of the sample data is $S_N(x)$, and $F(x)$ is the cumulative probability distribution function of the postulated probability density function. The Kolmogorov-Smirnov test relies on the fact that the value of the sample cumulative density function is asymptotically normally distributed. Hence the test is distribution free in the sense that the critical values do not depend on the specific probability distribution being tested. For a 10% significance level the critical value for the Kolmogorov-Smirnov test statistic is approximately $1.224/\sqrt{N}$, for 5% significance level it is approximately $1.358/\sqrt{N}$, and for a 1% significance level it is approximately $1.628/\sqrt{N}$.

Anderson-Darling goodness of fit test: The Anderson-Darling test statistic is given by

$$\hat{T} = -N - \frac{1}{N} \sum_{i=1}^{N} 2(i-1)\{\ln F(\tilde{x}_i) + \ln[1 - F(\tilde{x}_{N+1-i})]\}$$

where $\tilde{x}_i$ are the ordered by size sample data. It is a modification of the Kolmogorov-Smirnov test that is more sensitive to deviations in the tails of the postulated probability distribution. It achieves this added sensitivity by making use of the specific postulated distribution in calculating critical values. Unfortunately, this extra sensitivity comes at the cost of having to calculate critical values for *each* postulated distribution. For example, if we postulate a normal distribution for our data, then for a 10 percent significance level the critical value is approximately 0.631, for a 5 percent significance level it is 0.752, and for a 1 percent significance level it is 1.035. However, if we postulate a Weibull distribution, then the critical value for a 10 percent significance level the critical value is 0.637, for a 5 percent significance level it is 0.757, and for a 1 percent significance level it is 1.038.

CASE STUDY 7.1: MODELING SEVERITY OF LEGAL LIABILITY LOSSES

Table 7.3 shows the legal liability losses (measured in pounds Sterling) of a financial institution. Table 7.4 presents the statistical characteristics, and

TABLE 7.3 Legal Liability Losses for a Financial Institution

£45,457.72	£214,368.33	£55,008.91	£186,097.42	£260,375.11	£192,734.99
£319,574.15	£291,854.21	£677,797.15	£376,122.45	£11,020.21	£215,612.22
£13,476.34	£11,238.92	£375,798.31	£21,512.68	£22,005.92	£116,020.84
£239,542.60	£84,264.07	£7,695.82	£125,772.44	£46,965.45	£44,695.30
£49,852.51	£8,251.00	£191,892.23	£103,984.82	£73,633.52	£166,319.02
£112,367.19	£2,925.20	£64,517.17	£21,475.51	£460,861.10	£19,460.71
£112,964.44	£87,430.52	£68,867.22	£606,086.68	£51,541.79	£126,015.11
£121,936.07	£378,068.07	£22,209.74	£189,120.36	£40,925.99	£255,876.89
£331,168.35	£514,502.77	£7,164.50	£79,425.85	£183,104.87	£394,002.33
£186,043.30	£220,825.91	£213,582.12	£63,243.13	£70,100.90	£5,136.23
£188,713.75	£110,627.92	£114,511.58	£106,674.73	£13,584.55	£151,326.54
£545,837.15	£52,224.61	£27,940.46	£14,182.63	£4,707.90	£2,754.23
£51,668.72	£308,479.08	£707,734.82	£45,162.70	£199,784.16	£48,891.19
£102,553.18	£51,360.39	£42,013.46	£159,030.78	£109,489.79	£411,160.62
£1,255,736.19	£399,251.55	£66,681.67	£150,726.18	£279,630.93	£22,322.99
£25,615.32	£180,907.21	£241,691.87	£161,950.80	£171,992.38	£21,278.36
£35,143.21	£169,753.33	£276,554.41	£127,024.01	£83,209.51	£346,524.34
£129,854.17	£181,396.37	£39,293.09	£166,502.54	£68,929.68	£208,969.85
£6,155.91	£20,510.31	£144,190.61	£18,224.26	£149,043.99	£58,910.57
£22,456.23	£25,417.34	£13,590.82	£98,277.79	£82,322.75	£58,510.25
£30,178.48	£150,950.47	£93,453.08	£281,012.41	£76,766.50	
£64,264.76	£268,416.52	£103,060.97	£111,249.87	£261,539.04	
£7,117.74	£451,384.30	£59,260.91	£80,543.89	£326,492.18	
£56,025.11	£25,766.68	£108,325.56	£140,874.19	£36,622.85	

TABLE 7.4 Statistical Characteristics of Legal Liability Losses

Mean	£151,944.04
Median	£103,522.90
Standard deviation	£170,767.06
Skew	2.84
Kurtosis	12.81

Figure 7.12 illustrates the corresponding histogram. Several interesting points are evident. First, the mean of the sample is considerably larger than the median, which is reflected in a coefficient of skew equal to 2.83. Second, the losses are very fat tailed, with a kurtosis in excess of 12.

Since the losses are not symmetric, we would not expect them to come from a normal distribution. This is confirmed in the probability plot of Figure 7.13, for which the Anderson-Darling test statistic is 8.09. As the mean of the data lies close to the standard deviation, and given the shape of the histogram shown in Figure 7.12, we postulate that the data comes from an exponential distribution. This appears to be confirmed in the probability plot of Figure 7.14, for which the Anderson-Darling test statistic is 0.392. Therefore, we conclude that an exponential distribution with $\alpha = 151,944.04$ adequately describes this data. Figure 7.15 shows the fitted exponential distribution against a histogram of the actual data.

Is this the only distribution that can fit this data reasonably well? The answer is probably not. To see this, consider Figure 7.16, which shows a

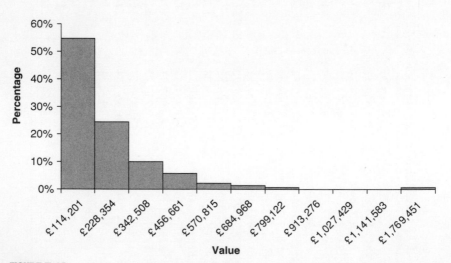

FIGURE 7.12 Histogram of legal event losses.

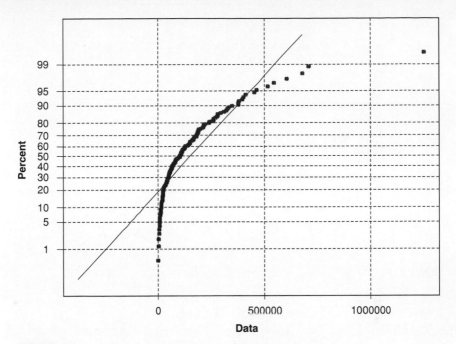

FIGURE 7.13 Normal Probability Plot for legal event losses.

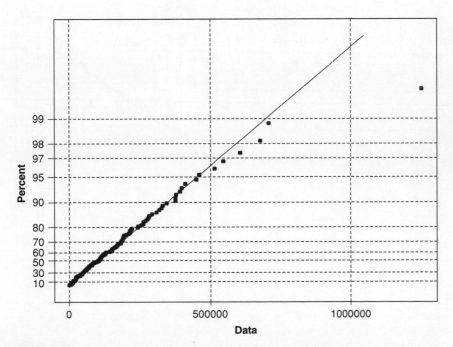

FIGURE 7.14 Exponential Probability Plot for legal event losses.

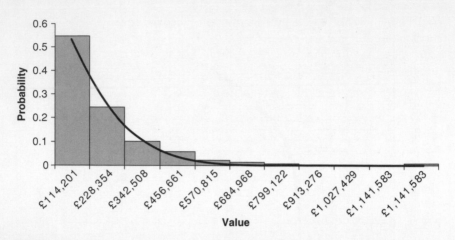

FIGURE 7.15   Fitted Exponential distribution(solid line) and legal event losses.

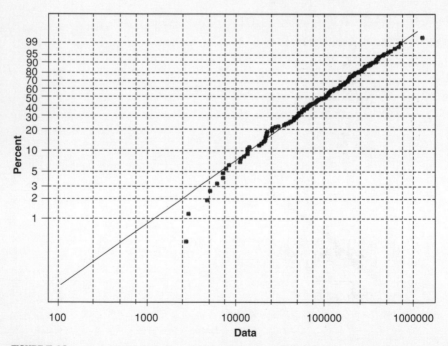

FIGURE 7.16   Weibull Probability Plot for legal event losses.

probability plot for the Weibull distribution. The plot appears to indicate that the Weibull distribution fits the data at least as well as the exponential distribution. Furthermore, the Anderson-Darling test statistic is only 0.267. Should we use the exponential distribution or the Weibull distribution? One argument in favor of the exponential distribution is that it depends on only one parameter and is therefore more parsimonious than a Weibull distribution. However, given that we have less than 200 observations (with more coming in the future), the added flexibility of the Weibull distribution provides an argument for choosing it.

SUMMARY

Fitting appropriate severity of loss probability models is a central task in operational risk modeling. It involves first selecting an appropriate probability distribution from a wide range of possible distributions and then assessing how well the selected model explains the empirical losses. Statistical or graphical methods can be used to assess model fit. Although much of this work can be carried out in Excel, it will also be necessary to write additional statistical functions and estimators in VBA. In the following chapter we continue with the theme of fitting probability distributions to empirical data, considering the frequency of events rather than their severity.

REVIEW QUESTIONS

1. Why is the normal probability distribution not necessarily a good choice for modeling severity of losses? Under what circumstances would you envisage using the normal distribution?
2. Given loss data which lies between the range of $0 and $75,000, what transformation do you need to apply before you could fit the standard beta distribution?
    ■ Calculate the mean, standard deviation, skew and kurtosis of the following loss data:

$ 4,695.11	$ 147.86	$24,757.17	$12,928.33
$ 9,073.66	$ 215.62	$13,647.10	$ 8,283.56
$19,353.32	$ 2,965.99	$ 9,510.18	$ 3,981.05
$15,669.64	$ 5,976.45	$ 1,643.43	$ 5,002.29
$ 4,354.27	$ 8,003.83	$ 664.28	$ 1,232.87
$13,817.18	$21,502.09	$ 5,128.66	$ 9,403.65
$ 384.13	$10,270.70	$ 7,993.91	$ 4,504.84
$ 8,386.20	$23,631.04	$ 1,690.75	$ 3,759.90
$17,237.93	$ 4,508.38	$ 1,915.58	$15,211.48
$ 745.39	$ 6,841.31	$ 3,385.31	$ 3,690.16

- Given your estimates, which probability models of those given in this chapter can you rule out as being unsuitable for modeling this data?
3. Fit the beta, lognormal, and normal probability functions to the above data and determine which (if any) of the fitted distributions is adequate for this data.
4. Explain the difference between an estimator and an estimate.
5. Suppose X follows a beta distribution. Create a worksheet to illustrate that using the following transformation $Y = aX + b$, we can get almost any shaped density on the interval $(b, a + b)$.

FURTHER READING

Details of the distributions given in this chapter and many others can be found in Gumbel (1954), Aitchison and Brown (1957), Ascher (1981), Hahn and Shapiro (1967), Johnson et al. (1994, 1995), and Lewis (2003). Further information on goodness of fit tests can be found in Press et al. (1995).

CHAPTER 8

Frequency of Loss Probability Models

In the previous chapter we learned how to estimate and assess severity of loss probability models. In this chapter we focus on frequency of loss models. The entity of interest for frequency of loss modeling will be a discrete random variable that represents the number of OR events observed. These events will occur with some probability p.[1]

Our discussion begins with three popular frequency of loss probability models: the binomial distribution, the Poisson distribution, and the negative binomial distribution. This is followed by a discussion of alternatives to these models. Since assessing the goodness of fit of a postulated frequency of loss probability model is an important issue, we introduce a formal test statistic known as the chi-squared goodness of fit test. This is followed by a detailed case study used to illustrate the process of building a frequency of loss probability model.

POPULAR FREQUENCY OF LOSS PROBABILITY MODELS

Three useful probability distributions for characterizing frequency of loss are the binomial distribution, the Poisson distribution, and the negative binomial distribution. We discuss the characteristics of these distributions and show how their parameters can be estimated.

Binomial Distribution

If x $(0 \leq x \leq N)$ is the number of successes over N trials, then the binomial probability function is given by

$$f(x) = \frac{N!}{x! \, (N - x)!} \, p^x \, (1 - p)^x$$

The mean is given by

$$\overline{X} = Np$$

and standard deviation by

$$\sigma = \sqrt{Np\,(1 - p)}$$

Figure 8.1 illustrates a binomial distribution with $N = 12$ and various values of p. You can experiment with differing values of N and p by open-

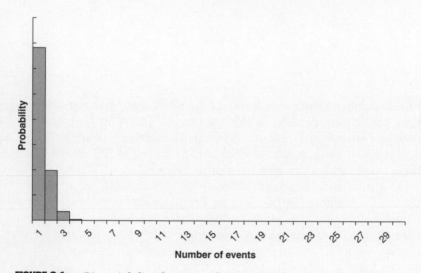

FIGURE 8.1a   Binomial distribution with $N = 12$ and various values of p.

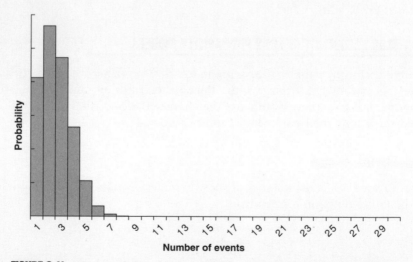

FIGURE 8.1b   Binomial distribution with $N = 12$ and various values of p.

ing the spreadsheet Operational Risk 08.xls and selecting the worksheet BINO. Notice that as N increases, the distribution becomes increasingly symmetric. Also note that for small values of N or very large (or very small) values of p, the distribution is skewed. The parameter p can be estimated by maximum likelihood:

$$\hat{p} = \frac{x}{N}$$

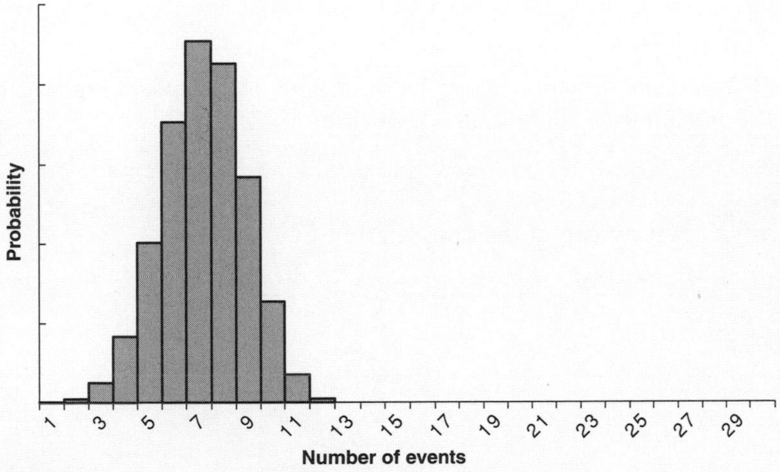

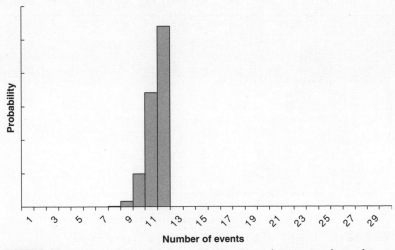

FIGURE 8.1c   Binomial distribution with $N = 12$ and various values of p.

FIGURE 8.1d   Binomial distribution with $N = 12$ and various values of p.

Poisson Distribution

The probability density function of the Poisson distribution is given by

$$f(x) = \lambda^x \frac{\exp\ (-\lambda)}{x!}$$

where $x \geq 0$ and the parameter $\lambda > 0$ can be interpreted as the arithmetic mean. Figure 8.2 illustrates this distribution for $\lambda = 4$ and $\lambda = 11$. You can investigate the impact of differing values of λ on the shape of the distribution by opening the spreadsheet Operational Risk 08.xls and selecting the worksheet POISSON.

The standard deviation is $\sqrt{\lambda}$. Estimation of the parameter can be carried out by maximum likelihood, in which case

$$\hat{\lambda} = \tilde{X}$$

where $\tilde{X}$ is the mean of the sample given by

$$\tilde{X} = \frac{\sum_{i=0}^{U_L} i n_i}{\sum_{i=0}^{U_L} n_i}$$

where n_i is the observed number of observations in category i and U_L is some empirically determined upper limit.

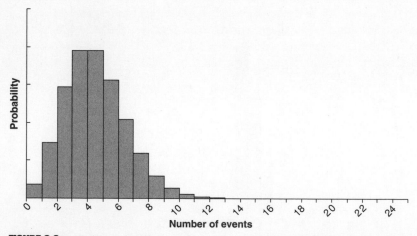

FIGURE 8.2a Poisson distribution for various parameter values.

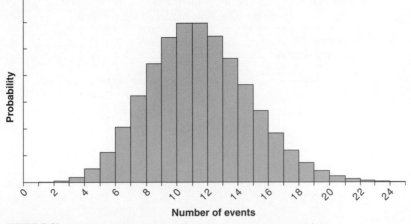

FIGURE 8.2b   Poisson distribution for various parameter values.

EXAMPLE 8.1 A FREQUENCY OF LOSS MODEL FOR CREDIT CARD FRAUD

To illustrate the estimation process for the Poisson model, consider the frequency of loss daily data for a specific type of credit card fraud, shown in Table 8.1. The first column shows the potential number of frauds of this type per day beginning at 0 and ending at 15. Thus, in this case $U_L = 15$. The second column shows the actual number of frauds. The third column is the kth row in the first column multiplied by kth row in the second column. For example, the second row of the first column is equal to 1 and the second row of the second column is equal to 16; therefore, the second row of the third column is equal to $16 \times 1 = 16$. Therefore, the sum of the third column is $\sum_{i=0}^{15} in_i = 352$. We also see that in total there are 124 observations; therefore, $\sum_{i=0}^{15} n_i = 124$ and thus the estimate of the parameter of the distribution is

$$\hat{\lambda} = \frac{\sum_{i=0}^{15} in_i}{\sum_{i=0}^{15} n_i} = \frac{352}{124} = 2.84$$

TABLE 8.1 Summary of Frequency of Loss Daily Data
for a Specific Type of Credit Card Fraud

Number of events per day	Observed frauds	$i \times n_i$
0	19	0
1	16	16
2	51	102
3	9	27
4	6	24
5	5	25
6	4	24
7	6	42
8	2	16
9	1	9
10	0	0
11	0	0
12	2	24
13	1	13
14	0	0
15	2	30

Negative Binomial Distribution

The negative binomial distribution is a popular alternative to the Poisson distribution. In fact, it is very closely related to the Poisson, Pascal, and geometric distributions. The probability function is given by

$$f(x) = \binom{x + y - 1}{y} p^x (1 - p)^y$$

This is similar to the binomial distribution except that the number of events is fixed and the number of trials (N in the binomial distribution) is variable. The Excel function Negbinomdist() can be used to calculate the probabilities of this distribution. The mean is $x(1-p)/p$, and the standard deviation

is $\sqrt{\dfrac{x(1 - p)}{p^2}}$. An unbiased estimator of the parameter p is

$$\hat{p} = \frac{x}{yx + x}$$

OTHER FREQUENCY OF LOSS DISTRIBUTIONS

Geometric, hypergeometric, Pascal, Polya-Aeplli, Poisson inverse Gaussian, Hofmann, Neymann Type A, and Neymann Type A plus Poisson are just

---

CHOOSING BETWEEN THE BINOMIAL, NEGATIVE BINOMIAL AND POISSON DISTRIBUTIONS

A useful rule of thumb for choosing between these popular distributions is to note that for the binomial distribution the variance is less than the arithmetic mean, for the Poisson distribution the variance is equal to the arithmetic mean and for the negative binomial distribution the variance is greater than the arithmetic mean. Thus, if we observe that our sample variance is much larger than the sample mean, the negative binomial distribution may be an appropriate choice.

some of a very large number of alternative distributions to the binomial, negative binomial, and Poisson distributions. In this section we review three of these that find occasional use. They are the geometric distribution, the hypergeometric distribution, and the Pascal distribution.

Geometric Distribution

For an integer random variable where $x \geq 1$, the probability density function of the geometric distribution is given by

$$f(x) = p(1 - p)^{x-1}$$

The mean is $1/p$ and standard deviation is $\sqrt{\dfrac{(1 - p)}{p^2}}$. A maximum likelihood estimator of the parameter p is

$$\hat{p} = \frac{1}{x}$$

Hypergeometric Distribution

The hypergeometric distribution is given by

$$f(x) = \frac{\dbinom{X}{n}\dbinom{N - X}{n - x}}{\dbinom{N}{n}}$$

where n is the sample size, N is the number of groups in the population of interest, and X is the number of events/ failures or other events of interest.

The mean is $\dfrac{nX}{N}$, and the standard deviation is $\sqrt{\dfrac{\left(n\,{}^{X}\!/\!_{N}\right)\left(1 - {}^{X}\!/\!_{N}\right)(N - n)}{(N - 1)}}$.

A maximum likelihood estimator of N is

$$\hat{N} = \frac{nX}{x}$$

Pascal Distribution

If the number of events is greater than or equal to 1, a Pascal probability distribution may be appropriate. The probability function is given by

$$f(x) = \binom{n - 1}{n - x} p^x (1 - p)^{n - x}$$

where x is the event parameter. The mean of the Pascal distribution is $\overline{X} = x\,/\,p$, and the standard deviation is $\sigma = \dfrac{\sqrt{xp}}{p}$. An unbiased estimator of the parameter is given by

$$\hat{p} = \frac{x - 1}{n - 1}$$

CHI-SQUARED GOODNESS OF FIT TEST

Too often, a particular frequency of loss distribution is chosen for no reason other than the risk manager's familiarity with it. As we have seen, a wide number of alternative distributions are always available, each generating a different pattern of probabilities. It is important, therefore, that the probability distribution be chosen with appropriate attention to the degree to which it fits the empirical data. The choice as to which distribution to use can be based on visual inspection of the fitted distribution against the actual data or a formal statistical test such as the chi-squared goodness of fit test. For the chi-squared goodness of fit test, the null hypothesis is

H_0: The data follow a specified distribution

and the alternative hypothesis is

H_1: The data do not follow the specified distribution

The test statistic is calculated by dividing the data into n bins and is defined as

$$\tilde{T} = \sum_{i=1}^{n} \frac{(O_i - E_i)^2}{E_i}$$

where O_i is the observed number of events, E_i is the expected number of events determined by the postulated frequency of loss probability distribution, and n is the number of categories. The test statistic is a measure of how different the observed frequencies are from the expected frequencies. It has a chi-squared distribution with $n - (k - 1)$ degrees of freedom, where k refers to the number of parameters that need to be estimated.

EXAMPLE 8.2 GOODNESS OF FIT TEST FOR FITTING FAILURES IN A CRITICAL BACK OFFICE SYSTEM

As a example of the calculation of this statistic consider Table 8.2, which shows the observed and actual number of failures per day of a critical back office transaction-processing system. Using this data, the chi-squared test statistic is calculated as

$$\tilde{T} = \sum_{i=1}^{n} \frac{(O_i - E_i)}{E_i} = \frac{(56 - 60)^2}{60} + \frac{(52 - 40)^2}{40} + \frac{(92 - 100)^2}{100}$$

Since $n = 3$ and there are no parameters to be estimated, the test statistic has a chi-squared distribution with 2 degrees of freedom. Thus, given a significance level of 5 percent, the critical value of this test statistic using the function Chiinv(0.05,2) = 5.99 (we could also look up the value in Table A2 in Appendix 1). Since the test statistic is less than the critical value, we fail to reject the null hypothesis and conclude that there is no evidence to support the alternative hypothesis that the observed distribution is significantly different from the expected distribution.

TABLE 8.2 Observed and Actual Number of Failures per Day of a Critical Back Office System

Number failures per day	Observed	Expected
0	56	60
1	52	40
2	92	100

TABLE 8.3 Number of Back Office Staff Leaving per Month

Numbers leaving per month	Observed
0	18
1	20
2	21
3	11
4	4
5	1

CASE STUDY 8.1: KEY PERSONNEL RISK

An important source of operational risk arises when there is high turnover in back office transaction-processing employees. High turnover may have an impact on the smooth processing of transactions. Table 8.3 lists the actual number of back office staff who left a particular company organized by category. This particular institution had a total back office staff of around 50 people over the period under consideration. Interestingly, over the 75 months for which measurements were available, there was one month in which five people left and 18 months in which nobody left.

In Figure 8.3 we fit a Poisson distribution to this data. The parameter λ is estimated as 1.55. What does this figure tell us? It reflects the observation that there has been a constant turnover in staff of between one or two people per month. In Figure 8.3 the Poisson distribution appears visually to fit the data fairly well. This is confirmed in the chi-squared test statistic $\hat{T} = 1.51$, which is less than the critical value of 3.84 at 5 percent significance (see Table A2 in Appendix 1). Thus, we conclude that the Poisson distribution with parameter of 1.55 is a suitable frequency model for the observed data.

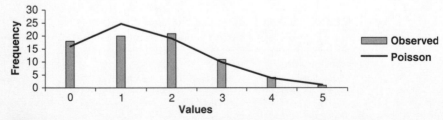

FIGURE 8.3 Actual Poisson fitted values for back office turnover risk.

SUMMARY

In this chapter we have considered how to model the frequency of loss arising from an operational loss. The discussion followed a similar approach to that taken in modeling the severity of loss. We begin by postulating a discrete probability distribution such as the Poisson or negative binomial distribution. Then we assess the goodness of fit of the postulated distribution against empirical observations. Goodness of fit can be assessed using formal test statistics such as the chi-squared goodness of fit test and/or visual inspection of the fitted distribution to the empirical data. In the next chapter we illustrate how to use the severity and frequency of loss distributions to obtain the aggregate loss distribution and thus to arrive at an estimate of operational value at risk.

REVIEW QUESTIONS

1. Create a spreadsheet using the Excel function Negbinomdist() that allows you to investigate how the shape of the negative binomial distribution changes as the values of its parameters are altered.
2. Write a VBA function to calculate the mean and variance of the hypergeometric probability distribution.
3. Why do you think the negative binomial distribution is popular for modeling frequency of loss?

FURTHER READING

Comprehensive details on the characteristics and estimation of a wide range of alternative probability distributions such as the Polya-Aeplli, with useful examples, can be found in Arbous and Kerrich (1951), Sharma (1988), Johnson et al. (1994, 1995), and Lewis (2003).

CHAPTER 9

Modeling Aggregate Loss Distributions

Even a cursory look at the operational risk literature reveals that measuring and modeling aggregate loss distributions are central to operational risk management practice. Since the daily operations of doing business have considerable risk, quantification in terms of an aggregate loss distribution is an important objective. A number of approaches have been developed to calculate the aggregate loss distribution. We begin this chapter by examining various approaches. We go on to give details of a practical Monte Carlo simulation–based approach from which we can also obtain an estimate of operational value at risk (OPVaR). However, OPVaR certainly is not the only risk measure of interest to operational risk managers and analysts. We discuss its limitations, outline the optimal criteria for a risk metric, and then introduce the risk measure known as expected shortfall (ES).

AGGREGATING SEVERITY OF LOSS AND FREQUENCY OF LOSS DISTRIBUTIONS

Even though in practice we may not have access to a historical sample of aggregate losses, it is possible to create sample values that represent aggregate OR losses given a severity and frequency of loss probability model. Using frequency and severity of loss data, we can simulate aggregate operational risk losses and then use these simulated losses to inform operational risk practice. The simplest way to obtain the aggregate loss distribution is to collect data on frequency and severity of losses for a particular operational risk type and then fit frequency and severity of loss models to the data. The aggregate loss distribution then can be found by combining the distributions for severity and frequency of operational losses over a fixed period such as a year. To see how this is accomplished, suppose N is a random variable representing the number of OR events between time t and $t + \delta$ with associated probability mass function $p(N)$; thus, $p(N)$ denotes the probability of exactly N losses in the time interval between t and $t + \delta$. Also, let X be a random variable representing the amount of loss arising from a single type of OR event with associated severity of loss probability density function $f(x)$. Provided we assume the frequency of events N is independent of the severity of events, the total loss from the specific type of OR event between time t and $t + \delta$ is

$$S = X_1 + X_2 + \cdots + X_N$$

The probability distribution function of S is a compound probability distribution:

$$G(x) = \begin{cases} \sum_{i=1}^{\infty} p(i) \times F^{i*}(x) & x > 0 \\ p(i) & x = 0 \end{cases}$$

where $F(x)$ is the probability that the aggregate amount of i losses is x, $*$ is the convolution operator on the functions F, and F^{i*} is the i-fold convolution of F with itself. For most distributions, $G(x)$ cannot be evaluated exactly and it must be evaluated numerically using methods such as Panjer's recursive algorithm or Monte Carlo simulation.

Panjer's recursive algorithm

If the frequency of loss probability mass function can be written in the form

$$p(k) = p(k-1)\left(a + \frac{b}{k}\right) k = 1, 2, 3\ldots, \ldots$$

where a and b are constants, Panjer's recursive algorithm can be used. The recursion is given by

$$g(x) = p(1)f(x) + \int_0^x (a + b\frac{y}{x})f(y)g(x-y)dy, x > 0$$

where $g(x)$ is the probability density function of $G(x)$.

Probability distributions that satisfy $p(k) = p(k-1)\left(a + \dfrac{b}{k}\right)$ include the Poisson distribution, binomial distribution, negative binomial distribution, and geometric distribution. For example, if our severity of loss is the Poisson distribution

$$p(n) = \frac{e^{-\lambda}\lambda^n}{n!}$$

then $a = 0$ and $b = \lambda$. If, on the other hand, we choose to use a binomial distribution

$$p(n) = \binom{K}{n} p^n (1 - p)^{K-n}$$

then $a = -\dfrac{p}{(1 - p)}$ and $b = \dfrac{(K + 1)^p}{(1 - p)}$.

A limitation of Panjer's algorithm is that it is only valid for *discrete* probability distributions. This implies that our severity of loss distribution, which is generally continuous, must be made discrete before it can be used. Another much larger drawback to the practical use of this method is that the calculation of convolutions is extremely time-intensive and rapidly becomes impossible as the number of losses in the time interval under consideration becomes large. Closely related adaptations to Panjer's algorithm include Kornya's algorithm and De Pril's algorithm. Other methods that take a slightly different approach are those based on the fast Fourier transform and the Heckman-Myers inversion method.

Monte Carlo method

Perhaps the simplest and often most direct approach is Monte Carlo simulation. The Monte Carlo method involves the following steps:

1. Choose a severity of loss and frequency of loss probability model.
2. Simulate the number of losses and individual loss amounts and then calculate the corresponding aggregate loss.
3. Repeat many times (at least 5,000) to obtain an empirical aggregate loss distribution.

EXAMPLE 9.1 MONTE CARLO SIMULATION OF AN AGGREGATE LOSS DISTRIBUTION

To illustrate the application of this method, open the worksheet MC Simulation in the workbook Operational Risk 09.xls. It generates a aggregate loss distribution using a Poisson frequency of loss model and a Weibull severity of loss model. Enter parameter values for each distribution and the number of simulations required; then press the <RUN SIMULATION> button. The aggregate values (results of simulation) are stored in column B starting at cell B6. Table 9.1 shows the descriptive statistics of the aggregate loss distribution for a simulation of 30,000. Figure 9.1 presents the associated histogram. The simulation parameters were $\lambda = 1.95$ for the Poisson distri-

TABLE 9.1 Summary Statistics for Simulation

Average loss (million $)	0.412
Standard deviation	0.839
Skew	3.943
Kurtosis	26.609

bution and $\beta = 0.25$ and $\alpha = 0.75$ for the Weibull distribution. The average loss is around \$412,000 with a standard deviation of \$839,000. The distribution is typical of operational loss distributions in that it is skewed and fat-tailed.

CALCULATING OpVaR

Operational value at risk offers a basis for risk managers to provide a consistent and integrated approach to the management of operational and other risks, leading to greater transparency and more informed management decisions. It provides a consistent and familiar measure of risk across different risk and asset types and is widely used in market risk (where it is known as value at risk), where it provides a common metric by which to

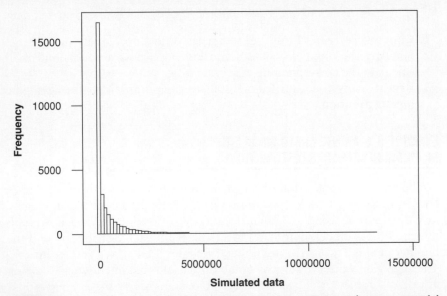

FIGURE 9.1 Simulated aggregate loss distribution using a Poisson frequency model and Weibull severity model.

compare risk in different portfolios. Furthermore, its calculation gives senior management the ability to set their overall operational risk target, and from that to determine the target risks for their various business divisions. Once the complete loss distribution has been obtained, OpVaR then can be evaluated by a given percentile of the empirical distribution. An alternative is to fit a probability distribution to the empirical loss distribution and then obtain OpVaR from the percentile function of the fitted probability distribution. Since OpVaR reflects large operational losses, it also can be used to determine operational economic capital and allocate it among various business lines.

EXAMPLE 9.2 CALCULATION OF OPVaR USING MONTE CARLO SIMULATION

To illustrate the calculation of OpVaR using Monte Carlo simulation open the workbook Operational Risk 09.XIS and select the worksheet `Legal Event Simulation`. This worksheet contains 30,000 legal liability losses simulated using the worksheet `MC Simulation`. Enter a confidence value in cell E6; typically, OR managers are interested in confidence values in the region 0.95 to 0.999. The worksheet uses the simulated data in column C and the Excel function `Percentile(loss_data,confidence_level)` to calculate the value of OpVaR. At 95 percent confidence, the OpVaR is equal to $15.99 million. Will the value of OpVaR differ significantly if we were to rerun the simulation? Since we used 30,000 in our simulation run, the OpVaR value should not be very different if you rerun the simulation. We ran it five times and obtained the values $16.03 million, $15.98 million, $16.04 million, $15.99 million, and $16.00 million. Thus, it appears that OpVaR for legal liability losses is around $16 million.

Operational value at risk also can be used in the calculation of an operational risk capital charge for a financial institution. To see how this might work, consider the classification of operational risk events proposed by the Risk Management Group of the Basle Committee. Their classification consists of eight standardized business lines and seven loss types. The eight business lines are:

1. Corporate finance
2. Trading and sales
3. Retail banking
4. Payment and settlement
5. Agency services
6. Commercial
7. Banking
8. Asset management and retail brokerage

The seven loss types are

1. Internal fraud
2. External fraud
3. Employment practices and workplace safety
4. Clients, products, and business practices
5. Damage to physical assets
6. Business disruption and system failure
7. Execution, delivery, and process management

For each line of business and operational risk type, we can calculate the severity and frequency of loss probability models over a particular time horizon (usually one year). Given the frequency and severity of loss model, we can compute the aggregate operational loss distribution for each risk type and business line. The total required capital is the sum of these OpVaRs. Adoption of Basle-type standards as a benchmark in operational risk management practice may enhance the focus and consistency of data collection and thereby make it possible for senior management to compare their loss experience across business lines, and for regulators to compare loss experience across regulated institutions.

COHERENT RISK MEASURES

We have emphasized throughout this book that in order to control operational risks, we must first be able to measure them. Operational value at risk gives us one way in which to measure risk. Is it the optimal measure? In order to answer this question, we need to outline the properties that a good risk metric should possess. We do this within the context of two random uncorrelated losses X and Y and a risk measure that we denote by $\rho()$. If $\rho()$ is an optimal risk measure, it will satisfy the following criteria:

1. *Subadditivity:* For all X and Y, $\rho(X + Y) \leq \rho(X) + \rho(Y)$. This implies that aggregating individual risks does not increase overall risk.
2. *Monotonicity:* If $X \leq Y$, then $\rho(X) \leq \rho(Y)$. This implies that if a portfolio X does better than portfolio Y under all scenarios, then the risk for X should be less than for Y.
3. *Positive homogeneity:* For all $\delta > 0$, $\rho(\delta X) = \delta \rho(X)$. This is the limiting case of subadditivity and informs us that combining perfectly correlated risks should not change the level of overall risk.
4. *Translation invariance:* For a constant θ, $\rho(X + \theta) = \rho(X) - \theta$. This implies if a nonrisky investment of \$$\theta$ is added to a risky portfolio, then the risk should decrease by \$$\theta$.

A risk measure which satisfies all of the above criteria is called a coherent measure of risk. Operational value at risk is not a coherent risk measure because it fails the first criteria. An alternative to OpVaR that is consistent is expected shortfall (ES). Expected shortfall is the average value of losses we can expect if we observe a loss in excess of OpVaR, or

$$ES = E[X \mid X > \text{OpVaR}]$$

where E[ ] is the expectation operator. Unlike OpVaR, which tells us how much we might expect to lose if a event in the tail of the loss distribution *does not occur*, ES informs us of how much we might expect to lose if an event in the tail of the distribution *does occur*.

Since ES is the probability weighted average loss beyond OpVaR, it is relatively easy to calculate. The simplest way to do this in Excel is to slice the tail of the aggregate loss distribution above the OpVaR confidence level into N slices and then use the Excel `Percentile(data, confidence_interval + Slice`$_i$` × d)` function to return the percentile of each slice. The average of these slices will give an estimate of ES.

EXAMPLE 9.3 CALCULATION OF EXPECTED SHORTFALL FOR LEGAL LOSSES

We illustrate this procedure using the in the worksheet `Legal Event Simulation`, which was previously discussed. Suppose we set $N = 10$ and $d = 0.005$ and choose a confidence level of 95 percent. The first percentile to be calculated will be the 95.5th. The function `Percentile(loss_data,confidence_level+ (1*d))` returns the value $17.2539. For the second slice we will use the 96th percentile and `Percentile(loss_data,confidence_level+(2*d))` returns the value $18.7905. The process is repeated 10 times, as shown in Table 9.2. The average of these 10 values provides an estimate of the expected shortfall; in this case it is $33.228. This value is much larger than the OpVaR value of $16 million because it reflects what you can expect to lose on average if an event beyond OpVaR occurs.

TABLE 9.2 Calculation of Expected Shortfall for Aggregate Loss Data

Slice	Percentile (%)	Value (million)
1	95.5	$17.2539
2	96.0	$18.7905
3	96.5	$20.4415
4	97.0	$22.5264
5	97.5	$24.7601
6	98.0	$27.5162
7	98.5	$31.3849
8	99.0	$35.9769
9	99.5	$44.3944
10	99.99	$91.1834

TABLE 9.3   Impact of Differing Numbers of Time Slices
on the Estimated Value of Expected Shortfall

N	ES
10	$33.4228
25	$30.2328
50	$29.2617
100	$28.7931
500	$28.4534
1,000	$28.4120
5,000	$28.3806

In practice, the number of slices, N, used in the calculation of ES needs to be reasonably large. Table 9.3 illustrates the impact of increasing N on the estimated value of ES for this data. In this case setting N at least equal to 1,000 produces a reasonably stable estimate of ES. The worksheet ES allows you to recalculate ES using different confidence levels and numbers of time slices.

SUMMARY

The assumption made in constructing the aggregate loss distribution is that the simulated losses are a realization of the combined frequency and severity of loss distributions. The process of generating aggregate loss distributions involves the specification of a number of probability distributions for the frequency and severity of loss models. For each frequency/severity of loss model the parameters need to be estimated and the adequacy of the model determined; only then can the loss distribution be simulated. A key objective in fitting the loss distribution is to obtain risk measures such as operational value at risk or expected shortfall.

REVIEW QUESTIONS

1. How useful do you think OpVaR is as a practical operational risk management tool?
2. Write a VBA function that calculates ES.
3. Is the fact that OpVaR is not coherent of any practical significance?
4. Rewrite the worksheet MC Simulation to use a negative binomial distribution instead of the Poisson distribution.

FURTHER READING

Further discussion of Panjer's approach with the alternative methods of Kornya and De Pril can be found in Kornya (1983) and De Pril (1986).

CHAPTER 10

The Law of Significant Digits and Fraud Risk Identification

In this chapter we discuss Benford's law of significant digits. Benford's law predicts the frequency of the leading digit in numbers met in a wide range of naturally occurring phenomena. In data following Benford's law, numbers start with a small leading digit more often than those with a large leading digit. Although the simplicity of the law is somewhat surprising, it has had some success in the field of fraud risk. In this chapter we illustrate, through a number of examples, how Benford's law can be used to help determine whether numerical data has been fabricated or altered.

THE LAW OF SIGNIFICANT DIGITS

Benford's law of significant digits states that a sample of the first significant and subsequent digits of numbers drawn from a wide variety of random probability distributions will have a certain form as the sample size becomes increasingly large. The law is actually based on a conjecture by the astronomer and mathematician Simon Newcomb. In a two-page article in 1881 in the *American Journal of Mathematics*, Newcomb conjectured that the probability that a number has first significant digit d is

$$\text{Prob}\ (X = d) = \log_{10}\left(1 + \frac{1}{d}\right) d = 1, \ 2, \ 3, \ 4, \ 5, \ 6, \ 7, \ 8, \ 9$$

Figure 10.1 plots this distribution. Notice how the probability of the first digit being 1 is much higher than the probability of it being 9. This may seem a counterintuitive result. What you might expect is for each digit to have a more or less equal chance of occurring, as shown in Figure 10.2.

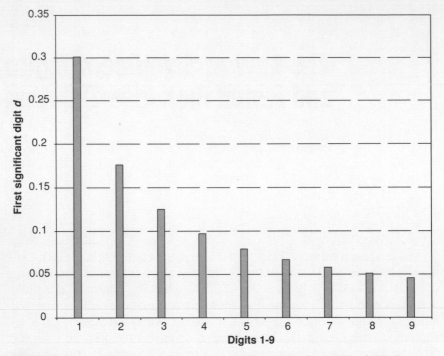

FIGURE 10.1   Probability distribution of first digits according to Benford's law.

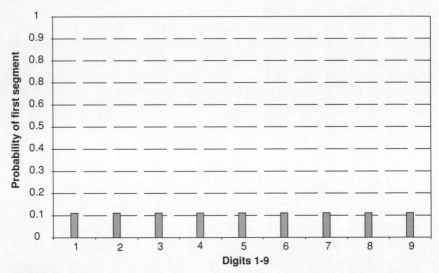

FIGURE 10.2   What we might expect the probability distribution of first digits to look like.

In fact, the significant digits are not uniformly distributed but obey Newcomb's logarithmic probability distribution. Unfortunately for Newcomb, his conjecture went largely unnoticed until the late 1930s when Benford, a physicist, tested the conjecture and found it did indeed hold on a very wide range of data sets. Thus, with the publication of Benford's results the Newcomb conjecture became widely known as Benford's law of significant digits.

EXAMPLE 10.1　SIMULATING BENFORD'S LAW

Let us investigate this law further using Excel. Open the file Operational Risk 10.xls. It contains the worksheet Benfords. The worksheet simulates 100 random numbers and then calculates Benford's law for the first significant digit. Press <F9> to start the simulation. Run it several times. The result is rather surprising. Benford's law is a good approximation for this data. The worksheet also makes use of the VBA function Benford(), which returns Benford's probability for any integer in the range 1 through 9. The code for the function is

```
Function Benford(d)   ' Returns the probability of d
        for the Benford distribution
    If d>9 Or d<1 Then
      Benford = -99   ' function only works with numbers 1-9
    Else
      Benford = (Log(1 + (1 / d))) / Log(10#)
    End If
End Function
```

For example, Benford(1) returns the value 0.301 and Benford(9) returns the value 0.0458.

STATISTICAL EXPLANATION OF BENFORD'S LAW

Why does Benford's law hold for so many empirical observations? The answer is related to the central limit theorem. Recall that the central theorem informs us that sums of random variables, under certain conditions, will follow the normal distribution. It turns out that if probability distributions are selected at random and then random samples are taken from each of these selected distributions, then the leading significant digits of the combined sample will be distributed according to Benford's law.

BENFORD'S LAW IN FINANCE

Empirical evidence in support of Benford's law has appeared in a wide variety of contexts, including newspaper articles, tables of physical constants, accounting data, and demographic data.

EXAMPLE 10.2 BENFORD'S LAW AND THE CLOSING PRICE OF IBM STOCK

To illustrate Benford's law with financial data, we consider the daily return of the closing price of IBM Corporation stock over the period January 1990 to the end of August 2002. Figure 10.3 plots Benford's distribution against the sample distribution calculated from IBM daily returns. Benford's distribution provides an excellent fit to the empirical observations.

Until recently empirical results such as those presented in Example 10.1 were regarded as little more than a statistical curiosity with no apparent application in risk management. However, in the mid-1990s, the law was applied successfully to detect fraud in accounting data. This proved the wake-up call to risk management.

CASE STUDY 10.1: ANALYSIS OF TRADER'S PROFIT AND LOSS USING BENFORD'S LAW

To illustrate the application of Benford's law in operational risk management, we consider the daily reported profit and loss of a foreign exchange options trading desk over the period January 10, 2000, to June 15, 2001. The

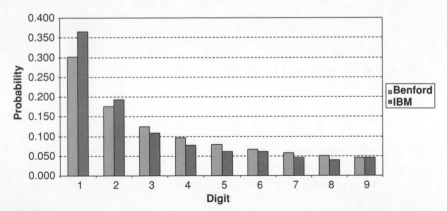

FIGURE 10.3 First significant digit of the daily return on the IBM stock price and Benford's distribution.

TABLE 10.1   Daily Profit and Loss of Five Traders

Trading Date	Trader 1	Trader 2	Trader 3	Trader 4	Trader 5
1/10/2000	−0.0336%	0.0669%	−0.0276%	−0.0125%	0.0456%
1/11/2000	−0.0166%	0.0368%	0.0527%	0.0114%	0.0433%
1/12/2000	−0.0419%	0.0866%	−0.0276%	0.0233%	−0.0170%
6/13/2001	−0.0247%	0.0132%	0.0697%	0.0242%	−0.0415%
6/15/2001	0.0104%	−0.0382%	0.0152%	−0.0276%	−0.0160%
6/15/2001	−0.0107%	−0.0421%	0.0259%	0.0527%	0.0309%

desk consists of five traders. Their typical profit and loss are shown in Table 10.1. For example, on January 10, 2000, trader 1 exhibited a loss of 0.0336 percent on his book, whereas trader 5 recorded a profit of 0.0456 percent. Table 10.2 gives the summary statistics for each of the traders. The standard deviations, maximum gain, and maximum loss are all very similar—around 0.046 percent, 0.099 percent, and −0.99 percent, respectively. We cannot discern anything unusual in these figures, except that on average over the period trader 2 and trader 4 lost money and might therefore be expected to seek alternative employment.

To conduct a first digit analysis of the entire trading desk we need to stack the daily returns of each trader on top of each other to give a single series upon which to perform the analysis. Figure 10.4 presents the empirical distribution of the first significant digit of the individual daily profit and loss for the five traders over a period of 18 months against Benford's distribution. The empirical observations fit Benford's distribution very well, in the sense that they agree with Table 10.2, which showed nothing untoward.

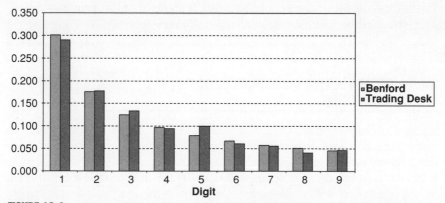

FIGURE 10.4   First significant digit of the daily profit and loss of trading desk.

TABLE 10.2 Summary Statistics for Each Trader

	Trader 1	Trader 2	Trader 3	Trader 4	Trader 5
Average	0.0046%	−0.0013%	0.0041%	−0.0001%	0.0025%
Stdev	0.0458%	0.0462%	0.0467%	0.0458%	0.0443%
Max gain	0.0991%	0.0997%	0.0995%	0.0998%	0.0995%
Max loss	−0.0978%	−0.0978%	−0.0998%	−0.0998%	−0.0998%

Although their appears little of concern in the data, it is always prudent to dig further. This can be achieved by plotting the absolute difference between the empirical distribution for each trader against the expected Benford frequency. For traders 1 to 4 this difference was close to 0 for each digit. The result for trader 5 was somewhat different and is shown in Figure 10.5. It reveals that the digit 5 occurs much more frequently than predicted by Benford's law. This was flagged as unusual and on further investigation it was discovered that trader 5, who had sole responsibility for inputting volatility into the pricing models, had been concealing losses by deliberately mispricing and overvaluing option contracts.

LIMITATIONS OF BENFORD'S LAW

Although Benford's law may seem almost miraculous, we caution that it is based on an empirical observation. There is no guarantee that all numerical data will follow this law; indeed, some does not. Examples include tables of square roots or lists of telephone numbers, which usually begin with the local area code. You also should be aware that the law is a large sample law, and it may not be true if the sample size is too small, say, less than 100 observations. However, Benford's law holds true in a surprising number of situations. It shows that OR processes can be remarkably resistant to complete randomness.

A STEP TOWARD BETTER STATISTICAL METHODS OF FRAUD DETECTION

There is a perception that the degree of fraud, in particular that related to money laundering, has increased dramatically with the expansion in modern telecommunications and computing technology. The loss to legitimate business from money laundering and other types of fraud must be counted in the billions of dollars annually. After the terrorist attack on the World

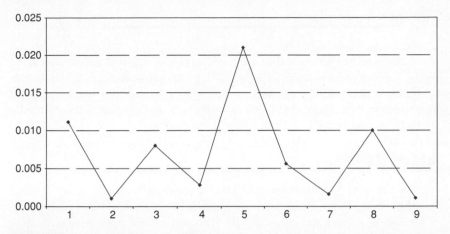

FIGURE 10.5 Absolute difference between the empirical observations and Benford's distribution for trader 5.

Trade Center on September 11, 2001, many operational risk managers have sought to reduce fraud risk by pursuing active strategies for fraud prevention and fraud detection. The idea behind the use of the Benford's law to detect anomalies in data is that fabricating data that agrees with the law is difficult. Since we know the distribution of the first significant digit (and subsequent digits—see box "Extending Benford's Law"), we may be able to detect erroneous and fraudulent data simply by comparing the observed distribution of digits with that expected by Benford's law.

EXTENDING BENFORD'S LAW

Benford's law also specifies the distribution of higher significant digits:

$$\text{Prob}\,(X_1 = d_1, X_2 = d_2, ..., X_k = d_k) = \log_{10}\left[1 + \left(\sum_{i=1}^{k} d_i \times 10^{k-i}\right)^{-1}\right]$$

where $d_1 = 1,\ 2,\ 3,\ 4,\ 5,\ 6,\ 7,\ 8,\ 9$ and
    $d_i = 0,\ 1,\ 2,\ 3,\ 4,\ 5,\ 6,\ 7,\ 8,\ 9$ for $i > 1$.

For example, the first three significant digits (3, 1, 4) occur with probability of approximately 0.0014.

SUMMARY

Benford's law is no "silver bullet". Deviation from Benford's law alone cannot provide absolute certainty that a operational risk event is definitely taking place. Rather, the objective of the method is to point out unusual observations. Used this way, Benford's law offers a powerful tool for seeking out anomalies in data and thereby assists in the task of fraud identification, and prevention and operational risk reduction.

REVIEW QUESTIONS

1. Generate 100, 500, 1000, and 10,000 random numbers in Excel using the Rand( ) function. Construct a histogram of the observations and comment. Compare the empirical distribution of the first significant digit with Benford's law. What do you conclude?
2. Generate 100, 500, 1000, and 10,000 random numbers in Excel using the combined functions Abs(Normsinv(Rand( ))). Construct a histogram of the observations and comment. Compare the empirical distribution of the first significant digit with Benford's law. What do you conclude?
3. Write a VBA function that extends Benford's law to the second and third significant digits. Use your VBA function to investigate the distribution of the second and third significant digits of the random numbers generated in Questions 1 and 2.

FURTHER READING

Details of the application of Benford's law in accountancy fraud can be found in Nigrini and Mittermaier (1997) and Nigrini (1999). Ley (1996) gives details of how well the Benford's distribution fits stock prices. For a discussion as to why the law holds and a derivation based on modern statistics, see Hill (1995, 1996, 1998).

CHAPTER 11

Correlation and Dependence

n risk management theory and practice the notion of correlation and dependence is central; for example, in market risk management, correlation is used as a measure of the relationship between different financial instruments in the calculation of value at risk. The complexity of OR events has led recently to increased interest in the modeling of correlation and notions of dependence. This is partly driven by the quest for a sound methodological basis for integrated risk management, which in itself also raises the issue of correlation and dependence, and partly because the correct modeling of OR events requires accurate and consistent measures of association and dependence. Correlation, as well as being one of the most ubiquitous concepts in modern risk management, is also one of the most misunderstood concepts. The main aim of this chapter is to collect together and clarify the essential ideas of correlation and dependence. In particular, we highlight a number of important empirical formulas for calculating correlation, explore common fallacies concerning the interpretation of correlation, and develop a notion of dependence that is relevant to operational risk management regression–based causal modeling to be introduced in the following chapters.

MEASURING CORRELATION

Correlation is a measure of association, whereas dependence is a measure of the presence or absence of a relationship between variables. In this chapter we provide empirical formulas for calculating correlation and discuss the concept of simple and stochastic dependence. There are many ways to calculate the correlation coefficient between two variables. We discuss some of the popular approaches here.

Sample Correlation Coefficient

Given a sample of n observations on two random variables S and T, the sample correlation coefficient (also known as the *Pearson correlation coefficient*) can be calculated as

$$\rho = \frac{\dfrac{1}{(n-1)} \sum_{i=1}^{n} \left(S_i - \bar{S} \right)\left(T_i - \bar{T} \right)}{\sigma_T \sigma_S}$$

where σ_S and σ_T are the sample standard deviations and $\bar{S}$ and $\bar{T}$ are the sample means. Since $0 \quad \rho \quad 1$, we see that if large values of S are associated with small values of T, then the correlation is negative. On the other hand, if large values of S are associated with large values of T, the correlation is positive.

EXAMPLE 11.1 CALCULATION OF PEARSON CORRELATION BETWEEN INCOME GENERATION AND SALARY

Table 11.1 lists the gross income generation and salary as a proportion of the sector median for 10 foreign exchange options traders. We can calculate the Pearson correlation coefficient in Excel using the `Pearson()` or `Correl()` functions. Using `Pearson()`, we estimate the correlation as 0.717.

The key assumption underlying the Pearson correlation coefficient is that the joint probability distribution of the variables is the bivariate normal distribution. If this assumption is untenable, an alternative measure of correlation known as the *Spearman rank correlation coefficient* can be calculated.

CORRELATION RULES OF THUMB

In empirical work we consider an absolute correlation in the range of 1.0 to 0.7 as indicating that the two variables are strongly correlated, 0.7 to 0.3 as weakly correlated, and less than 0.3 as indicative of weak or very little correlation.

Spearman Rank Correlation Coefficient

The Spearman rank correlation coefficient retains all of the assumptions of the Pearson correlation coefficient *except* the assumption of joint normal-

TABLE 11.1   Gross Income Generation and Salary Ratio for 10 Traders

Trader	Gross income generation ($)	Salary ratio (%)
Trader 1	114,110.75	90.66
Trader 2	828,113.51	182.84
Trader 3	74,596.96	114.18
Trader 4	994,182.19	167.46
Trader 5	405,435.58	151.55
Trader 6	414,132.38	144.58
Trader 7	307,932.27	187.85
Trader 8	208,949.86	150.67
Trader 9	23,011.67	69.78
Trader 10	844,090.39	166.44

ity between the two variables. Spearman correlation is calculated using the ranks of the original data, rather than the actual values. Provided that there are no tied ranks, we can use the following formula

$$\rho = 1 - \frac{6 \sum\limits_{i=1}^{n} d_i^2}{\left(n^2 - 1\right)n}$$

where d_i are the differences of the ranked pairs.

EXAMPLE 11.2 CALCULATION OF SPEARMAN RANK CORRELATION BETWEEN INCOME GENERATION AND SALARY

Table 11.2 presents the steps involved in calculating the Spearman rank correlation coefficient for the data of Table 11.1. The fourth column gives the rank of gross income, and the fifth column gives the rank of salary. The sixth column gives the difference between the ranks, and the final column gives this difference squared. The sum of the final column is 46, and hence the estimated value of the Spearman rank correlation is therefore given by

$$\rho = 1 - \frac{276}{\left(10^2 - 1\right) 10} = 0.721$$

This value is very close to the estimate of 0.717 given by the Pearson correlation coefficient.

TABLE 11.2 Calculation of Spearman Rank Correlation for Gross Income Generation and Salary Ratio

Trader	Gross income generation ($)	Salary ratio (%)	Rank gross income	Rank salary	$d_i = ($Rank gross income − rank salary$)$	$d_i \times d_i$
Trader 1	114,110.75	90.66	8	9	−1	1
Trader 2	828,113.51	182.84	3	2	1	1
Trader 3	74,596.96	114.18	9	8	1	1
Trader 4	994,182.19	167.46	1	3	−2	4
Trader 5	405,435.58	151.55	5	5	0	0
Trader 6	414,132.38	144.58	4	7	−3	9
Trader 7	307,932.27	187.85	6	1	5	25
Trader 8	208,949.86	150.67	7	6	1	1
Trader 9	23,011.67	69.78	10	10	0	0
Trader 10	844,090.39	166.44	2	4	−2	4

EXAMPLE 11.3 SIMULATION OF PEARSON AND SPEARMAN CORRELATIONS

In this example we take a moment to reflect on the calculation of the Spearman correlation coefficient, and contrast its value using simulation with the Pearson correlation coefficient. Open the file Operational Risk 11.xls and select the worksheet entitled Spearman & Pearson. This calculates the Spearman and Pearson correlation coefficients for the data in Table 11.1. In the calculation of the Spearman coefficient it uses the Excel function Rank() in order to obtain the d_i values. Spend a moment familiarizing yourself with the worksheet. Now select the worksheet Spearman & Pearson Simulation. You can use this worksheet to investigate the differences via simulation between the Spearman and Pearson estimates of correlation. Press <F9> to run a simulation. Make a note of the values obtained for 10 simulations. What do you conclude?

PARAMETRIC AND NONPARAMETRIC CORRELATION COEFFICIENTS

Correlation coefficients that make assumptions about the joint distributions of the correlated variables are known as *parametric correlation metrics*. The most popular is the Pearson correlation coefficient. The Spearman rank correlation coefficient is nonparametric because it does not make any assumption about the joint distribution of the variables.

Point Biserial Correlation

When one of the variables is binary and the other continuous, we can use the point biserial correlation coefficient. If S is a continuous variable and Y a binary variable taking the values 0 and 1, the point biserial correlation is calculated as

$$\rho = \frac{\left(\bar{S}_1 - \bar{S}_0\right)\sqrt{p(1 - p)}}{\sigma_S}$$

where $\bar{S}_1$ = mean of S when $Y = 1$

S_0 = mean of S when $Y = 0$

σ_s = sample standard deviation of S

ρ = proportion of values where $Y = 1$

A VBA function to estimate the biserial correlation coefficient is given below. Note that the first column passed to the function should be the continuous variable and the second column the binary variable.

```
Function Biserial(data As Range)
    ' Calculate Biserial correlation

    Dim number_columns As Double
      Dim number_rows As Double
        Dim row As Integer
          Dim x1 As Double
            Dim x0 As Double
          Dim s As Double
        Dim p As Double
      Dim average_x As Double
    Dim all_x() As Double

    number_columns = data.Columns.Count
      number_rows = data.Rows.Count

      If (number_columns <> 2) Then    'check no more than
            2 columns Biserial = "2 columns only"
      ElseIf (number_rows< 4) Then    'We should use at least 4
              ' observations although the more the better
        Biserial = "need at least 4 rows"

      Else

        x0 = 0
          x1 = 0
          p = 0
```

```
            s = 0
              average_x = 0
    Dim number_ones As Integer
    number_ones = 0
  ReDim all_x(number_rows)
    For row = 1 To number_rows    ' calculate averages and
            sum of binary variable
      Dim is_one As Integer
        is_one = data(row, 2).Value
          p = p + is_one
      If (is_one = 0) Then

        x0 = x0 + data(row, 1).Value

        Else
          x1 = x1 + data(row, 1).Value
          number_ones = number_ones + 1
        End If

    average_x = average_x + data(row, 1).Value
    all_x(row) = data(row, 1).Value
  Next row

    x0 = x0 / (number_rows - number_ones)
      x1 = x1 / number_ones
        average_x = average_x / number_rows
    p = p / number_rows
    For row = 1 To number_rows 'calculate standard deviation
      s = s + (all_x(row) - average_x)^2

    Next row

    s = (s / (number_rows-1))^0.5
      Dim temp As Double

    Biserial = ((x1 - x0) * (p * (1 - p))^0.5) / s
     ' Return Biserial correlation
    End If
End Function
```

EXAMPLE 11.4 CORRELATION BETWEEN OPERATIONAL RISK AND GROSS INCOME OF BUSINESS LINES

An application of this function is given in the worksheet Biserial in the workbook Operational Risk 11.xls. The worksheet is based on the follow-

TABLE 11.3 OR Risk and Gross Income across Business Lines

Business line	Operational risk	Gross income (millions $)	Risk coding
Corporate finance	Low	117.78	0
Trading and sales	High	161.84	1
Retail banking	Low	117.11	0
Commercial banking	High	161.91	1
Payment and settlement	High	162.11	1
Agency services and custody	High	80.45	1
Asset management	Low	50.57	0
Retail brokerage	High	172.88	1

ing example: Let us imagine that the level of operational risk in an institution's business lines is graded as high or low based on the opinion of an OR analyst. Suppose we are interested in assessing the degree of correlation between OR risk and gross income of the business lines. Since in this case OR risk is a binary variable and gross income a continuous variable, we can use the biserial coefficient to estimate correlation. Table 11.3 provides a typical example. The final column gives the mapping of high or low into a binary variable. Using the above `Biserial()` function in the worksheet `Biserial`, the estimate of correlation is 0.57.

Tetrachoric Correlation

Tetrachoric correlation measures the association between two binary variables. Assume T and S are dichotomized at unknown threshold values θ_S and θ_T, respectively. Our observable measurements on S and T are denoted by S^d and T^d, where $T^d = 1$ if $T \geq \theta_T$ (otherwise $T^d = 0$), and $S^d = 1$ if $S \geq \vartheta_S$ (otherwise $S^d = 0$). The joint distribution of (S^d, T^d) can be summarized as

TABLE 11.4 The General Situation for Outcomes of a Binary Variables S and T with Probability of Occurrence

	$T = 1$	$T = 0$	
$S = 1$	P_{11}	P_{01}	P_S
$S = 0$	P_{10}	P_{00}	$1 - P_S$
	P_T	$1 - P_T$	1

Note P_{kj} is the probability that $T = k$ and $S = j$ where $j, k = 0$ or 1

a 2×2 contingency table. The general situation is outlined in Table 11.4, where $Pij = $ Prob $(T^d = i, S^d = j)$. Each cell is a bivariate normal integral. For example:

$$P_{00} = \text{Prob}\,(T^d = 0,\ S^d = 0) = \text{Prob}\,(T < \theta_T,\ S < \theta_S)$$

$$= \int_{-\infty}^{\theta_T} \int_{-\infty}^{\theta_S} \Phi\,(t, s, r)\,dt ds$$

The actual formula for the tetrachoric correlation coefficient is complex and contains an infinite series of terms. However, Pearson[1] provides an easy-to-use approximation[2] given by

$$\hat{\rho} = \cos\left[\frac{180°}{\left(1 + \sqrt{bc/ad}\right)}\right]$$

where a, b, c, and d refer to the frequencies in a fourfold table in cells 11, 12, 21, and 22, respectively, and where row 1 and column 2 designate presence.

Consider Table 11.5, which provides information concerning whether a reputational risk event has occurred alongside an internal OR audit score.

TABLE 11.5 Reputational Risk Events and OR Internal Audit Score for 12 Fictional Banks

Bank	Recorded Reputational risk event	Data OR audit score	Data Reputational risk event	Mapping OR Audit Score
XYZ Bank	No	Low	0	1
GIA Financials	No	Low	0	1
City FG Holdings	Yes	High	1	0
Financial Street Bank	Yes	High	1	0
FPG	No	Low	0	1
Boston Regal	Yes	High	1	0
Imperial Crown	No	Low	0	1
Market DG	Yes	Low	1	1
Coventry Provincial	No	High	0	0
Bank 10	Yes	High	1	0
AG Swift Inc	Yes	Low	1	1
High Street Holdings	Yes	Low	1	1

For this table the tetrachoric correlation coefficient is equal to 0.58. A VBA function to calculate tetrachoric correlation is

```
Function Tetra(S As Range, T As Range)' Function
     takes two binary ranges S and T
' Error checks
If (S.Columns.Count > 1 Or T.Columns.Count > 1) Then
Tetra = "Need only 1 column"
ElseIf (S.Rows.Count < 10 Or T.Rows.Count < 10) Then
Tetra = "Need at least 10 rows"
ElseIf (S.Rows.Count <> T.Rows.Count) Then
Tetra = "Need at equal number of rows"
Else ' correlation calculation starts here
Dim a As Integer
Dim b As Integer
Dim c As Integer
Dim d As Integer
Dim i As Integer
a = 0
b = 0
c = 0
d = 0
Dim pi As Double
pi = 3.14159265358979
For i = 1 To S.Rows.Count
If (S(i, 1) = 1 And (T(i, 1) = 1)) Then a = a + 1
If (S(i, 1) = 1 And (T(i, 1) = 0)) Then b = b + 1
If (S(i, 1) = 0 And (T(i, 1) = 1)) Then c = c + 1
If (S(i, 1) = 0 And (T(i, 1) = 0)) Then d = d + 1
Next i
Tetra = Cos(pi / (1 + (Sqr((b * c) / (a * d)))))
End If
End Function
```

The function Tetra() takes two columns which must be of equal length and have at least 10 rows. An example of the use of this function is given in the worksheet Tetrachoric. The worksheet combines the Tetra() function with a simulation of the two binary variables "OR Audit Score" and "Reputational Risk Event" for 12 fictional financial institutions. Press <F9> to run the simulation.

UNDERSTANDING THE PEARSON TETRACHORIC APPROXIMATION

Note that when $bc = ad$, the fraction under the radical is unity, which means that the overall denominator is 2, and that the overall fraction is 90° so that $\hat{\rho} = 0$ and therefore there is no correlation between S and T. When bc dominates over ad, the overall denominator is greater than 2, which means that the overall fraction is less than 90°, and the resulting estimate of $\hat{\rho}$ is negative.

Confidence Intervals and Hypothesis Testing

Occasionally, we will wish to conduct a hypothesis test or construct a confidence interval around our correlation estimate. To do this, we will need to draw on two properties introduced by Fisher[3] and discussed in detail by Cramér[4]:

Property 1: If the population correlation (which we refer to as r) = 0, then

$$\hat{\rho}\sqrt{\frac{(N-2)}{(1-\hat{\rho}^2)}}$$ has a t distribution on $N - 2$ degrees of freedom.

Property 2: As the sample size N increases, the distribution of

$0.5 \ln\left[(1 + \hat{\rho}) \Big/ (1 - \hat{\rho})\right]$ approaches a normal distribution with a mean of

$0.5 \ln\left[(1 + r) \Big/ (1 - r)\right]$ and variance $1 \Big/ N - 3$.

These properties can be used to test hypotheses and construct confidence intervals for r, the population correlation coefficient. We illustrate this by assuming the correlation of interest between two variables S and T is estimated as $\hat{\rho} = 0.156$ from a sample size of 339. The question now is: Does the data provide good evidence that there is weak positive correlation between the S and T? To answer this question, we must test the null hypothesis (H_0) that $r = 0$ against the alternative (H_1) that $r > 0$. Since $\hat{\rho} = 0.156$ and $N = 339$, using property 1 we see that

$$\hat{\rho}\sqrt{\frac{(N-2)}{(1-\hat{\rho}^2)}} = 0.156\sqrt{\frac{(337)}{1-(0.156)^2}} = 2.899$$

If H_0 is true, then this should be an observation from a t distribution on 337 degrees of freedom. But the upper 5 percent significance point of this t distribution is 1.65, and since the test is one-tailed we therefore reject H_0 at the 5 per cent significance level. In fact, the upper 1 per cent and 0.1 per cent are 2.33 and 2.68, respectively, so there is highly significant evidence in favor of the alternative hypothesis, $r > 0$. We would also like to find a 95 percent confidence interval for $\hat{\rho}$. To do this, we need to use property 2.

Now

$$0.5 \ln \left. (1 + \hat{\rho}) \middle/ (1 - \hat{\rho}) \right. = 0.1573 \tag{11.1}$$

and

$$\frac{1}{\sqrt{N - 3}} = 0.0546 \tag{11.2}$$

but if $0.5 \ln \left[(1 + \hat{\rho}) \middle/ (1 - \hat{\rho}) \right]$ is normally distributed with mean

$0.5 \ln \left[(1 + r) \middle/ (1 - r) \right]$ and variance $\dfrac{1}{N - 3}$, then

$$\text{Prob} \left\{ -1.96 \leq \sqrt{N - 3} \left[0.5 \ln \left[\frac{(1 + \hat{\rho})}{(1 - \hat{\rho})} \right] - 0.5 \ln \left[\frac{(1 + r)}{(1 - r)} \right] \right] \leq 1.96 \right\}$$
$$= 0.95$$

so that

$$\text{Prob} \left\{ 0.5 \ln \left[\frac{(1 + \hat{\rho})}{(1 - \hat{\rho})} \right] - 1.96 / \sqrt{N - 3} \leq 0.5 \ln \left[\frac{(1 + r)}{(1 - r)} \right] \\ \leq 0.5 \ln \left[\frac{(1 + \hat{\rho})}{(1 - \hat{\rho})} \right] + 1.96 / \sqrt{N - 3} \right\} = 0.95$$

Using the values obtained in Equation 11.1 and Equation 11.2, therefore

$$\text{Prob} \left\{ \begin{array}{l} 0.1573 - 1.96 \times 0.0546 \leq 0.5 \\ \ln \left[\frac{(1 + r)}{(1 - r)} \right] \leq 0.1573 + 1.96 \times 0.0546 \end{array} \right\} = 0.95$$

From this value we see that

$$\text{Prob} \left\{ 0.0503 \leq 0.5 \ln \left[\frac{(1 + r)}{(1 - r)} \right] \leq 0.2643 \right\} = 0.95 \text{ and}$$

$$\text{Prob} \left\{ 0.1006 \leq \ln \left[\frac{(1+r)}{(1-r)} \right] \leq 0.5286 \right\} = 0.95$$

which on exponentiation throughout gives

$$\text{Prob} \left\{ 1.1058 \leq \frac{(1+r)}{(1-r)} \leq 1.697 \right\} = 0.95$$

Now if $\frac{(1+r)}{(1-r)} \geq c$, where c is a constant, and $r \neq 1$, then $(1+r) \geq c$

$(1-r)$ so that $r \geq \frac{(c-1)}{(c+1)}$; similarly, $\frac{(1+r)}{(1-r)} \leq c$

implies $r \leq \frac{(c-1)}{(c+1)}$.

Setting c successively equal to 1.1058 and 1.697, we therefore obtain

$$\text{Prob} \left\{ 0.050 \leq \hat{\rho} \leq 0.258 \right\} = 0.95$$

Hence an approximate 95 percent confidence interval for $\hat{\rho} = 0.156$ is (0.05, 0.258).

Coefficient of Determination

The coefficient of determination is the square of the correlation coefficient and therefore takes values in the range 0 to 1. The magnitude of the coefficient of determination indicates the proportion of variance in one variable, explained by the second variable. For example, a correlation between S and T of 0.33 implies that around 10 percent of the variance of S can be explained by T (or vice versa). If the correlation is 0.71, the proportion explained rises to 50 percent. A deterministic linear relationship between S and T gives a coefficient of determination of 1, whereas no relationship gives a coefficient of determination of 0.

DEPENDENCE

We explore the notion of simple dependence by considering the relationship between a group of continuous variables T, S, and X, where S and T are different types of OR losses (due to systems failure, legal costs, etc.) and X is an OR indicator. Let us further assume T and S are linear functions of X given by

$$T = \alpha + \beta X \tag{11.3}$$

and

$$S = \alpha_s + \beta_s X \tag{11.4}$$

CORRELATION DOES NOT IMPLY CAUSATION

It is tempting to conclude that a strong correlation between two variables implies a causal relationship between them. This is not necessarily the case. Just because two variables are highly correlated does not mean that one causes the other. In statistical terms, we say that correlation does not imply causation. Why? First, the high correlation may be through chance alone. As an illustration consider European storks, which breed over parts of central Europe. In such areas there is an increase in the number of new babies born in the spring, precisely when the storks, appear and begin nesting. The correlation between babies and the appearance of the storks is high but spurious. Second, even if the particular observed correlation is not due to chance, the fact that storks and babies occur together does not imply causality. Causality requires the addition of time.

To explore this argument further, consider two variables S and T. If S is always followed by T, then it might be arguable that the appearance of S causes T. However, even if S is always followed by T, there is the possibility that S and T are both caused by a third event, R, and it is just that R always causes S more rapidly than T.

As a simple illustration of a common causal event consider the correlation between the dollar cost of damage in London and the number of fire engines attending the fire. The correlation is high, not because the number of fire engines causes the dollar cost or vice versa, but because both variables are caused by a third variable, "severity of the fire." In this example, assuming that a high correlation implies causation leads to a logical fallacy. The causal argument that the number of fire engines causes the dollar cost or vice versa is a false categorical syllogism. The fallacy ignores the possibility that the correlation is coincidence or the result of a third common causal variable. The fallacy is ignoring something besides coincidence. The statement "correlation does not imply causation" is given as a warning *not* to deduce causation from a statistical correlation alone. Knowledge of the operational processes under consideration, logic, and statistical modeling are all required.

The parameters α and α_s are the intercept terms. We can interpret β and β_s as the slope of the line between T and X, and the slope of the line between S and X, respectively. Since a slope measures the change in one variable as the other changes, we can write $\beta = \dfrac{\Delta T}{\Delta X}$ and $\beta_S = \dfrac{\Delta S}{\Delta X}$, where Δ represents a finite increment. Taking limits as $\Delta X \to 0$, we have

$$\underset{\Delta X \to 0}{Limit}\left[\frac{\Delta T}{\Delta X}\right] = \frac{dT}{dX} \tag{11.5}$$

and

$$\underset{\Delta X \to 0}{Limit}\left[\frac{\Delta S}{\Delta X}\right] = \frac{dS}{dX} \tag{11.6}$$

which are the derivatives of T with respect to X and S with respect to X, respectively.

Given risk indicator X, we are generally interested in assessing the dependence of operational loss T on X. Since $T = \alpha$ if, $\beta = 0$, it should be clear that we can use $\beta \neq 0$ to signify dependence of operational loss T on X. Similarly, $\beta_s \neq 0$ would signify dependence of operational loss S on risk indicator X. This type of dependence can be estimated using regression models. We investigate this further in the following chapters.

STOCHASTIC DEPENDENCE

What dependence characteristics would we like our related variables to satisfy? To begin to answer this question, let S and T be two dependent random variables representing OR events or risk indicators of interest. Let F, a right continuous function on the real line, be the corresponding cumulative density function, such that $Lim_{s \to -\infty} F(S, T) = 0$ and $Lim_{s \to \infty, T \to \infty} F(S, T) = 1$, so that $F(S,T)$ *is* the joint cumulative distribution function. We denote the bivariate probability density function as P_{11} with marginal densities P_T and P_S for T and S, respectively.

Stochastic Increase

If T is more likely to take on larger values as the value of S increases, we say that T is *stochastically increasing.*[5] More formally, this is written as

$$\text{Prob}\,(T > t \mid S > s) \;=\; 1 - \; F_{T|S}(t \mid s) \;\uparrow\; s \text{ for all } t \tag{11.7}$$

where $F_{T|S}$ is the conditional distribution function of T given S. By reversing the direction of monotonicity in Equation 11.7 from $\uparrow$ to $\downarrow$, T is said to be stochastically decreasing in S. The reason why Equation 11.7, is a positive dependence condition is that T takes on larger values as S increases.

Positive and Negative Quadrant Dependence

If S is independent of T then

$$P_{11} (S > s, T > t) = P_s (S > s) P_T (T > t)$$

On the other hand, if S and T are dependent in some way, we may expect S to be large when T is large and small when T is small; thus

$$P_{11} (S > s, T > t) = P_S (S > s) P_T (T > t) \tag{11.8}$$

or alternatively

$$\text{Prob } (S \le s, \ T \le t) \ \ge \ \text{Prob } (S \le s) \text{ Prob } (T \le t) \tag{11.9}$$

If Equation 11.8 holds, then S and T are said to be *positive quadrant dependent*.[6] If the inequalities in Equation 11.8 are reversed, then S and T are said to be *negative quadrant dependent*.[7] The reason why Equation 11.8 is a relevant positive dependence concept is that S and T are likely to be large together when they are dependent compared to the situation when they are independent.

Totally Positive of Order 2

We may expect dependent variables S and T to be more likely to have two pairs matching high-high and low-low than two pairs matching high-low and low-high. This idea is captured in the dependence concept of *totally positive of order 2*.[8] The joint probability P_{11} is totally positive of order 2 if for all $t_1 < t_2$ and $s_1 < s_2$ $P_{11}(s_1, t_1) P_{11}(s_2, t_2) \ge P_{11}(s_1, t_2) P_{11}(s_2, t_1)$.

Dependence Properties

Three dependence properties[9] are worth noting:

Dependence property 1: The joint density function of the standardized bivariate normal distribution is total positive of order 2.

Dependence property 2: If S and T are bivariate normally distributed and positively (negatively) correlated, then T is stochastically increasing (decreasing) in S.

Dependence property 3: If T is stochastically increasing (decreasing) in S, and S and T are bivariate normally distributed, then S and T are positive (negative) quadrant dependent.

SUMMARY

The concept of correlation and dependence permeates operational risk management in a most profound manner. Examples of correlated and interdependent OR events and indicators are too numerous to be cited individually. As such, operational risk management calls for an understanding of the distinction between correlation and dependence. It also requires tools that allow us to measure correlation and dependence beyond the situation in which both variables are continuous. The point biserial and tetrachoric coefficient are useful in this situation. Dependence and causal modeling using linear and logistic regression will be discussed in the following two chapters.

REVIEW QUESTIONS

1. What is the difference between correlation and dependence?
2. In what circumstances would you prefer to use the Pearson coefficient over the Spearman coefficient?
3. Use the coefficient of determination to explain the values for the rules of thumb for assessing the strength of correlation.
4. Explain the concept of simple and stochastic dependence.

FURTHER READING

Further discussion on the relationship between correlation and dependence can be found in Mari and Katz (2001). Castellan (1966) provides a superb discussion on the estimation of the tetrachoric correlation coefficient.

CHAPTER 12

Linear Regression in Operational Risk Management

How should we characterize the relationship between the size of operational losses and computer system downtime? We might speculate that the longer is the computer system downtime, the larger are the operational losses. Although we might not expect the relationship to be perfect, if we could establish its approximate validity this knowledge would provide us with useful risk management information. Linear regression is one way we can investigate this relationship. It offers a tried and tested way to determine the relationship between operational risk factors. It involves finding the best-fitting line through a data sample. In most circumstances, the slope of this line and the intercept have a clear operational risk interpretation. In other cases, we can use linear regression to forecast future values of operational risk factors. In this chapter we introduce aspects of the applied use of linear regression.

THE SIMPLE LINEAR REGRESSION MODEL

Suppose we observe a sample of n pairs $\{(y_1, x_i), \ldots, (y_n, x_n)\}$ on the operational risk factors X and Y. If we wish to use X to help explain Y, we can use simple linear regression. Simple linear regression models the relationship between X and Y by

$$y_i = \alpha + \beta x_i + \varepsilon_i$$

where x_i is known as the *independent* (or explanatory) variable, and y_i is known as the *dependent* (or response) variable. The realized value y_i is the observed response for the ith observation and x_i is the corresponding known constant level of the independent variable. The coefficients α and β are unknown model parameters and ε is known as the *residual* (or random) error, generally assumed to be an independent identical normally distributed random variable with mean 0 and variance σ^2.

EXAMPLE 12.1 POSTULATING A SIMPLE LINEAR REGRESSION MODEL FOR OPERATIONAL LOSSES

Table 12.1 presents the format of daily data (102 observations in total) over a number of months on the size of operational losses and system downtime. We are interested in investigating whether the size of operational loss is related to system downtime. A scatter plot of the two variables is shown in Figure 12.1.

Since the relationship appears fairly linear, we postulate the simple linear regression model

```
Operational_loss day i = [intercept] + [slope × system
            downtime day i] + [random error day i]
```

Interpretation of Model and Parameters

What is the meaning of the regression equation? To gain some insight, consider the linear equation

$$y = a + bx$$

The coefficient b is the slope of the line and the coefficient a is the intercept. As shown in Figure 12.2 , when $b > 0$ the line has positive slope, for $b < 0$ it has negative slope, and for $b = 0$ it has zero slope. The linear regression parameters α and β are interpreted in an analogous fashion. The regression model of the relationship between Y and X can be interpreted as

$$y_i = [\text{intercept}] + [\text{slope} \times x_i] + [\text{random error}] = \alpha + \beta \quad x_i + \varepsilon_i$$

LINEAR REGRESSION AND EXPECTATIONS

In Chapter 2 we gave the expectation of a risk factor Y as $E(Y)$ and the conditional expectation of Y given the risk factor X as $E(Y|X)$. We can interpret linear regression as a conditional expectation. To see this, assume the random error has an expected value of 0; then we can write $E(Y|X) = \alpha + \beta X$. Therefore, simple linear regression is essentially a conditional expectation, where the intercept α tells us the value of Y that is expected when $X = 0$. The slope parameter β measures the relationship between X and Y. It is interpreted as the expected change in Y for a 1-unit change in X. For example, if we estimate a regression and find $E(Y|X) = 2.75 + 0.35X$, a 1-unit change in X is expected to lead to a 0.35-unit change in Y.

TABLE 12.1 Operational Losses and System Downtime

Date	Operational losses ($)	System down time (minutes)
1-Jun	1,610,371	9
2-Jun	25,677	0
3-Jun	1,504,852	11
4-Jun	0	
5-Jun	913,881	7
6-Jun	2,352,458	18
7-Jun	3,549,325	19
8-Jun	0	0
9-Jun	0	0
10-Jun	1,649,917	13

Estimators of parameters

As yet, we have only a postulated model between two risk factors Y and X of the form

$$y_i = \alpha + \beta \quad x_i + \varepsilon_i$$

We will need to estimate the value of the intercept and slope from our data. These model parameters can be estimated using the method of ordinary least squares (OLS) or maximum likelihood estimation (MLE).

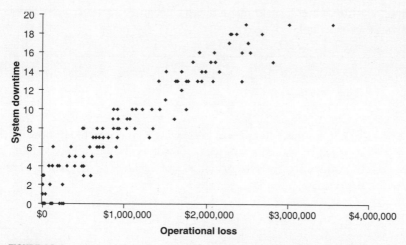

FIGURE 12.1 Scatter plot of system downtime against amount of operational loss.

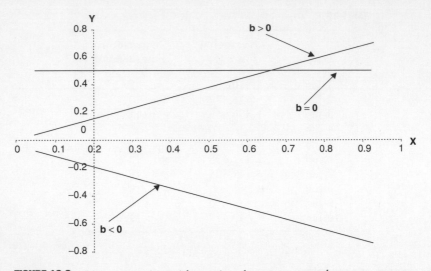

FIGURE 12.2 Linear equation with varying slope parameter b.

Ordinary least squares estimators of the parameters are given by

$$\hat{\alpha} = \bar{y} - \beta\bar{x} \quad \text{and} \quad \hat{\beta} = \frac{\sum_{i=1}^{n}(x_i - \bar{x})(y_i - \bar{y})}{\sum_{i=1}^{n}(x_i - \bar{x})^2}$$

where $\bar{y}$ and $\bar{x}$ are the arithmetic mean of Y and X, respectively. The sample variance is calculated as

$$\hat{\sigma}^2 = \frac{\sum_{i=1}^{n}(y_i - \bar{y})^2}{n-1}$$

We also can estimate the parameters using maximum likelihood. In this case we assume the residual $\varepsilon \sim N(0, \sigma^2)$, so, as shown in Figure 12.3, the individual y_i values are $y_i \sim N(\mu_i, \sigma^2)$, where $\mu_i = \alpha + \beta x_i$. The likelihood equation is given by

$$L(\mu_i, \sigma^2) = \prod_{i=1}^{n} f(y_i \mid \mu_i, \sigma^2)$$

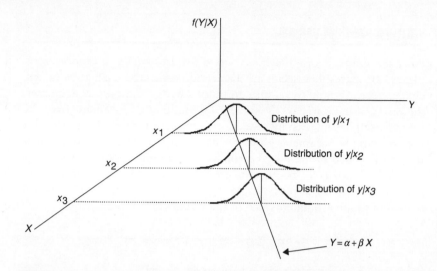

FIGURE 12.3 Distribution of dependent variable given independent variable in linear regression.

Taking logs, we have the log likelihood

$$\log L\left(\alpha, \beta, \sigma \mid \left\{(y_1, x_i), \ldots, (y_n, x_n)\right\}\right) = -\frac{1}{2} n \log 2\pi - \frac{1}{2} n \log \sigma^2$$
$$- \frac{1}{2} \sum_{i=1}^{n} \left(y_i - \alpha - \beta x_i\right)^2 / \sigma^2$$

This can be be solved to give

$$\hat{\alpha} = \bar{y} - \beta \bar{x} \qquad \hat{\beta} = \frac{\sum\limits_{i=1}^{n} (x_i - \bar{x})(y_i - \bar{y})}{\sum\limits_{i=1}^{n} (x_i - \bar{x})^2} \qquad \hat{\sigma}^2 = \frac{\sum\limits_{i=1}^{n} (Y_i - \bar{Y})^2}{n}$$

The only difference between the ordinary least squares and maximum likelihood estimations is that the divisor for the sample variance is n in MLE and $n - 1$ for OLS. In fact, the MLE estimator of sample variance is biased, although as n becomes large this bias becomes less of an issue.

ANOTHER RANDOM VARIABLE

Since the sample from which we derive the estimates is a random sample, the estimates themselves are also random variables. Their value will change from sample to sample. In theory, as the sample size increases, the variation measured by the standard deviation in the estimate from the sample becomes increasingly small. In empirical studies we estimate this variation in the parameter estimates using the standard deviation, more frequently called the standard error. We do not give an explicit formula for the standard error because its precise algebraic form is rather complicated. For practical purposes, you should interpret it as the standard deviation in the estimated value of the parameter of interest.

EXAMPLE 12.2 OLS ESTIMATION OF THE REGRESSION OF OPERATIONAL LOSSES ON SYSTEM DOWNTIME

Continuing with Example 12.1, we estimate the regression equation using OLS as

$$\text{Operational\_Loss} = -\$34,815 + [\$136,205 \times \text{system downtime}]$$

These estimates provide us with useful operational risk management information because they inform us that the longer is system downtime, the higher are the operational losses. Furthermore, a 1-minute change in system downtime is expected to lead to a \$136,205 change in operational losses. Thus, the cost of an additional 1 minute of system downtime is approximately \$136,205. Such information is very useful for managing operational risk; if average downtime can be reduced by 2 minutes a day, we can expect to reduce daily average operational losses by around \$272,410.

Assumptions of Simple Linear Regression

Linear regression requires that a number of assumptions hold for the data. The first is that the relationship between X and Y is linear. If this assumption is not met, the model will not be adequate and the OLS estimates will be biased. Second, we assume homoscedasticity in variance. This implies the variance of the residual term σ^2 is constant across all values of X. Third, we require the independence of ε_i and ε_j for all $i \neq j$ so that errors associated with different observations are independent of one another. For a similar reason we also require the residual to be uncorrelated with the x_i values.

Finally, we assume the residual is normally distributed. If all of these assumptions are met, then the OLS estimates are known as the *best linear unbiased estimators*.

WHAT ARE BEST LINEAR UNBIASED ESTIMATORS?

We have seen that estimators can be derived by the method of maximum likelihood, the method of ordinary least squares, and various other methods. We know that a good estimator should be unbiased, and for simple linear regression the MLE estimator of the variance is biased and the OLS estimator is unbiased. A best linear unbiased estimator is an estimator that has the *smallest variance* in the class estimators that are linear in the dependent variable Y. Why is this important? Because apart from wanting an estimator that is unbiased, we also would like an estimator that is always close to the population parameter we are trying to estimate. One way to measure this closeness is through the variance of the estimator. If we have two unbiased estimators, one with a large variance and the other with a small variance, we always choose to use the estimator with the small variance.

Coefficient of Determination

Before we make inferences about parameters from our sample estimates, we would like to determine how well the regression model fits our risk factor data. The coefficient of determination (R^2) is the most commonly cited measure to achieve this. In the simple linear regression model, R^2 is the square of the correlation between X and Y. For a poor fitting model, R^2 will be small. For a good fitting model, R^2 will be large. In fact, for a very poor model, $R^2 = 0$, and for a perfect fit, $R^2 = 1$. Since R^2 is the square of the correlation between X and Y, it lies between 0 and 1.

An important interpretation of R^2 is as the proportion of the variation in the dependent variable Y explained by the linear regression. To see this, recall that our OLS parameter estimates were $\hat{\alpha}$ and $\hat{\beta}$, and our estimated linear regression equation was

$$y_i = \hat{\alpha} + \hat{\beta} x_i + \varepsilon_i$$

The estimated value of y_i can also be written as

$$y_i = \hat{y}_i + \varepsilon_i$$

where $\hat{y}_i = \hat{\alpha} + \hat{\beta}x$ and is the expected value for y_i. If we square both sides and take the sum, we have

$$\sum_{i=1}^{n} y_i^2 = \sum_{i=1}^{n} (\hat{y}_i + \varepsilon_i)^2 = \sum_{i=1}^{n} (\hat{y}_i^2 + 2\varepsilon_i\hat{y}_i + \varepsilon_i^2) = \sum_{i=1}^{n} \hat{y}_i^2 + \sum_{i=1}^{n} \varepsilon_i^2$$

because $\displaystyle\sum_{i=1}^{n} 2\varepsilon_i\hat{y}_i = 0$.

If we now use the fact that the average value of the residual is zero and express the above result in deviation form, we obtain

$$\sum_{i=1}^{n} (y_i - \bar{y})^2 = \sum_{i=1}^{n} (\hat{y}_i - \bar{y})^2 + \sum_{i=1}^{n} (y_i - \hat{y})^2$$

If we recall the formula for sample variance, $\displaystyle\sum_{i=1}^{n} \frac{(Y_i - \bar{Y})^2}{n-1}$, we see that

the equation measures the total variation explained by the model and residual. In fact, $\displaystyle\sum_{i=1}^{n} (y_i - \bar{y})^2$ is known as the total sum of squares (TSS),

$\displaystyle\sum_{i=1}^{n} (\hat{y}_i - \bar{y})$ is known as the explained sum of squares (ESS), and $\displaystyle\sum_{i=1}^{n} (y_i - \hat{y})$

is known as the residual sum of squares (RSS). The difference between TSS and RSS represents the improvement obtained by adjusting Y to account for X. This difference is, of course, ESS, which measures the amount of variability in Y that is eliminated by including X in the model. So we see that TSS = ESS + RSS.

THINKING ABOUT ESS AND R^2

You should think of ESS as measuring the "value added" by including the operational risk factor X in the model compared to a model that does not include X. The measure of fit R^2 can be constructed by taking the ratio of the explained variance to the total variance, that is, $\dfrac{\text{ESS}}{\text{TSS}} = 1 - \dfrac{\text{RSS}}{\text{TSS}}$. Therefore, R^2 is simply the proportion of total variation in Y explained by regression model. However, it will only have this interpretation provided an intercept term is included in the regression. If this is the case for a poor-fitting model, we would expect RSS to be large and ESS to be small and consequently R^2 will be small. For a good-fitting model ESS will be large and RSS small and therefore R^2 will be large. It is easy to see that for a very poor model ESS = 0 and therefore $R^2 = 0$. For a perfect fit RSS = 0 and therefore ESS = TSS and $R^2 = 1$.

EXAMPLE 12.3 CORRELATION AND COEFFICIENT OF DETERMINATION BETWEEN OPERATIONAL LOSSES AND SYSTEM DOWNTIME

To illustrate the calculation of R^2 we return to Example 12.2. We calculate the correlation between operational losses and system downtime as 0.970, and thus $R^2 = (0.970)^2 = 0.941$. Therefore, around 94 percent of the variation in the data is explained by the regression model. This is quite high and provides information that the model may have some value. Figure 12.4 presents the fitted regression line for this model.

A t Test and Confidence Interval for Simple Regression

Our objective in using linear regression is to determine if the value of the dependent variable can be explained by the independent variable. In this case, for a two-sided hypothesis test and given the standard error of $\hat{\beta}$ [denoted by S.E. $\hat{\beta}$], the test statistic is

$$t_{\alpha/2} = \frac{\hat{\beta} - \beta_0}{s.e.(\hat{\beta})}$$

A $100(1 - \alpha)$ confidence interval is given by

$$\hat{\beta} \pm s.e.(\hat{\beta}) \times t_{\alpha/2}$$

where t is the t distribution with $n - 2$ degrees of freedom.

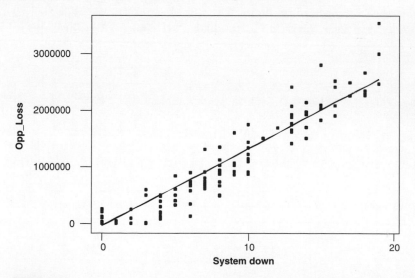

FIGURE 12.4 Fitted regression line for operational loss dependent on system downtime.

EXAMPLE 12.4 A t TEST FOR THE REGRESSION OF THE EFFECT OF SYSTEM DOWNTIME ON THE AMOUNT OF OPERATIONAL LOSSES

In Example 12.3, does system downtime affect the amount of operational losses? It appears that the answer is yes since the slope of the regression line $\hat{\beta} = 136205$, which is clearly not 0. We may, if we wish, test this formally with $H_0: \beta_0 = 0$ against $H_0: \beta_0 > 0$.

The standard error of $\hat{\beta} = 2,132$ and $t = 63.90$ with a resulting p value less than 0.001. Therefore, we reject the null hypothesis and conclude there is a positive relationship between operational losses and system downtime.

Checking the Assumptions of the Regression Model

Checking that the assumptions of the regression model are satisfied is an important part of regression modeling. In general we check for unusual observations, homoscedasticity of variance, independence, and normality.

Standardizing the residuals by dividing them by their standard deviation is a quick and simple way to check for unusual observations. Values grater than 2 or less than −2 are considered significant outliers. Occasionally, values outside of these ranges may be due to a transcription or data collection error or random chance. However, if there are a large number of such values, the regression model may be misspecified.

Analysis of homoscedasticity and normality may also be carried out using the standardized residuals. A simple check for homoscedasticity is to visually inspect a standardized residual plot. Figure 12.5 illustrates what

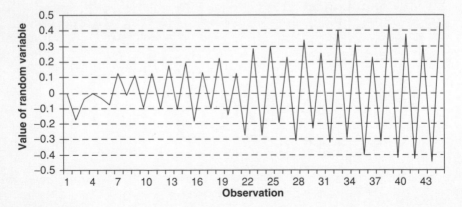

FIGURE 12.5   Random variable with increasing variance.

such a plot might look like for a random variable with increasing variance. For a homoscedastic standardized residual we would expect the scatter of points to be distributed randomly around 0, with no discernable trend. We can investigate normality of the residual by building a histogram; alternatively, we can construct a normal probability plot. If normality holds, the residuals should lie along a 45° line. We can check visually for independence by plotting the standardized residuals against the fitted values and against time to see if any nonrandom patterns emerge. We illustrate some of these ideas with the following example.

EXAMPLE 12.5 MISSPECIFICATION TESTING SIMPLE LINEAR REGRESSION OF OPERATIONAL LOSSES ON SYSTEM DOWNTIME

Figure 12.6 plots the standardized residuals for the regression model of Example 12.4. The vast majority of residuals lie within –2 to 2, although there are three points which lie considerably above –2 and three points which lie considerably below –2. Further checking revealed these six observations

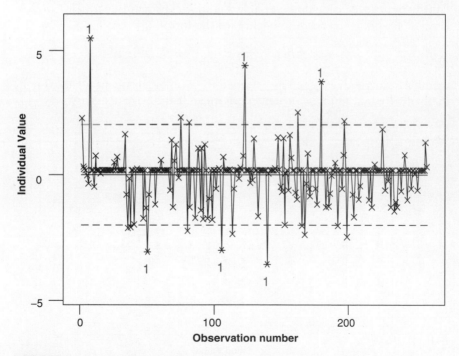

FIGURE 12.6 Standardized residuals for operational loss dependent on system downtime simple linear regression.

were recorded correctly, and therefore their large values were assigned to chance. A visual inspection of Figure 12.6 does not reveal any violations in the homoscedasticity or the independence assumption. As a further check of independence, in Figure 12.7, we plot the residuals against the fitted values; no discernable nonrandom pattern is obvious. In Figure 12.8 we construct a histogram of the standardized residuals. It clearly shows evidence of non-normality. This is confirmed in Figure 12.9, in which the standardized residuals appear to form two separate lines. The assumption of normal residuals appears to have failed in this model. This failure indicates that an alternative specification may be more appropriate. We investigate this further in the next section.

MULTIPLE REGRESSION

In many operational risk applications the relationship proposed by a simple linear regression model, with only one independent variable, may not adequately explain the variation in the dependent variable. This is because in practice there will be many influences on the dependent variable. In such cases, we can extend simple linear regression to multiple linear regression. Given the dependent random variable Y and k explanatory variables $X^1, X^2, \ldots, X^k$, multiple regression model takes the form

$$y_i = \alpha + \beta_1 x_i^1 + \beta_2 x_i^2 + \cdots + \beta_k x_i^k + \varepsilon_i$$

where ε is the residual generally assumed to be an independent identical normally distributed random variable with mean 0 and variance σ^2.

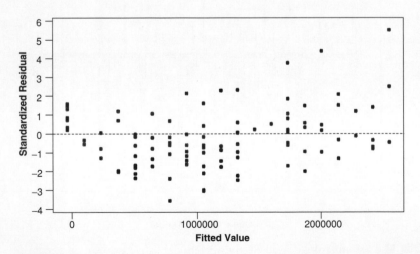

FIGURE 12.7 Standardized residuals versus fitted values for linear regression of operational losses on system downtime.

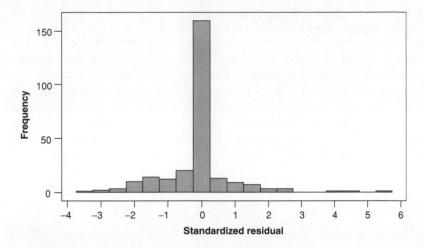

FIGURE 12.8 Histogram of standardized residuals for linear regression of operational losses on system downtime.

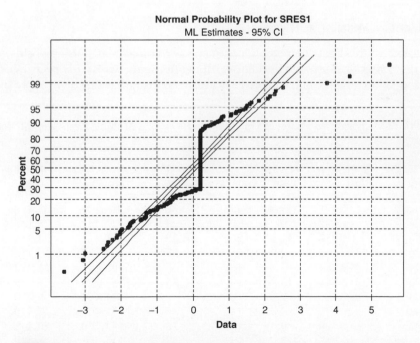

FIGURE 12.9 Normal probability plot for the standardized residuals for linear regression of operational losses on system downtime.

EXAMPLE 12.6 MULTIPLE LINEAR REGRESSION OF OPERATIONAL LOSSES

Recall Example 12.1 in which system downtime was the sole independent variable and operational losses were the dependent variable. We might expect a more accurate model if we included a number of other independent variables. Table 12.2 provides details on other independent variables that also might be relevant. They include the number of trainees employed in the back office on a particular day, number of experienced staff, volume of transactions and number of transaction errors. Therefore, we might postulate

$$y_i = \alpha + \beta_1 x_i^1 + \beta_2 x_i^2 - \beta_3 x_i^3 + \beta_4 x_i^4 + \beta_5 x_i^5 + \varepsilon_i$$

where Y is operational losses, x^1 is system downtime, x^2 is the number of trainees working in the back office, x^3 is the number of experienced staff, x^4 is the volume of transactions, and x^5 is the number of transaction errors. We might expect the coefficient on β_3 to be negative—the more experienced the staff working in the back office on a particular day, the less likely is an operational loss. All the other independent variables are expected to have a positive sign.

Estimation, Model Fit, and Hypothesis Testing

As with simple linear regression, parameters can be estimated using ordinary least squares or maximum likelihood. Model fit cannot necessarily be assessed using R^2 because it can be inflated towards its maximum value of 1 simply by

TABLE 12.2   Postulated Causes of Operational Losses for a Multiple Regression Model

Date	Operational loss ($)	System down-time	Trainees	Experienced staff	Transactions	Transaction errors
1-Jun	1,610,371	9	15	30	389,125	38,456
2-Jun	25,677	0	7	21	327,451	28,372
3-Jun	1,504,852	11	6	29	258,321	23,916
4-Jun	0	0	5	37	209,124	17,456
5-Jun	913,881	7	16	33	198,243	15,912
6-Jun	2,352,458	18	4	33	152,586	7,629
7-Jun	3,549,325	19	0	3	121,411	9,070
8-Jun	0	0	16	34	127,407	7,370
9-Jun	0	0	14	28	144,760	10,238
10-Jun	1,649,917	13	9	32	116,548	7,827

adding more independent variables to the regression equation. The adjusted coefficient of determination [$R^2(\text{adj})$] takes into account the number of explanatory variables in the model:

$$R^2(\text{adj}) = 1 - \left[\frac{\dfrac{\text{RSS}}{n-k}}{\dfrac{\text{TSS}}{n-1}} \right]$$

Notice that when $k = 1$:

$$R^2(\text{adj}) = 1 - \left[\frac{\dfrac{\text{RSS}}{n-k}}{\dfrac{\text{TSS}}{n-1}} \right] = 1 - \frac{\text{RSS}}{\text{TSS}} = R^2$$

The value of the estimated coefficients can be investigated using the t test described in the previous section. We may also be interested in the joint test of the null hypothesis that none of the explanatory variables have any effect on the dependent variable. In this case, provided our regression model has an intercept, we would use the test statistic

$$F = \frac{\left[\dfrac{\left(\text{TSS} - \text{RSS} \right)}{k} \right]}{\left[\dfrac{\text{RSS}}{\left(n - k - 1 \right)} \right]}$$

This test statistic has an F distribution with k and $n - k - 1$ degrees of freedom. Rejection of the null hypothesis implies that at least one of the explanatory variables has an effect on the dependent variable.

EXAMPLE 12.7 ESTIMATION OF PARAMETERS OF MULTIPLE LINEAR REGRESSION OF OPERATIONAL LOSSES

The parameter estimates for Example 12.1 are shown in Table 12.3. The first thing to notice is that the signs are more or less as expected. Second, the coefficient on system downtime is only slightly different from the value estimated in simple linear regression. However, R^2 is higher, indicating that the model fits the data slightly better than simple linear regression. The t statistic and F test statistic, with their corresponding p values, are also listed.

TABLE 12.3 Multiple Linear Regression for Operational Loss

The regression equation is
Opp_Loss = 153165 + 135950 System down time + 5506 Trainees − 11286
  Exp_Staff + 0.888 Transactions − 0.52 Trans_errors

Predictor	Coef	SE Coef	T	p	VIF
Constant	153165	46611	3.29	0.001	
Sys_down	135950	1864	72.93	0.000	1
Trainees	5506	2335	2.36	0.019	1.7
Exp_Staf	−11286	1416	−7.97	0.000	1.7
Transact	0.8883	0.3135	2.83	0.005	1.4
Trans_err	−0.520	1.826	−0.28	0.776	1.4

R^2(adj) = 95.4%
S = 160556
F joint test = 4082 (p < 0.001)

All of the independent variables, except transaction errors are significantly different from zero. The coefficients shown in Table 12.3 allow us to assess the impact on operational losses of a change in the independent variables. For example reducing the number of trainees on a particular day by 1 individual will lead to a reduction in operational losses of around $5,506, whilst reducing the number of trained staff by 1 individual increases operational losses by $11,286. Knowledge of this type is important in assessing the operational impact of decisions to change the trainee/experienced staff mix.

Checking the Assumptions of the Multiple Regression Model

We can use the same procedures mentioned for simple linear regression. The only additional concern is that the independent variables are uncorrelated. If this is not the case, the regression model may suffer from multicollinearity. Multicollinearity occurs when a linear relationship exists among the independent variables. If this occurs, the estimated regression coefficients become unreliable. There are a number of quantitative ways to detect multicollinearity. The simplest involves inspecting the sample correlation matrix constructed from the independent variables. Another way to detect multicollinearity, available in most regression software packages, involves the calculation of variance inflationary factors (VIFs) for each variable. VIFs are used to detect whether one predictor has a strong linear association with the remaining predictors (the presence of multicollinearity among the predictors). VIFs measure how much the variance of an estimated regression coefficient increases if the independent variables are highly correlated. It is generally accepted that a value greater than 5 indicates multicollinearity may be a serious problem, and therefore the regression coefficients, particularly those with high VIFs, may be unreliable.

EXAMPLE 12.8 MISSPECIFICATION TESTING THE SIMPLE LINEAR REGRESSION OF OPERATIONAL LOSSES ON SYSTEM DOWNTIME

Figure 12.10 plots the standardized residuals for the multiple regression model of Example 12.7. The vast majority of residuals lie within −2 to 2. Table 12.3 also reports that the variance inflation factors all are less than 2. Multicollinearity should not be a problem. Inspection of Figure 12.10 does not reveal any violations in homoscedasticity, although the pattern of observations seems to indicate failure of the independence assumption. The standardized residuals appear approximately normal, as shown in Figure 12.11.

PREDICTION

Regression occasionally is used to predict future values of the dependent variable. In the case of simple regression our predicted value $\hat{y}_{i+1}$ is

$$\hat{y}_{i+1} = \hat{\alpha} + \hat{\beta}\, x_{i+1}$$

and in the case of multiple regression we have

$$\hat{y}_{i+1} = \alpha + \hat{\beta}_1\, x_{i+1}^1 + \hat{\beta}_2\, x_{i+1}^2 + \cdots + \hat{\beta}_k\, x_{i+1}^k$$

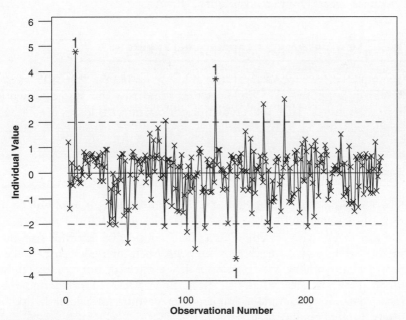

FIGURE 12.10　Standardized residuals for operational loss dependent on system downtime in multiple linear regression model.

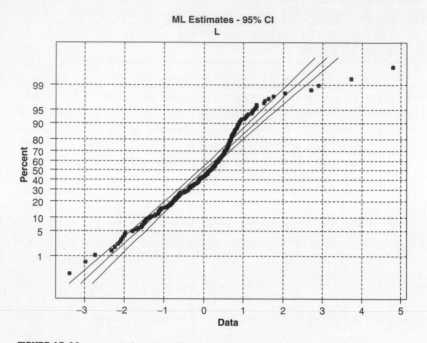

FIGURE 12.11   Normal probability plot for the standardized residuals for multiple linear regression of operational loss.

EXAMPLE 12.9   PREDICTION OF OPERATIONAL LOSSES

In Example 12.1 we found Operational loss = − 34815 + [136,205 × system downtime]. Suppose today we know that tomorrow our system downtime will be 10 minutes. Then our prediction for operational losses is − 34,815 + [136,205 × 10] = $1,327,235.

PREDICTIONS ARE RANDOM VARIABLES

Since a prediction is a function of a random variable, it, too, will be a random variable and will have an underlying probability distribution. We can, if we wish, calculate analytical confidence intervals for our prediction, known as *prediction intervals*. Such intervals can be interpreted along similar lines to a confidence interval, but are generally much wider because of the inherent uncertainty of predicting the future. Details of a simple-to-implement procedure for calculating such intervals numerically are given in Lewis (2003).

POLYNOMIAL AND OTHER TYPES OF REGRESSION

On occasion, the relationship between a dependent variable and independent variable may have considerable curvature. Polynomial regression offers a way to deal with this. For example, suppose you were considering the regression of Y on X and found the linear model is inadequate. You might then choose to model the relationship using a quadratic regression model, such as

$$y_i = \alpha + \beta_1 x_i + \beta_2 x_i^2 + \varepsilon_i$$

If this model proved unsatisfactory, you might then consider the model that includes x^3:

$$y_i = \alpha + \beta_1 x_i + \beta_2 x_i^2 + \beta_3 x_i^3 + \varepsilon_i$$

Polynomial regression analysis is sequential. We first evaluate a linear model. If this is inadequate, we add a quadratic term and then decide whether the addition of such a term is justified.

Other frequently specified forms of the relationship between the dependent and independent variable are the logarithmic regression, in which $y_i = \alpha + \beta_1 \ln(x_i) + \varepsilon_i$, and the exponential regression, in which $y_i = \alpha \exp(\beta_1 x_i) + \varepsilon_i$. Figure 12.12 shows these nonlinear relationships alongside the linear relationship between a dependent Y and independent variable X.

MULTIVARIATE MULTIPLE REGRESSION

In some circumstances the relationship between various types of operational risk factors will depend on a common set of explanatory variables. Where this is the case, we can estimate a multivariate multiple linear regression. As an illustration, suppose we have n measurements on q classes of operational losses $Y^1, \ldots, Y^q$ that are believed to be influenced by a common set of explanatory variables $X^1, X^2, \ldots, X^k$. The multivariate multiple regression model takes the form

$$\begin{cases} y_i^1 = \alpha_1 + \beta_{11} x_i^1 + \beta_{12} x_i^2 + \cdots + \beta_{1k} x_i^k + \varepsilon_{1i} \\ y_i^2 = \alpha_2 + \beta_{21} x_i^1 + \beta_{22} x_i^2 + \cdots + \beta_{2k} x_i^k + \varepsilon_{2i} \\ \quad \cdot \\ \quad \cdot \\ \quad \cdot \\ y_i^q = \alpha_q + \beta_{q1} x_i^1 + \beta_{q2} x_i^2 + \cdots + \beta_{qk} x_i^k + \varepsilon_{qi} \end{cases}$$

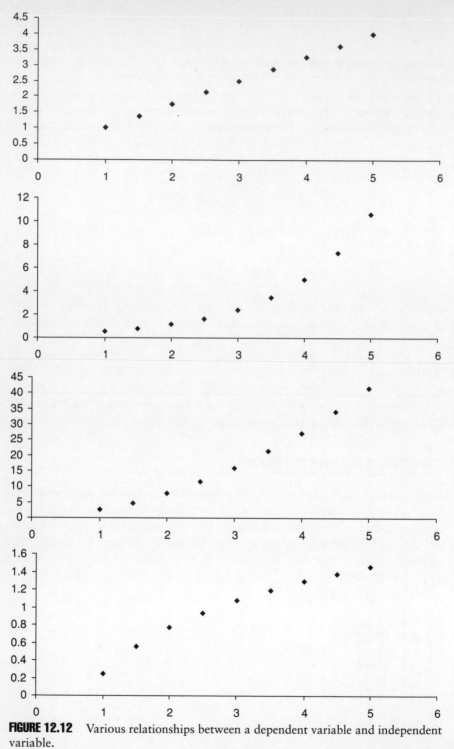

FIGURE 12.12 Various relationships between a dependent variable and independent variable.

The model parameters are estimated simultaneously using a procedure such as univariate least absolute deviation or coordinate rank regression.[1] Provided the model is correctly specified, it will have smaller standard errors than if we estimated each regression equation separately. We can check the validity of the regression assumptions using the methods previously outlined.

REGIME-SWITCHING REGRESSION

When an operational risk event is subject to regime shifts, the parameters of the statistical model will be time-varying. For example, consider the time series of minutes of system downtime per month for a particular business unit shown in Figure 12.13. In June 2003 total downtime fell sharply as a result of the business unit outsourcing its IT administration. Thus, the change in management policy had a direct impact on the stochastic behavior of the OR event "system downtime."

There are five issues that arise when we consider modeling shifts in regime:

1. How to extract the information in the data about regime shifts in the past
2. How to estimate the parameters of the model consistently and efficiently
3. How to detect recent regime shifts
4. How to correct the models at times when it is known that the regime has occurred
5. How to incorporate the probability of future regime shifts into forecasts

In general, these issues are tackled in a linear regression model by characterizing the process generating the dependent variable as piecewise linear. This

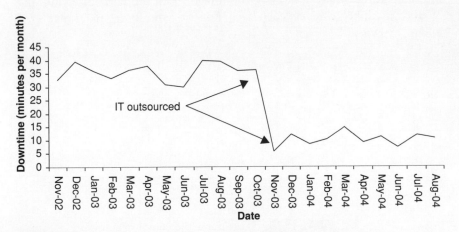

FIGURE 12.13 A structural break in minutes of system downtime.

is achieved by restricting the process to be linear in each regime. Although the importance of taking into account regime shifts in the OR analysis is widely appreciated, there is no established statistical theory offering a unique approach for specifying regression models that embed changes in regime. Indeed there are numerous models[2] that differ in their assumptions concerning the stochastic process generating the regime. One simple approach for the above example would be to model each regime separately:

$$Y_t = \alpha_1 + \beta_1 X_t$$
$$Y_t = \alpha_2 + \beta_2 X_t$$

where α_1 is the intercept term before the change in management policy and α_1 the intercept term after the IT function has been outsourced. This illustrates the basic idea of regime-switching models—that the process is time-invariant conditional on the regime prevailing at time t. An alternative approach is to consider regime shifts not as singular deterministic events, but governed by an exogenous stochastic process. Thus, regime shifts of the past are expected to occur randomly in the future.

THE DIFFERENCE BETWEEN CORRELATION AND REGRESSION

Correlation analysis compares how two random variables vary together. In regression we assume the values taken by the dependent variable are influenced or caused by the independent variables. Therefore, regression provides us with a cause-and-effect modeling framework. Correlation, on the other hand, informs us that two variables may be related, but it tells us nothing about causation. For example, in Figure 12.14 we consider two random variables, W and X, and a dependent variable Z. If increasing values of W and increasing values of X tend to influence Z in the same direction, then W and X will be positively correlated, *but* not causally related; however, W and X *do cause* Z.

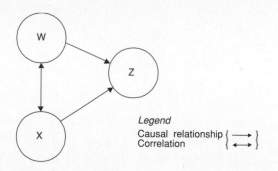

FIGURE 12.14 Correlation and causal relationship between three variables.

A STRATEGY FOR REGRESSION MODEL BUILDING IN OPERATIONAL RISK MANAGEMENT

A general strategy for successful regression model building consists of three stages. In the first stage we postulate a causal model between a dependent variable and at least one explanatory variable. The relationship between each explanatory variable and the dependent variable can be explored using a scatter plot and correlation. For each independent variable we may then visually examine the relationship with the dependent variable. Questions to bear in mind at this stage include:

- What does the scatter plot of the dependent variable indicate about the relationship between the two variables?
- What is the direction of causation? Is it positive or negative?
- What is the shape of the relationship? Linear or nonlinear?
- What is the correlation between the two variables?

The second stage involves estimation of the regression equation and interpreting the output. In this stage we are interested in what proportion of the variance in the dependent variable is explained by the regression model and the interpretation and statistical significance of the regression coefficients. Are the signs of these coefficients as expected?

The third stage of analysis involves checking that the assumptions of the regression model are met. This can be achieved informally by looking at graphs of the residuals, including the histogram, the normal probability plot, and the scatter plot of the standardized residuals as a function of the standardized predictions. If serious failure is evident, formal hypothesis testing can be carried out.

SUMMARY

Linear regression is intuitive and easy to calculate and presents risk management information in a clear and unambiguous fashion. A thorough understanding of its applicability and use will enhance your operational risk management planning and practice.

REVIEW QUESTIONS

1. What is the difference between the simple linear regression model and linear multiple regression?
2. Define and explain the coefficient of determination.

   - What is its relationship to the correlation coefficient?
   - What is its relationship to the adjusted coefficient of determination?

3. Give the form of the *t*-test statistic for testing the regression parameter estimates. How would you calculate a confidence interval around the regression parameter estimates?
4. What are the key misspecification tests you should carry out when using linear regression?
5. Why are predictions from linear regression models random variables?
6. Correlation is about association and regression about dependence. Discuss.
7. For the simple linear regression model ordinary least squares is a better estimator than maximum likelihood. Do you agree or disagree and why?

FURTHER READING

Further details on the linear regression model, including measures for detecting unusual observations such as leverage and Cook's distance, and formal hypothesis tests for normality such as the Kolmogorov-Smirnov test, are discussed in Montgomery and Peck (1982). Lewis (2003) gives details of how to calculate confidence intervals for any parameter using a simple numerical procedure.

CHAPTER 13

Logistic Regression in Operational Risk Management

ogistic regression is a useful tool for analyzing data that includes binary re-sponse variables, such as presence or absence of a fraud and success or failure of a back office process or system. The models work by fitting the probability of successes to the proportions of successes observed. For instance, "computer system failure today?" is an observed response (or, in the language of linear regression, the dependent variable). The observed number of failures are converted to proportions, which are then fitted by models that determine the probability that the computer system will fail today. In fact, logistic regression is a simply nonlinear transformation of the linear regression model. However, unlike linear regression, discussed in the previous chapter, logistic regression does not require assumptions about normality. We show in this chapter how it can be used in a univariate setting and then develop in detail a model for bivariate binary data.

BINARY LOGISTIC REGRESSION

Given a binary dependent variable Y, where $Y = 1$ if an event of interest occurs and 0 otherwise. Assume the event occurs with probability p and that we have k explanatory or independent variables $X^1, X^2, \ldots, X^k$. The binary logistic regression model takes the form

$$\ln\left[\frac{p}{(1-p)}\right] = \alpha + \beta_1\, x_i^1 + \beta_2\, x_i^2 + \cdots + \beta_k\, x_i^k + \varepsilon_i$$

ε is the residual, or error. This is very similar to the linear regression introduced in the previous chapter. To see this, recall that the linear regression specification is given by

$$Y = \alpha + \beta_1\, x_i^1 + \beta_2\, x_i^2 + \cdots + \beta_k\, x_i^k + \varepsilon_i$$

Since Y is binary, the above linear regression model cannot be used because we would encounter difficulties ensuring that the predicted value of Y lies between 0 and 1.

The ratio $\left[p \big/ (1-p) \right]$ is known as the *odds ratio*. The log of the odds ratio, $\ln\left[p \big/ (1-p) \right]$ is known as the *log odds ratio* or *logit*. An odds ratio equal to 1 implies that p, the probability of the event, equals 0.5 Therefore, there is a 50–50 chance the event will occur. Table 13.1 illustrates the relationship between p and the odds and log odds ratios. For $p > 0.5$, the odds ratio is greater than 1 and the log odds ratio is greater than 0; for $p < 0.5$ the odds ratio is less than 1 and the log odds ratio is negative.

Since p is a probability, the logistic regression model is constructed so that $0 \leq p \leq 1$. To see that this is so, note that as

$$\alpha + \beta_1 x_i^1 + \beta_2 x_i^2 + \cdots + \beta_k x_i^k$$

becomes very large, p approaches 1, and as

$$\alpha + \beta_1 x_i^1 + \beta_2 x_i^2 + \cdots + \beta_k x_i^k$$

becomes very small, p approaches 0. Furthermore, if

$$\alpha + \beta_1 x_i^1 + \beta_2 x_i^2 + \cdots + \beta_k x_i^k = 0$$

then $p = 0.5$. As with linear regression, the logistic regression coefficients can be estimated by maximum likelihood.

TABLE 13.1 Relationship between p, Odds Ratio, and Log Odds Ratio

p	Odds ratio	Log odds ratio
0.9	9.000	2.197
0.8	4.000	1.386
0.7	2.333	0.847
0.6	1.500	0.405
0.5	1.000	0.000
0.4	0.667	−0.405
0.3	0.429	−0.847
0.2	0.250	−1.386
0.1	0.111	−2.197

EXAMPLE 13.1 MODELING COMPUTER SYSTEM FAILURE RISK WITH LOGISTIC REGRESSION

Processing risk covers losses from back office operations. It includes, among other factors, the failure of computer systems such as order routing or electronic quote systems. Logistic regression allows us to calculate the probability associated with such a failure, given assumed risk indicators. Suppose (given the data) we postulate that the probability of computer failure is related to the ratio of available staff (systems support and maintenance) to all available staff on a particular day and the volume of computer-related business activity as a proportion of the recommended maximum capacity of the computer system. Table 13.2 shows how the data might be coded. We can model the probability of a computer system failure as

$$\ln\left[\frac{p}{(1-p)}\right] = \alpha + \beta_1 \left(\text{staff ratio}_i\right) + \beta_2 \left(\text{volume}_i\right) + \varepsilon_i$$

Interpretation and Model Fit

We interpret $\exp(\hat{\beta}_i)$ as the effect of the independent variable on the odds ratio. For example, if we postulate the logistic regression

$$\ln\left[\frac{p}{(1-p)}\right] = \alpha + \beta_1 x_i + \varepsilon_i$$

and on estimation find that $\hat{\beta}_1 = 0.963$, then $\exp(\hat{\beta}_1) = 1.999$ and a 1-unit change in X would make the event Y about twice as likely. Positive coefficients lead to an odds ratio greater than 1 and negative coefficients to a

TABLE 13.2 Example of Coding Daily Data Computer System Failure

Date	System failure	Coding of system failure	Staff ratio (%)	Volume (%)
1-Feb	Yes	1	3.0	79.5
2-Feb	No	0	18.0	53.6
3-Feb	Yes	1	4.5	21.9
4-Feb	No	0	5.0	52.3
5-Feb	Yes	1	1.4	10.3
⋮	⋮	⋮	⋮	⋮
12-Dec	No	0	12.3	45.1

odds ratio less than 1. As with linear regression, our objective is to determine if the value of the dependent variable can be explained by the independent variables. In this case, given the standard error of $\hat{\beta}_i$ [denoted by $s.e. (\hat{\beta}_i)$], the test statistic is

$$C = \left[\frac{\hat{\beta}_i}{s.e.(\hat{\beta}_i)} \right]^2$$

which has a chi-squared distribution with 1 degree of freedom. We also may be interested in the joint test of the null hypothesis that none of the explanatory variables have any effect on the dependent variable. In this case we use the test statistic

$$G = -2[LL(\hat{\alpha}) - LL(\hat{\alpha}, \hat{\beta}_1, \hat{\beta}_2, \cdots, \hat{\beta}_k)]$$

where $LL(\hat{\alpha}$ is the maximized log likelihood function of the model with only the intercept term and $LL(\hat{\alpha}, \hat{\beta}_1, \hat{\beta}_2, \cdots, \hat{\beta}_k)$ is the maximized log likelihood function with all the independent variables. G has a chi-squared distribution with k degrees of freedom. Rejection of the null hypothesis implies that at least one of the explanatory variables has an effect on the dependent variable.

Measuring overall model fit is not quite as straightforward as with linear regression. This is because there is no comparable measure of R^2, the proportion of variance in the dependent variable explained by the independent variables. However, there are quite a few number of "pseudo-R^2" statistics. Typical is McFadden's R^2 (McR^2) statistic

$$McR^2 = 1 - \frac{LL(\hat{\alpha}, \hat{\beta}_1, \hat{\beta}_2, \cdots, \hat{\beta}_k)}{LL(\hat{\alpha})}$$

MCFADDEN'S R^2

McFadden's R^2 (McR^2) is called a pseudo-R^2 statistic because unlike R^2, which takes on a minimum value of 0 and a maximum value of 1, $0 \leq McR^2 < 1$. In fact, McR^2 *can only be used* to determine the optimal number of independent variables given a specific data set. It cannot be used to compare the adequacy of models constructed using a different data set. Nevertheless, within these limitations, higher values of McR^2 are supposed to be indicative of a better-fitting model.

EXAMPLE 13.2 ESTIMATION AND INTERPRETATION OF LOGISTIC REGRESSION COEFFICIENTS FOR SYSTEMS FAILURE

Continuing with Example 13.1, we estimate the logistic regression equation (p values in brackets) as

$$\ln\left[\frac{p}{(1-p)}\right] = -1.9936\,(0.001) + 1.416\,(0.002) \times Staff\_ratio$$
$$+ 1.3917\,(.003) \times Volume$$

The estimates indicate that both explanatory variables are significant. Thus, the higher the staff absence ratio and volume, the more likely is a system failure. Furthermore, the estimated odds ratio on staff absence is 4.12 (95 percent confidence interval 1.71 to 9.91), which informs us that a 1-unit change in this ratio makes a system failure about four times as likely. We get a similar figure for volume, with an odds ratio of 4.05 (95 percent confidence interval 1.60 to 10.10). The test statistic $G = 18.75$, $p < 0.001$, and therefore we reject the joint test of the null hypothesis that none of the explanatory variables have any effect on the dependent variable.

BIVARIATE LOGISTIC REGRESSION

In some circumstances we may wish to model bivariate binary data with two binary dependent variables T and S. For example, T might be whether there has been a nostro break at the London office and S whether there has been a nostro break in the New York office during a particular time period. The model we develop is specified in such a way that the correlations between the binary dependent variables and the logistic regression coefficients are model parameters. In addition, the dependent variables T and S are assumed to be latent variables from a bivariate normal distribution. Latent variable constructions have been widely used in the social sciences as a means of characterizing the relationship between different outcomes.[1] We shall assume we have a data set with N paired binary outcomes on a dependent variable S and dependent variable T. Observations within pairs are correlated, but observations from different pairs are independent. The marginal outcome probabilities are denoted by P_S and P_T for S and T, respectively. The general situation is outlined in Table 13.3.

In 1970 Ashford and Sowden[2] introduced the multivariate probit model for modeling bivariate normally distributed random variables. Le Cessie & Van Houweligen,[3] in an analysis of neonatal mortality and morbidity in twins, replaced the probit marginals in the Ashford and Sowden bivariate probit model with identical logistic marginals. We adopt the Ashford and

TABLE 13.3 Outcomes for Two Binary Dependent Variables with Probability of Occurrence, Where P_{kj} Is the Probability that $T = k$ and $S = j$, Where j, k = 0 or 1

	$T = 1$	$T = 0$	
$S = 1$	P_{11}	P_{01}	P_S
$S = 0$	P_{10}	P_{00}	$1 - P_S$
	P_T	$1 - P_T$	1

Sowden bivariate framework and adjust the Le Cessie & Van Houweligen model to use nonidentical logistic marginals.

We assume the marginal outcome probabilities P_S and P_T are logistic and dependent upon an independent variable (also known as a covariate) x. For example, P_S and P_T might be the probabilities of a nostro break in the London or New York office, respectively, and x might be the total volume of activity. Thus, the marginal probabilities have a direct interpretation in terms of the logarithm of the odds in favor of success for the S and T endpoints, respectively. Therefore

$$P_S = \frac{\exp[\alpha_s + \beta_s x]}{1 + \exp[\alpha_s + \beta_s x]} \quad (13.1)$$

and

$$P_T = \frac{\exp[\alpha + \beta x]}{1 + \exp[\alpha + \beta x]} \quad (13.2)$$

where α, β, α_s, β_s, are unknown model parameters and x is the independent variable vector. P_S and P_T represent the logistic regression models discussed in the previous section.

Latent variables provide a useful and intuitive way to characterize the underlying distribution giving rise to the observable dependent variables. Such models presuppose the existence of unobservable continuous variables and assume that S and T enter a particular state when their associated latent variable exceeds a certain threshold. We model dependence by regarding the dichotomous outcome as realizations of a pair of associated continuous latent bivariate standard normally distributed variables S_n^L and T_n^L with correlation ρ. We capture this situation in the assumptions that

$$S_n = 1 \text{ if } S_n^L < g_S, \text{ with } g_S = \phi^{-1}(P_S) \quad (13.3)$$

and

$$T_n = 1 \text{ if } T_n^L < g_T, \text{ with } g_T = \phi^{-1}(P_T) \quad (13.4)$$

The function ϕ is the standard normal cumulative distribution function.

THE VALUE OF A LATENT VARIABLE SPECIFICATION

Now we can begin to see why the latent variable idea offers a natural model for the underlying mechanisms that are manifest, perhaps only roughly, in the realization of jointly distributed dichotomous dependent variables S and T. The joint probability is given by

$$\text{Prob }(S_n^L < g_S, T_n^L < g_T) = \int_{-\infty}^{g_S} \int_{-\infty}^{g_T} f(s, t, \rho)\, ds\, dt$$

where the function $f(s, t, \rho)$ is the joint density function of the standardized bivariate normal distribution. In this context ρ is the tetrachoric correlation[4] between S and T.

Using the above and the notation in Table 13.3, we can write the full model as

$$P_{11} = \int_{-\infty}^{g_S} \int_{-\infty}^{g_T} f(s, t, \rho)\, ds\, dt$$

$$P_{01} = P_S - P_{11}$$

$$P_{10} = P_T - P_{11}$$

$$P_{00} = 1 - P_{01} - P_{10} - P_{11}$$

The advantage of this particular latent variable formulation is that it leads to a set of intuitively appealing parameters. First, β_S and β have the same interpretation as they do in the marginal setting. Second, ρ gives us a measure of association between the dependent variables. Also, since $P_{11} \geq P_S P_T$, our model guarantees that if S and T are related, then they are at least positive quadrant–dependent. In addition, the dependence properties discussed in Chapter 11 inform us that the joint density function of the standardized bivariate normal distribution is totally positive of order 2. Therefore, if S and T are positively correlated, it follows, from the dependence properties of discussed in Chapter 11, that they are positively associated, and that T is stochastically increasing in S. Thus, a positive correlation implies dependence between S and T.

Parameter Estimation

In order to estimate the parameters of the model, we can use the method of maximum likelihood. For this we will need to define the associated likelihood equation. To achieve this, let ϑ be a $5*1$ vector of the unknown parameters α α_s, β, β_s and ρ given by:

$$\theta = \begin{bmatrix} \alpha_s \\ \alpha \\ \beta_s \\ \beta \\ \rho \end{bmatrix}$$

The log likelihood function is given by

$$LL(\theta) = \sum_{i=1}^{N} Y_{11i} \log P_{11i} + Y_{01i} \log P_{01i} + Y_{10i} \log P_{10i} + Y_{00i} \log P_{00i}$$

where Y_{jki} is an indicator variable such that

$$Y_{jki} \begin{cases} = 1 \text{ if } S_i = k \text{ and } T_i = j \\ = 0 \text{ otherwise} \end{cases}$$

Estimates of the parameters can be obtained by differentiating the log likelihood equation with respect to each parameter to obtain the efficient scores, and then solving the resulting simultaneous equations:

$$\frac{\partial LL(\theta)}{\partial \alpha_s} = \sum_{i=1}^{N} \left(\frac{Y_{11i}}{P_{11i}} \frac{\partial P_{11i}}{\partial \alpha_s} + \frac{Y_{10i}}{P_{10i}} \frac{\partial P_{10i}}{\partial \alpha_s} \right.$$
$$\left. + \frac{Y_{01i}}{P_{01i}} \frac{\partial P_{01i}}{\partial \alpha_s} + \frac{Y_{00i}}{P_{00i}} \frac{\partial P_{00i}}{\partial \alpha_s} = 0 \right)$$

$$\frac{\partial LL(\theta)}{\partial \alpha} = \sum_{i=1}^{N} \left(\frac{Y_{11i}}{P_{11i}} \frac{\partial P_{11i}}{\partial \alpha} + \frac{Y_{10i}}{P_{10i}} \frac{\partial P_{10i}}{\partial \alpha} \right.$$
$$\left. + \frac{Y_{01i}}{P_{01i}} \frac{\partial P_{01i}}{\partial \alpha} + \frac{Y_{00i}}{P_{00i}} \frac{\partial P_{00i}}{\partial \alpha} \right) = 0$$

$$\frac{\partial LL(\theta)}{\partial \beta_s} = \sum_{i=1}^{N} \left(\frac{Y_{11i}}{P_{11i}} \frac{\partial P_{11i}}{\partial \beta_s} + \frac{Y_{10i}}{P_{10i}} \frac{\partial P_{10i}}{\partial \beta_s} \right.$$
$$\left. + \frac{Y_{01i}}{P_{01i}} \frac{\partial P_{01i}}{\partial \beta_s} + \frac{Y_{00i}}{P_{00i}} \frac{\partial P_{00i}}{\partial \beta_s} \right) = 0$$

$$\frac{\partial LL(\theta)}{\partial \beta} = \sum_{i=1}^{N} \left(\frac{Y_{11i}}{P_{11i}} \frac{\partial P_{11i}}{\partial \beta} + \frac{Y_{10i}}{P_{10i}} \frac{\partial P_{10i}}{\partial \beta} \right.$$

$$\left. + \frac{Y_{01i}}{P_{01i}} \frac{\partial P_{01i}}{\partial \beta} + \frac{Y_{00i}}{P_{00i}} \frac{\partial P_{00i}}{\partial \beta} \right) = 0$$

For the unknown correlation coefficient note that

$$\frac{\partial P_{10i}}{\partial \rho} = \frac{\partial (P_{si} - P_{11i})}{\partial \rho} = -\frac{\partial P_{11i}}{\partial \rho} \text{ and}$$

$$\frac{\partial P_{01i}}{\partial \rho} = \frac{\partial (P_{yi} - P_{11i})}{\partial \rho} = -\frac{\partial P_{11i}}{\partial \rho}$$

Thus we can simplify $\dfrac{\partial LL(\theta)}{\partial \rho}$ slightly by writing

$$\frac{\partial LL(\theta)}{\partial \rho} = \sum_{i=1}^{N} \left(\frac{Y_{11i}}{P_{11i}} - \frac{Y_{10i}}{P_{10i}} - \frac{Y_{01i}}{P_{01i}} + \frac{Y_{00i}}{P_{00i}} \right) \frac{\partial P_{11i}}{\partial \rho} = 0$$

Taking the expectation of the second order derivatives, we have

$$E\left[\frac{\partial^2 LL(\theta)}{\partial \alpha_s^2} \right] = \sum_{i=1}^{N} \left(\frac{1}{P_{11i}} \frac{\partial P_{11i}}{\partial \alpha_s} \frac{\partial P_{11i}}{\partial \alpha_s} + \frac{1}{P_{10i}} \frac{\partial P_{10i}}{\partial \alpha_s} \frac{\partial P_{10i}}{\partial \alpha_s} \right.$$

$$\left. + \frac{1}{P_{01i}} \frac{\partial P_{01i}}{\partial \alpha_s} \frac{\partial P_{01i}}{\partial \alpha_s} + \frac{1}{P_{00i}} \frac{\partial P_{00i}}{\partial \alpha_s} \frac{\partial P_{00i}}{\partial \alpha_s} \right)$$

$$E\left[\frac{\partial^2 LL(\theta)}{\partial \alpha^2} \right] = -\sum_{i=1}^{N} \left(\frac{1}{P_{11i}} \frac{\partial P_{11i}}{\partial \alpha} \frac{\partial P_{11i}}{\partial \alpha} + \frac{1}{P_{10i}} \frac{\partial P_{10i}}{\partial \alpha} \frac{\partial P_{10i}}{\partial \alpha} \right.$$

$$\left. + \frac{1}{P_{01i}} \frac{\partial P_{01i}}{\partial \alpha} \frac{\partial P_{01i}}{\partial \alpha} + \frac{1}{P_{00i}} \frac{\partial P_{00i}}{\partial \alpha} \frac{\partial P_{00i}}{\partial \alpha} \right)$$

$$E\left[\frac{\partial^2 LL(\theta)}{\partial \beta_s^2} \right] = -\sum_{i=1}^{N} \left(\frac{1}{P_{11i}} \frac{\partial P_{11i}}{\partial \beta_s} \frac{\partial P_{11i}}{\partial \beta_s} + \frac{1}{P_{10i}} \frac{\partial P_{10i}}{\partial \beta_s} \frac{\partial P_{10i}}{\partial \beta_s} \right.$$

$$\left. + \frac{1}{P_{01i}} \frac{\partial P_{01i}}{\partial \beta_s} \frac{\partial P_{01i}}{\partial \beta_s} + \frac{1}{P_{00i}} \frac{\partial P_{00i}}{\partial \beta_s} \frac{\partial P_{00i}}{\partial \beta_s} \right)$$

$$E\left[\frac{\partial^2 \, \text{LL}(\theta)}{\partial \beta^2}\right] = -\sum_{i=1}^{N}\left(\frac{1}{P_{11i}}\frac{\partial P_{11i}}{\partial \beta}\frac{\partial P_{11i}}{\partial \beta} + \frac{1}{P_{10i}}\frac{\partial P_{10i}}{\partial \beta}\frac{\partial P_{10i}}{\partial \beta}\right.$$
$$\left. + \frac{1}{P_{01i}}\frac{\partial P_{01i}}{\partial \beta}\frac{\partial P_{01i}}{\partial \beta} + \frac{1}{P_{00i}}\frac{\partial P_{00i}}{\partial \beta}\frac{\partial P_{00i}}{\partial \beta}\right)$$

$$E\left[\frac{\partial^2 \, \text{LL}(\theta)}{\partial \rho^2}\right] = -\sum_{i=1}^{N}\left(\frac{1}{P_{11i}} - \frac{1}{P_{10i}} - \frac{1}{P_{01i}} + \frac{1}{P_{00i}}\right)\frac{\partial P_{11i}}{\partial \rho}\frac{\partial P_{11i}}{\partial \rho}$$

where $E[.]$ is the expectation operator discussed.

For notational ease in writing out the expectation of the cross derivatives, we denote

$$\theta = \begin{bmatrix} \alpha_s \\ \alpha \\ \beta_s \\ \beta \\ \rho \end{bmatrix} = \begin{bmatrix} \theta_1 \\ \theta_2 \\ \theta_3 \\ \theta_4 \\ \theta_5 \end{bmatrix}$$

so that $\vartheta_1 = \alpha_s$ etc. Using this notation, we have

$$E\left[\frac{\partial^2 \, \text{LL}(\theta_j)}{\partial \theta_j \theta_5}\right] = -\sum_{i=1}^{N}\left(\frac{1}{P_{11i}}\frac{\partial P_{11i}}{\partial \theta_j} + \frac{1}{P_{10i}}\frac{\partial P_{10i}}{\partial \theta_j} + \frac{1}{P_{01i}}\frac{\partial P_{01i}}{\partial \theta_j}\right.$$
$$\left. + \frac{1}{P_{00i}}\frac{\partial P_{00i}}{\partial \theta_j}\right)\frac{\partial P_{11i}}{\partial \theta_5} \quad \text{for } j = 1 \text{ to } 4$$

and

$$E\left[\frac{\partial^2 \, \text{LL}(\theta_j)}{\partial \theta_j \theta_k}\right] = -\sum_{i=1}^{N}\left(\frac{1}{P_{11i}}\frac{\partial P_{11i}}{\partial \theta_j}\frac{\partial P_{11i}}{\partial \theta_k} + \frac{1}{P_{10i}}\frac{\partial P_{10i}}{\partial \theta_j}\frac{\partial P_{10i}}{\partial \theta_k}\right.$$
$$+ \frac{1}{P_{01i}}\frac{\partial P_{01i}}{\partial \theta_j}\frac{\partial P_{01i}}{\partial \theta_k}$$
$$\left. + \frac{1}{P_{00i}}\frac{\partial P_{00i}}{\partial \theta_j}\frac{\partial P_{00i}}{\partial \theta_k}\right) \quad \text{for } j, k = 1 \text{ to } 4$$

In practice, the above equations are highly nonlinear and do not yield an explicit solution for the parameter estimates. A straightforward approach to finding the solution numerically involves assembling the efficient scores into a $5*1$ vector

$$U(\theta) = \begin{bmatrix} \dfrac{\partial LL(\theta)}{\partial \theta_1} \\ \cdot \\ \cdot \\ \cdot \\ \dfrac{\partial LL(\theta)}{\partial \theta_5} \end{bmatrix}$$

so that the jth component of this vector $\dfrac{\partial LL(\theta)}{\partial \theta_j} = 0 \; (j = 1, \cdots, 5)$ is the jth efficient score.

Define $U(\hat{\vartheta})$ as the vector of efficient scores evaluated at the maximum likelihood estimate $L(\hat{\vartheta})$ of the estimated parameters. Let $H(\vartheta)$ be the observed matrix of negative second derivatives associated with $U(\vartheta)$ such that its (i, j)th element is given by

$$-\frac{\partial^2 LL(\theta)}{\partial \theta_i \, \theta_j} \quad i = 1, \cdots, 5; j = 1, \cdots, 5$$

by definition at the maximized value of the likelihood function $U(\hat{\vartheta}) = 0$.

A first-order Taylor series expansion of $U(\hat{\vartheta})$ around ϑ_0 gives

$$U(\hat{\theta}) \approx U(\theta_0) + H(\theta_0)(\hat{\theta} - \theta_0)$$

from which it follows that

$$\hat{\theta} \approx \theta_0 - H^{-1}(\theta_0) \, U(\theta_0)$$

which suggests an iterative scheme, such as the Newton-Raphson procedure,[5] for estimating $\hat{\vartheta}$. The estimate of ϑ at the $(m+1)$th cycle of the iteration is given by

$$\hat{\theta}_{m+1} = \hat{\theta}_m - H^{-1}(\hat{\theta}_m) U(\hat{\theta}_m) \quad m = 0, \; 1, \; 2, \; 3, \; \ldots$$

where $\hat{\vartheta}_0$ is the parameter vector of initial (first guess) estimates of ϑ.

In practice, the algorithm you should implement to estimate the above is a slight modification of this scheme. We replace the observed matrix of negative second derivatives with the expected information matrix:

$$I(\theta) = -E\left[\frac{\partial^2 LL(\theta)}{\partial \theta_i \theta_j}\right] \quad i = 1, \cdots, 5; j = 1, \cdots, 5$$

so that the iterative scheme we use is given by

$$\hat{\theta}_{m+1} = \hat{\theta}_m - kI^{-1}(\hat{\theta}_m)U(\hat{\theta}_m) \quad m = 0, 1, 2, 3, \ldots$$

where k is a positive constant used to improve optimization.[6] To remove the restriction that $-1 < \rho < 1$ in our computations, we use the transformation $\log\left(\dfrac{1 + \rho}{1 - \rho}\right)$ in place of r. Maximization of the likelihood function occurs where $|L(\hat{\theta}_{m+1}) - L(\hat{\theta}_m)| < \varepsilon$, where ε is a small positive constant. In addition to obtaining the parameter estimates, I-1(^qm) provides an estimate of the asymptotic variance-covariance matrix evaluated at the maximum likelihood estimate.

CASE STUDY 13.1: NOSTRO BREAKS AND VOLUME IN A BIVARIATE LOGISTIC REGRESSION

We postulate that nostro breaks in the London office and New York office are dependent on the volume of activity. We code breaks in the London office (S) and New York office (T) as binary variables, whereas volume (X) is takes the values low, medium, and high. Table 13.4 shows the joint model and individual logistic model parameter estimates. The relevant regression coefficients for the marginal models of Equations 13.1 and 13.2 are $\tilde{\beta} = -0.2542$ (s.e $= 0.2119$, $p = 0.230$) and $\tilde{\beta}_s = -0.1478$ (s.e $= 0.2192$, $p = 0.500$), and for the joint model $\hat{\beta} = -0.2569$ (s.e $= 0.2119$, $p = 0.225$) and $\hat{\beta}_s = -0.1414$ (s.e $= 0.2191$, $p = 0.519$). Thus, there is little evidence in this sample of dependence between T or S on X, and we conclude that nostro breaks are not dependent on volume. Further investigation is clearly required. Perhaps we might include other variables in the model such as the absence or presence of key systems and back office staff.

TABLE 13.4 Table 13.4 Joint model parameter estimates $(\hat{\beta}, \hat{\beta}_s, \hat{\rho})$ and marginal logistic regression parameter estimates $(\tilde{\beta} \quad \tilde{\beta}_s)$ for bivariate logistic regression of Nostro Breaks against volume

$\hat{\rho}$	s.e $\hat{\rho}$	$\hat{\beta}$	$\tilde{\beta}$	s.e $\hat{\beta}$	s.e $\tilde{\beta}$	$\hat{\beta}_s$	$\tilde{\beta}_s$	s.e $\hat{\beta}_s$	$\tilde{\beta}_s$
0.095	0.058	−0.2569	−0.2542	0.2119	0.2119	−0.1414	−0.1478	0.2191	0.2192

OTHER APPROACHES FOR MODELING BIVARIATE BINARY ENDPOINTS

As always in statistical modeling, there are many ways to achieve our objectives. In this section we highlight a number of alternative models.

Bivariate Bernoulli Model and Bivariate Binomial Model

The bivariate Bernoulli distribution is natural starting point for modeling bivariate binary data. It is parameterized by two marginal parameters (P_S and P_T) and one bivariate parameter (P_{11}). The correlation between S and T (ρ) is given by[7]

$$\rho = \frac{(P_{11} - P_S P_T)}{\sqrt{P_S(1 - P_S)P_T(1 - P_T)}}$$

It can also be shown that

$$\mathrm{Max}\left\{\frac{P_S P_T}{\sqrt{(1 - P_S)(1 - P_T)}}, \frac{(1 - P_S)(1 - P_T)}{\sqrt{P_S P_T}}\right\} \le r \le$$
$$\sqrt{\frac{\min[P_S, P_T](1 - \max[P_S, P_T])}{\max[P_S, P_T] - (1 - \min[P_S, P_T])}}$$

from which it can be seen that ρ is only an adequate measure of association, in the sense that we get the full range of correlation $-1 \le \rho \le 1$ when the S and T marginal probabilities are the same in the sense that $P_s = P_T$. An alternative would be to use the bivariate binomial model

$$\frac{n!}{\sum s! \sum t! \, [\, n - \sum s - \sum t\,]!} \, P_S^{\sum s} P_T^{\sum t} \left\{1 - n - P_S^{\sum s} P_T^{\sum t}\right\}$$

Gumbel-type Models

An alternative to the bivariate binomial distribution was introduced by Gumbel.[8] Gumbel developed several bivariate logistic distributions with the property that their marginal distributions were also logistic. His first distribution is given by

$$F(s, t) = [1 + \exp^{-s} + \exp^{-t}]^{-1} \tag{13.5}$$

where $F(s, t)$ is the cumulative probability function.

Gumbel showed that the logistic distribution implied by Equation 13.5 is asymmetric. In particular, the probability at the center $F(0,0) = 0.3333$ instead of 0.25 as implied by the bivariate normal probability function used in the bivariate logistic model discussed in Case Study 13.1. The author goes on to show that Equation 13.5 cannot be split into the product of the marginal distributions; therefore, it implies a priori that the variables are dependent. In addition, Gumbel showed that Equation 13.5 can be used in cases where the marginal distributions are symmetrical and resemble the normal distribution if the sample coefficient correlation is of the order 0.5.

Gumbel's second logistic distribution is given by

$$F(s,t) = [1 + \exp^{-s}]^{-1}[1 + \exp^{-t}]^{-1}[1 + \alpha \exp^{-s-t}$$
$$[1 + \exp^{-s}]^{-1}[1 + \exp^{-t}]^{-1}] \qquad (13.6)$$

where the unknown parameter α is subject to the restriction $-1 < \alpha < 1$. The author shows that the correlation (ρ) between S and T is a function of α given by

$$\rho = \frac{3\alpha}{\pi^2}$$

where $\pi = 3.1415927\ldots$. Equation 13.6 is more flexible than Equation 13.5 due to the addition of the dependence parameter α. The probability at the center $F(0,0) = 0.25\left[1 + \dfrac{\alpha}{4}\right]$ Independence occurs when $\alpha = 0$.

Grizzle-type Models

Following Gumbel's proposal, a number of authors introduced covariates into the bivariate logistic framework. An early marginal modeling approach was developed by Grizzle,[9] who analyzed data on coal miners in nine five-year-wide age groups reporting either, neither, or both of the respiratory symptoms, breathlessness and wheeze. For each age category the author considered only the marginal data of how many had or did not have breathlessness and how many or did not have wheeze. Two marginal models were developed for each symptom:

1. $\ln\left[\dfrac{P_S}{1 - P_S}\right] = \alpha_{\text{wheeze}_i} + \beta_{\text{wheeze}_i} x_i \ i = 1, \ldots, 9$

2. $\ln\left[\dfrac{P_S}{1 - P_S}\right] = \alpha_{\text{breathlessness}_i} + \beta_{\text{breathlessness}_i} x_i \ i = 1, \ldots, 9$

where x is an indicator variable for wheeze or breathlessness. Mantel and Brown along with Nerlove and Press[10] extended this model into the multivariate setting.

Generalization of the Ashford-Sowden Probit Model

Morimune,[11] in a discussion of the differences between the bivariate logistic and bivariate normal distribution, developed a generalization of the Ashford-Sowden probit model in which the correlation coefficient is made a function of X:

1. $P_{11} = \dfrac{\exp\ (\beta_S X + \beta X + \kappa X)}{1 + \exp\ (\beta_S X + \beta X + \kappa X)}$

2. $P_{01} = \dfrac{\exp\ (\beta_S X)}{1 + \exp\ (\beta_S X + \beta X + \kappa X)} - P_{11}$

3. $P_{10} = \dfrac{\exp\ (\beta X)}{1 + \exp\ (\beta_S X + \beta X + \kappa X)} - P_{11}$

4. $P_{00} = 1 - P_{01} - P_{10} - P_{11}$

This was extended into a fully logistic version of the Ashford-Sowden model by Maddala,[12] given by

1. $P_{11} = \dfrac{\exp\ (\beta_S X + \beta X + \kappa X)}{1 + \exp\ (\beta_S X + \beta X + \kappa X)}$

2. $P_{01} = \dfrac{\exp\ (\beta_S X)}{1 + \exp\ (\beta_S X)} - P_{11}$

3. $P_{10} = \dfrac{\exp\ (\beta X)}{1 + \exp\ (\beta X)} - P_{11}$

4. $P_{00} = 1 - P_{01} - P_{10} - P_{11}$

Copula-based Models

An alternative framework for developing multivariate models is based on the use of copula functions. Let P_S and P_T represent two univariate marginal distribution functions. Let $H(u, v)$ denote a bivariate distribution function concentrated on the unit square having uniform marginal distributions, so that $H(1,1) = 1$, $H(0,0) = 0$, $H(u,1) = u$, and $H(1,v) = v$. Such bivariate distribution functions are called *copulas*. We can define a bivariate distribution for random variables S and T by

$$\text{Prob} \quad (S < s, \ T < t) = H[P_s(s), P_T(t)]$$

Since H has uniform marginal distributions, S and T have marginal distribution functions P_S and P_T. All that remains is to choose an appropriate distribution for H. There are a wide variety of one-parameter and two-parameter parametric families of multivariate copulas. The choice between one-parameter and two-parameter families will depend on how many types of dependence you wish to capture in your model. One-parameter families, in particular the Plackett family,[13] have been popularized by Dale,[14] and Le Cessie and Van Houwelingen.[15] For $0 \leq \delta < \infty$, the Placket copula is given by

$$H(s, t, \delta) = \frac{1}{2}(\delta - 1)^{-1}\{1 + (\delta - 1)(s + t) - [(1 + (\delta - 1)(s + t)^2)$$
$$- 4(\delta - 1)st]^{1/2}\}$$

where δ is the dependence parameter such the marginal distributions are independent if $\delta = 1$.

The Plackett copula is considered by Dale,[16] who investigates the problem of correlated ordinal outcomes. Dale quantified the dependence parameter δ in the Plackett copula as the "cross ratio" between outcomes defined as

$$\delta = \frac{P_{11}P_{00}}{P_{01}P_{10}}$$

When the responses are binary, the cross ratio reduces to the odds ratio. Le Cessie and Van Houweligen,[17] who used the Plackett copula, with the dependence parameter given by the Dale cross ratio, to model correlated binary outcomes in such a way that the marginal response probabilities are logistic.

SUMMARY

There are many important research topics in OR for which the dependent variable is limited (discrete, not continuous). OR managers may wish to analyze whether some event occurred, such as failure of a system or fraud. Binary logistic regression is a type of regression analysis where the dependent variable is a coded 0 or 1. Logistic regression has many analogies to linear regression, the logistic regression coefficients correspond to coefficients in the linear regression equation, and a pseudo-R^2 statistic such as McFadden's R^2 can be used to summarize the strength of the relationship. Unlike linear regression, logistic regression does not assume linearity of relationship between the dependent and independent variables, nor does it require normally distributed random variables or homoscedasticity. We can easily extend logistic regression into the bivariate setting. Indeed, the bivariate model developed in this chapter allows us to explore the relationships between the independent and binary dependent variables. The model is simple to apply and easy to implement. The parameters in the joint model have the same interpretation as they do in the standard logistic regression setting. In the following chapter we discuss how we can generate multivariate regression–type models where the dependent variables may be all binary, all continuous, or an arbitrary combination.

REVIEW QUESTIONS

1. Outline the differences between logistic and linear regression.
2. Can we estimate the logistic regression parameters using ordinary least squares?
3. How can we assess model fit in logistic regression?
4. What is the odds ratio?
5. Write a function in VBA that returns the parameter estimates for the bivariate logistic model introduced in this chapter.

   ■ Test the model on a range of simulated and real binary data.
   ■ Is the latent variable assumption of normality generally valid for your data?

FURTHER READING

Details of estimation of ordinal logistic regression parameters using an iterative reweighted least squares algorithm to obtain maximum likelihood estimates are given in McCullagh and Nelder (1992).

CHAPTER 14

Mixed Dependent Variable Modeling

In the previous two chapters we have discussed how to use linear regression and logistic regression when we have continuous or binary dependent variables. In some other situations we might wish to model jointly dependent variables that are a mixture of binary and continuous variables. For example, an OR manager might be interested in developing a joint model with the binary dependent variable "transaction completed" alongside the continuous dependent variable "transaction time." In this chapter we outline a general and easily implemented approach for multivariate regression modeling of this type.

A MODEL FOR MIXED DEPENDENT VARIABLES

The general challenges in constructing multivariate models that cater for mixed dependent variables (which we also refer to as *endpoints*) have been well documented.[1] Our primary concern as OR managers and analysts is to obtain accurate estimates of model parameters for use in management decision making. For parsimony we shall focus on the situation where we wish to model jointly binary and continuous dependent variables in a regression framework. We assume T is a continuous variable and measures the time to failure of a back office system. We assume a specific parametric distribution is known, possibly up to a vector parameter β and that there is available for inference about β a sample of uncensored observations and an independent variable vector X of relevant risk indicators. Also suppose for a binary dependent variable S a specific parametric distribution is known possibly up to a vector parameter β_S and that there is available for inference about β_S a complete sample of observations, given the dependent variable vector X. We also assume we have n paired outcomes on S and T. Furthermore, observations within pairs are correlated, but observations from different pairs are independent.

Since S is binary, the probability of a response to X can be modeled using the logistic regression given by

$$P_S = \text{Prob}\,\{e_S\} = \frac{\exp[\alpha_S + \beta_S X]}{1 + \exp[\alpha_S + \beta_S X]}$$

where α_S and β_S are unknown model parameters. Similarly, as T is a time to failure variable, the probability of failure at $T = t$ is conditional upon survival to time t and the dependent variable X is given by

$$P_T = \lim_{\delta \to 0^+} \frac{\text{Prob}\,(t \le T < t + \delta \mid T \ge t, X = x)}{\delta}$$

If we were only interested in P_S or P_T, we could quite easily specify a marginal model for P_S (logistic) and P_T (lognormal, exponential, etc.). Misspecification testing (goodness of fit, omitted variables, etc.) can be carried out on these marginal models. Returning to the framework and notation introduced in the previous chapter, we write

1. P_{11}
2. $P_{01} = P_S - P_{11}$
3. $P_{10} = P_T - P_{11}$
4. $P_{00} = 1 - P_{01} - P_{10} - P_{11}$

where we denote the bivariate probability density function as P_{11} with marginal densities P_T and P_S for T and S, respectively. In the context of our example, P_{01} can be interpreted as the probability of only observing a response in the dependent variable S and P_{10} can be interpreted as the probability of only observing a failure in the time to failure endpoint T during the time interval $t \ge T \ge t + \delta$ ($\delta > 0$).

Notice that the above framework is essentially the same as that discussed in the previous chapter; however, in this case we interpret P_{11}, P_{01}, P_{00}, and P_T as probability density functions. Furthermore, since S is discrete, P_S and P_{01} can be interpreted as probability mass functions. Thus, in this example we have a joint probability density function (P_{11}) whose marginal probabilities are generated by a marginal probability density function (P_T) for the dependent variable T and a marginal probability mass function (P_S) for the dependent variable S. If P_{11}, P_S, and P_T are known, a likelihood function can be specified and parameter estimates obtained. Unfortunately, P_{11} is generally unknown and T may be heavily censored.

As the exact form of P_{11} is generally unknown, a variety of parametric models from which we could obtain an estimate of the model parameters have been proposed. For example Catalano and Ryan,[2] for binary and continuous outcomes, used the concept of a latent variable to derive the joint distribution of a discrete and continuous variable. The Catalano model is parameterized such that the joint distribution is the product of a standard linear model for the continuous variable and a correlated probit model for the discrete variable. It involves specifying a model for association between the binary and continuous outcomes and a model for the means. Unfortunately, the regression parameters in their probit model do not have the same interpretation as the parameters in the marginal model. In addition, if the model for the mean has been correctly specified, but the model for the association between the binary and continuous outcomes is misspecified, the regression parameters in their probit model are not consistent.

Olkin and Tate,[3] for a continuous and discrete outcome, assumed a multinomial model for discrete outcomes and a multivariate normal model for continuous outcomes, given the discrete outcome. Fitzmaurice and Laird[4] described a likelihood-based extension to the approach of Olkin and Tate. O'Brien,[5] and Pocock et al.,[6] among others, discussed methods for combining outcomes in a general testing context. Lefkopoulou et al.[7] considered multiple outcomes in the developmental toxicity context but deal only with binary endpoints. Recently, Molenberghs et al.[8] used a latent variable probit model and a Plackett-Dale bivariate density to model mixed discrete and continuous endpoints. Although it may be possible to use any of the above models to obtain an estimate of parameters, the assumed structure for the association between endpoints in the above models is complex.

In many situations the OR manager will not know the nature of the relationship between S and T, and is unlikely to have any information on the form of the joint distribution. What is required is a generally applicable approach to estimating the parameters that is suitable for arbitrarily mixed endpoints. One solution is to use a bootstrap procedure.[9] Indeed, for many situations this will prove adequate. However, where there are few events in T (that is, few failures), bootstrapping will be infeasible. An alternative that works well in this situation is to obtain the parameters using the asymptotic distribution via a working assumption of independence (WAI). We discuss WAI in the next section.

WORKING ASSUMPTION OF INDEPENDENCE

A working assumption of independence (WAI)[10] offers a pragmatic solution to the complex estimation problem, especially where we have no information on the joint distribution of the dependent variables. Huster et al.[11] and Wei et al.[12] considered the relative effects of one or more explanatory variables, such as treatment assignments, on the distribution of multivariate failure times. Their estimation approach ignores the form of association between endpoints. They use instead a WAI, in which failure times are formulated independently for each endpoint. The general appeal of WAI formulation is that all modeling is done independently within margins. Where appropriate, marginal forms can be drawn from well-studied models. Misspecification testing (goodness of fit, omitted variables, etc.) can be carried out on these marginal models, and thus the inherent complexity of carrying out misspecification testing on a joint model is avoided.

A WAI leaves the nature of dependence between endpoints completely unspecified. To appreciate the consequence of this, consider some asymptotic results under separate marginal analysis of S and T. Given a model for P_T and P_S, under standard regularity conditions,[13] and given the consistent maximum likelihood estimators of the marginal models $\hat{\beta}$ and $\hat{\beta}_S$ of the true values of the parameters β and β_S, respectively, then $I[\hat{\beta}]^{1/2}(\hat{\beta}_N - \dot{\beta})$ and $I[\hat{\beta}_S]^{1/2}(\hat{\beta}_{S_N} - \dot{\beta}_S)$ both converge asymptotically in distribution to the standard normal distribution,[14] where $I[\beta]$ and $I[\beta_S]$ are the information matrices obtained from the associated marginal likelihood functions of P_T and P_S. This allows us to set the usual approximate confidence interval of $\hat{\beta} \pm z\ I[\beta\ ]^{-1/2}$ and $\hat{\beta}_S \pm z\ I[\beta_S]^{-1/2}$.

The asymptotic validity of these intervals depend on three properties:

Property 1: Consistency of $\hat{\beta}$ for estimating β and $\hat{\beta}_S$ for estimating β_S

Property 2: Asymptotic normality of $N^{1/2}\left\{ \hat{\beta}_N - \dot{\beta} \right\}$ and $N^{1/2}\left\{ \hat{\beta}_{S_N} - \dot{\beta} \right\}$

Property 3: Consistency of $n\ I[\hat{\beta}]^{-1}$ and $n\ I[\hat{\beta}_S]^{-1}$ for estimating the variance

of the respective limiting distributions

Under the WAI the joint likelihood is the product of the likelihood of the marginal models. Parameters are estimated by maximizing separately the likelihood from each of these models. Of course, in reality, there is dependence between S and T. Thus the WAI likelihood is misspecified and we should be concerned that property 1 will not hold, that is, that the estimates of the marginal parameters may not be consistent for those of the true (unknown) bivariate distribution. Fortunately, the key feature of WAI is the result that consistent parameter estimates are obtained, despite the possible misspecification of the joint distribution, as long as the marginal models are correctly specified with respect to the true margins of the unknown joint distribution. The trade-off is a potential loss of efficiency for not making full use of information contained in the true joint distribution of the endpoints.

Although parameter estimates for well-specified models will be consistent, in general, the likelihood estimates of the variance will not be consistent unless the WAI assumption is true and our dependent variable S contains no information about the outcome on the final endpoint. Royall[15] discusses the WAI adjustment to variance estimation that is robust to the failure of this type. For notational ease, we write

$$\hat{\theta} = \begin{bmatrix} \hat{\beta} \\ \hat{\beta}_S \end{bmatrix} \text{ and } \theta = \begin{bmatrix} \dot{\beta} \\ \dot{\beta}_S \end{bmatrix}$$

and denote the vector pth derivatives at the maximum likelihood as

$$U^p(\hat{\theta}) = \begin{bmatrix} \dfrac{\partial^p LL(\beta, \beta_S)}{\partial (\beta)^p} \\ \dfrac{\partial^p LL(\beta, \beta_S)}{\partial (\beta)^p s} \end{bmatrix}$$

Royall notes that it is possible to approximate $U^1[\hat{\vartheta}]$, the score vector, using a first-order Taylor series expansion around ϑ so that

$$0 = U^1[\hat{\vartheta}] \approx U^1[\vartheta] + U^2[\vartheta](\hat{\vartheta} - \vartheta)$$

from which we see that

$$-\frac{U^1[\dot{\theta}]}{U^2[\dot{\theta}]} = (\hat{\theta} - \dot{\theta}) \tag{14.1}$$

Royall shows that $n^{1/2}\{\hat{\vartheta} - \vartheta\}$ converges as $n \rightarrow \infty$ to a normal distribution (by the central limit theorem because $U^1[\vartheta]$ and $U^2[\vartheta]$ are sums of independent random variables) with mean zero [since $E(\hat{\vartheta} - \vartheta) = 0$, as $n \rightarrow \infty$, where $E(.)$ is the expectations operator] and variance covariance matrix Σ given by

$$\psi = n U^2[\hat{\theta}]^{-1} \left\{ \sum_{i=1}^{n} U_i^1[\hat{\theta}] U_i^1[\hat{\theta}]^T \right\} U^2[\hat{\theta}]^{-1} \tag{14.2}$$

where $U_i^1[\hat{\theta}]$ is the contribution of the ith pair to the vector of first derivatives.

Therefore, by using a postestimation correction to the information matrix, an asymptotic estimate of the variance-covariance matrix that is robust to the WAI is obtained.[16] Hence, given $I[\hat{\vartheta}]$, the joint model information matrix

$$I[\hat{\theta}] = -E\left[\begin{matrix}\left[\dfrac{\partial^2\,LL(\beta,\beta_S)}{\partial\beta^2}\right] & \left[\dfrac{\partial\,LL(\beta,\beta_S)}{\partial\beta_S\beta}\right] \\[3mm] \left[\dfrac{\partial\,LL(\beta,\beta_S)}{\partial\beta\,\beta_S}\right] & \left[\dfrac{\partial^2\,LL(\beta,\beta_S)}{\partial\beta_S^2}\right]\end{matrix}\right]$$

ψ rather than $nI[\hat{\vartheta}]^{-1}$ could be used for estimating the variance of the limiting distribution.

UNDERSTANDING THE BENEFITS OF USING A WAI

Our use of WAI is essentially pragmatic; if we have a large number of events in T, we could use a bootstrap procedure. However, OR managers will frequently collect data on dependent variables when there are a very limited number of events. If we had knowledge of the joint distribution of T and S, a joint model could have be specified. Unfortunately, in OR practice, such knowledge is rarely available.

CASE STUDY 14.1: MODELING FAILURE IN COMPLIANCE

In April 2003 the UK Financial Services Authority (FSA) fined Lincoln Assurance Limited £485,000 for the misselling of 10-year savings plans by its appointed representative, City Financial Partners Limited (CFPL), between September 1, 1998 and August 31, 2000. The misselling occurred because Lincoln Assurance Limited did not adequately monitor CFPL and so failed to ensure that CFPL only recommended 10-year savings plans where they were suitable for their customers' needs. We can use our WAI model to investigate the joint likelihood of a similar failure in compliance and the time before a hefty fine is imposed. Suppose we denote an internally detected serious failure in compliance as S, where S is 1 if there is a serious failure, and 0 otherwise. Ideally, all such failures will be detected internally, although this is not necessarily the case. We assume the marginal outcome probabilities for S (P_S) are logistic, dependent upon the amount of staff training (X), given by

$$P_S = \frac{\exp\,[\alpha_S + \beta_S X]}{1 + \exp\,[\alpha_S + \beta_S X]} \tag{14.3}$$

where α_S and β_S are unknown model parameters. We assume X is categorical, representing "none," "very low," "low," "average," "high," or "very high."

TABLE 14.1 Parameter Estimates for the Marginal Logistic Regression, Marginal Weibull Regression, and Joint WAI Model, with Standard Errors in Parentheses

	$\hat{\alpha}_S$	$\hat{\beta}_S$	$\hat{\alpha}$	$\hat{\beta}_S$	$\hat{\kappa}$
Marginal	3.5316	−0.7747	10.5226	−0.7943	1.3517
	(0.5501)	(0.3212)	(0.8464)	(0.3569)	(0.2420)
Joint WAI	3.5587	−0.7850	10.5670	−0.8099	1.3728
	(0.5662)	(0.3282)	(0.7690)	(0.3827)	(0.1288)

We assume the time to a serious fine by the regulatory authorities (T) follows a Weibull distribution, such that

$$\lambda_i = \exp\{-(\alpha + \beta X)\} \text{ and } w_i = \kappa \ln(\lambda_i t_i)$$

where β, α, and κ are unknown model parameters.

We will use maximum likelihood to estimate the model parameters. The WAI log likelihood is given by

$$\sum_{i=1}^{n} \left\{ \delta_i \ln f(w_i) + (1 - \delta_i) \right\} \left[\ln G(w_i) S_i \log(P_S) + (g_i - S_i) \log(1 - P_S) \right. $$
$$\left. + \log \binom{g_i}{S_i} \right\}$$

where δ_i is a censoring indicator ($\delta_i = 0$ for censored observations), $f(w_i)$
$= \dfrac{1}{\sigma} \exp\{w_i - \exp(w_i)\}$, $G(w_i) = \dfrac{1}{\sigma} \exp\{-\exp(w_i)\}$, $\sigma = \dfrac{1}{\kappa}$, and g_i is the number of categories in X.

The marginal logistic regression of S on X yields a log odds ratio of $\hat{\beta}_S$ $= -0.7747$ (s.e 0.3212, $p = 0.016$), whereas the marginal Weibull regression yields $\hat{\beta} = -0.7943$ (s.e 0.3569, $p = 0.026$). In this case there is a significant effect on both endpoints. From Table 14.1 we see that the WAI estimates of the model parameters (standard errors in parentheses) are comparable with the marginal models.

SUMMARY

Whether our dependent variables are binary or mixed, it is possible to build a joint or multivariate model and easily obtain parameter estimates using

WAI. The principle disadvantages of WAI are that it tends to be biased downward in very small samples[17] and, as the number of parameters estimated per marginal model increases, it tends to underestimate the finite sample variance, with the magnitude of bias growing as the number of parameters estimated per marginal model increases.[18] This is not really a drawback in OR practice because the number of parameters per marginal model tends to be small. Thus, WAI provides a solution to the problem of estimating model parameters when the joint distribution of S and T is unknown and bootstrapping proves infeasible. It gives the OR manager the ability to construct models simply by specifying the marginal distributions. Furthermore, the parameters in the joint model have the same interpretation as they do in the marginal setting.

REVIEW QUESTIONS

1. Why would we use WAI rather than develop a joint model?
2. What are the key drawbacks of using WAI? Are these drawbacks of practical concern to the OR manager?
3. Write VBA code to estimate a joint binary model using WAI and compare your parameter estimates using the bivariate binary model discussed in the previous chapter.
4. Under what conditions would you prefer to build a true joint model rather than an approximate WAI model?

FURTHER READING

Further details on WAI can be found in Huster et al. (1989) and Wei et al. (1989). Details on the application of the bootstrap in risk management are given in Lewis (2003).

CHAPTER 15

Validating Operational Risk Proxies Using Surrogate Endpoints

Over the past decade there has been much interest in the scientific literature in the replacement of so-called final endpoints with surrogate variables.[1] A *final endpoint* is a dependent variable of direct interest. A *surrogate endpoint* is a dependent variable used as a proxy for the final endpoint. For example, we might be interested in large operational losses above $2 million due to failure in information systems but because they occur very rarely, we might use operations staff experience, turnover, or days of training as a surrogate or proxy. In this chapter we illustrate the potential of surrogate endpoints in OR analysis, examine the key ideas of surrogate modeling, and discuss the major validation techniques and their limitations.

THE NEED FOR SURROGATE ENDPOINTS IN OR MODELING

Operational risk practice is dogged by limited data availability and missing observations. Operational risk studies investigating the effects of various risk indicators or key OR events, such as serious operational losses and costly legal cases or reputation damage, require extended periods of time to collect the data, are costly, and may take many years to complete. Fortunately, some of the tools required to draw useful conclusions about the cause of OR events as soon as possible from surrogate endpoints have been developed in the medical statistics field. Here, researchers are required to explore events or biological markers that may be observed and assessed prior to the appearance of the clinical outcome measure of primary interest. The occurrence of these surrogate events, sometime between a given exposure or intervention that affects the disease process and the time of the clinical outcome, allows medical researchers to speculate that they may serve as a surrogate for the final endpoint. The notion of surrogate endpoints is clearly relevant in OR modeling.

MEDICAL STATISTICS METHODS DOMINATE THE SURROGATE ENDPOINT LITERATURE

Much of the reported work in the literature about the use and validation of surrogate endpoints has been motivated by the need to increase the speed by which results for new medical treatments can be obtained. Progress has been so swift that there are now numerous surrogate endpoint techniques developed in the medical statistics literature that are *directly* relevant to OR modeling and practice. The replacement of a rare final endpoint with a surrogate variable that can be measured earlier, more conveniently, or more frequently can lead to substantial reductions in sample size, study duration, and cost.[2] Piantadosi[3] illustrated the potential benefits using a simple medical example (p. 141):

> *Suppose we wish to test the benefit of a new anti-hypertensive agent against standard therapy in a randomised trial. Survival is a definitive endpoint and blood pressure the surrogate. If it were practical and ethical to follow patients long enough to observe overall mortality, such a trial would need to be large. For example, the difference between 95% and 90% overall mortality at five years requires 1162 subjects to detect a statistically significant difference with 90% power and a two sided 0.05 significance level test. In contrast, if we use diastolic blood pressure as the endpoint, we could detect a reduction of as little as ½ of a standard deviation using 170 patients with a trial duration of a few weeks or months.*

In order to be consistent with the medical literature and to assist your reading of this literature, we refer to an independent variable as the *treatment*. Our objective in assessing the value of a surrogate variable lies in assessing how the final endpoint and surrogate variable respond to the treatment. Before we can replace a final endpoint with a surrogate, we need to be sure that it has a causal relationship with the final endpoint; that is, we need to validate surrogate endpoints prior to their use. One criteria for doing this is know as the Prentice criterion.

THE PRENTICE CRITERION

The practical use of surrogate variables is founded in notions of dependence and causality. In the language of statistics this relationship requires that we test for dependence by specifying a null hypothesis of no causal link between the surrogate variable and the final endpoint. Of course, non-counterfactual tests of this type prove difficult to construct.[4] In practice, we need to couch all notions of causality in much weaker hypotheses that may be more easily subjected to statistical testing. An influential series of applied papers published in 1989 on the role of surrogate variables in cancer[5] and ophthalmic conditions[6] provided the necessary basis from which such a hypothesis could be generated. These papers offered empirical support for the idea that the strength of association between a surrogate variable and final endpoint offers a plausible criteria for assessing dependence. Prentice,[7] in a published commentary on these papers, used this result to propose a formal criteria for surrogate variables (p. 432):

> *In considering criteria for use of the term "surrogate" it is natural to ask what we require of a treatment comparison based on a surrogate response variable. Even though a range of endpoint comparisons may have relevance to an understanding of the effects of treatments under study, it seems logical to restrict the use of surrogate to response variables that can substitute for a true response variable for certain purposes. Equivalently, it seems reasonable to require a surrogate for some true endpoint to have potential to yield unambiguous information about differential treatment effects on the true endpoint. While one could attempt to require a surrogate response to provide some quantitative information on the comparison of true endpoint rates among treatments, a criterion involving only a qualitative link will be much more readily applied. Hence, I define a surrogate endpoint to be a response variable for which a test of the null hypothesis of no relationship to the treatment groups under consideration is also a valid test of the corresponding null hypothesis based on the true endpoint.*

Prentice captured this idea more formally within a failure time setting as follows: Let T be a non-negative random variable representing the failure time of an individual from the population of interest. T is the event of primary interest (final endpoint). Let $x = (x_1, x_2, \ldots, x_p)$ consist of the indicator variates (independent variables in the language of regression) for p (≥ 1) of the $p + 1$ levels to be compared. In addition, denote $S(t) = \{Z(u); 0 \leq u \leq t\}$ as the history prior to t of a possibly vector-valued stochastic process $Z(u) = \{z_1(u), z_2(u), \ldots\}$, which is to be used as the surrogate variable for the final endpoint T. The survivor function for T is given by

$$F_T(t) = \text{Prob } (T \geq t)$$

where: $F_T(0)$ s $= 1$ and $\lim_{t \to \infty} F_T(t) = 0$.

The instantaneous hazard function specifies the rate of failure at $T = t$ conditional upon survival to t. It is given by

$$\lambda_T(t) = \lim_{\delta \to \infty} \frac{\text{Prob}(t \le T < t + \delta \mid T \ge t)}{\delta}$$

By the rule of conditional probabilty and the log function rule of calculus it is easy to see that

$$\lambda_T(t) = \frac{f_T(t)}{F_T(t)} = \frac{-d \log F_T(t)}{dt} \tag{15.1}$$

Prentice establishes a link between the surrogate variable and final endpoint by assuming

$$\lambda_T(t \mid x) = E[\lambda_T\{t \mid x, S(t)\}] = \int \lambda_T\{t \mid x, S(t)\}d\text{Prob}\{S(t) \mid x, F(t)\}$$

where $\lambda_T(.\mid.)$ is the conditional failure rate at t, $E[.]$ is the expectation over the distribution of $S(t)$ given x, Prob $(.\mid.)$ is a conditional probability, and $F(t)$ represents the final endpoint failure distribution function and censoring histories prior to t.

Prentice now makes a critical assumption that provides a direct link to the unconditional instantaneous hazard function of Equation 15.1. He assumes that the final endpoint and treatment are conditionally independent, given the surrogate variable, so that

$$\lambda_T(t \mid x, S(t)) = \lambda_T(t \mid S(t)) \tag{15.2}$$

This is directly related to Equation 15.1 because

$$\lambda_T(t \mid x) = \int \lambda_T\{t \mid S(t)\} \, d\text{Prob}\{S(t) \mid F(t)\} = \lambda_T(t) \tag{15.3}$$

To ensure the surrogate variable has some prognostic value for the final endpoint, Prentice additionally assumes

$$\lambda_T(t \mid S(t)) \ne \lambda_T(t \mid x) \tag{15.4}$$

and

$$\lambda_T(t \mid x) = \lambda_T(t) \tag{15.5}$$

Equations 15.2, 15.4, and 15.5 have become known as the *Prentice criterion*.[8]

Using a Cox proportional hazards model,[9] we can investigate whether Equation 15.2 holds by specifying

$$\lambda_T(t \mid S(t), x) = \lambda_{0T}(t)\exp\left[\beta_1 x S(t) + \beta_2 x\{1 - S(t)\} + \beta_3 S(t)\right]$$

The parameters can be estimated using partial likelihood or marginal likelihood procedures.[10] We could then investigate whether:

$\beta_1 = 0$, which examines the interaction between the dependent variable and the surrogate and is known as the *treatment effect*.

$\beta_2 = 0$, which examines the relationship between those who do not show a surrogate response and the final endpoint.

$\beta_3 \neq 0$, indicating a relationship between the surrogate and the final endpoint.

LIMITATIONS OF THE PRENTICE CRITERION

Freedman et al.[11] highlight a conceptual difficulty with Equation 15.2. It requires the treatment effect on the true endpoint to be 0 after adjustment for the surrogate variable. This seems reasonable to test the hypothesis of rejecting a poor surrogate variable when in fact the surrogate variable is poor. However, it is certainly inadequate when considering a good surrogate variable because failing to reject the null hypothesis may be due to either insufficient power or that requiring such a perfect surrogate variable is really too hopeful.

The Prentice criterion defines a surrogate endpoint as a surrogate variable[12] that fully captures the relationship between the dependent variable and the final endpoint in the sense that any information the dependent variable gives about the final endpoint failure rate is also contained in the surrogate endpoint. The Prentice notion of a surrogate endpoint has been a persistent one in the medical statistical literature. The nature of the debate surrounding the validation and use of surrogate variables seems to have been much influenced by his basic premise.[13] Buyse and Molenberghs[14] show that the criterion is neither necessary or sufficient for the Prentice definition, except for binary endpoints, and the criterion continues to provide motivation for many surrogate variable validation techniques.[15]

The general acceptance within the statistics community of the Prentice criterion as the de facto benchmark against which potential surrogate variables should be compared came under attack in a Royal Statistical Society paper[16]. The debate was focused around the issue of whether the Prentice criterion is appropriate for deciding whether or not to use a surrogate variable, or for distinguishing the merits of alternative candidates. At the core of the debate is an argument about the generic applicability of a surrogate variable (p. 28)[17]:

> *Another point of contention is the issue of whether or not a surrogate endpoint should be considered for its generic applicability, as opposed to being evaluated specifically for the trial being planned. In our expe-*

rience we know of no surrogate endpoint that has any unique features that would make it specifically applicable to a particular treatment contrast. Widely used surrogate endpoints in medical research, such as prostate-specific antigen failure in prostate cancer, or viral load in studies of acquired immune deficiency syndrome or, indeed, factors related to incidence as opposed to mortality in cancer screen trials, are all inherently generic.

We should mention that Prentice himself was quite aware that his criterion was not a particularly realistic one. Indeed, he laments (p. 439)[18]:

> ...*I am somewhat pessimistic concerning the potential of the surrogate endpoint concept, as it is interpreted in this paper. One interpretation...is that the surrogate endpoint must have precisely the same relationship to the true endpoint under each of the treatment strategies being compared. We need only look as far as the Multiple Risk Factor Intervention Trial for an example in which important differences in prominent risk factors—namely blood pressure levels, smoking habits, and blood cholesterol—between intervention and control subjects evidently did not convey the anticipated difference in coronary heart disease mortality.*

This raises the question as to why Prentice and subsequent authors[19] have spent so much time and effort in developing approaches to investigate a line of inquiry founded on a criterion that Prentice himself believed to be false. The issue is not why such a criterion should be employed in making precise the notion of a surrogate endpoint (the nature of the inquiry makes this inevitable), but why choose to focus on criterion which appears to require such a strong relationship between the surrogate variable and final endpoint? Part of the answer, as far as Prentice is concerned, can be found in his more recent comments that (p. 26)[20]:

> *The purpose in setting out these criteria was not to encourage their adoption in any particular setting...but rather to reinforce that it is only in very special circumstances that treatment information on an early surrogate endpoint will convey direct information concerning a treatment effect on a true later endpoint.*

We agree with Prentice; his criterion will be too restrictive for nearly all purposes. However, in the rare situations where surrogate variables can be shown to satisfy his criterion, the implications provide some interesting insights and are worth studying for this reason alone.

THE REAL VALUE ADDED OF USING SURROGATE VARIABLES

The fundamental proposition of the advocates of surrogate variables is that they have the potential to add value to statistical inference about the treatment effect on a final endpoint. No matter what side of the controversy is in question, no matter what statistical techniques have been adopted, the proposition that surrogate variables add value is central. It would be premature to say that the theory surrounding this subject is complete. But it is clear that enough has been done to warrant our taking this central proposition as established. Therefore we proceed to inquire under what conditions value added is attainable. This is a matter of some intricacy that deserves attention, not only for its own sake, but for the light it casts upon surrogate variable validation methods in general.

Cox's Study of the Information Gain from Using Auxiliary Endpoints

Cox[21] developed a theoretical study on how information contained in a surrogate variable can be used to strengthen the data analysis of the treatment effect on the final endpoint. Following Flemming et al.[22] a surrogate used for this purpose is known as an *auxiliary endpoint*. Some consideration of the potential of this approach has appeared more recently in the statistical literature.[23]

Cox asks the question, *How can information on a surrogate variable S be used and what gain in information is potentially achievable?* To this end, the author assumes there exists a surrogate variable *S* measured on all censored individuals that is related to the final endpoint of interest. Cox makes the simple assumption that if V_i is the unobserved remaining lifetime of the *i*th individual on the final endpoint and W_i is an independent noise component having some fixed distribution independent of the censoring time and treatment, then

$$S_i = V_i / W_i$$

He takes a parametric approach by assuming W_i to have a gamma distribution, with parameters β, φ and λ, given by $\dfrac{\beta(\beta\omega)^{\lambda-1}\exp(-\beta\omega)}{\Gamma(\lambda)}$ and that V_i is exponential with parameter q so that S_i has the density $\dfrac{q_i \lambda \beta^\lambda}{(\beta + q_i s)^{\lambda+1}}$.

Cox then goes on to show that if l and b are known so that S is directly calibrated to relate to the final endpoint, a proportion $\lambda/(\lambda + 2)-1$ of the loss of information from the censored variables can be recovered by the incorporation of information on S into the likelihood function.

Augmenting the Final Endpoint Likelihood with Surrogate Information

The approach of Cox suggests there could be benefits from incorporating surrogate information directly into the estimation of the treatment effect on the final endpoint, where the final endpoint is a time to event with right censoring. We explore this issue further in this section. We begin by considering how information contained in a surrogate variable could be used to strengthen the data analysis of the treatment effect on the final endpoint. Note that it is the fact that the final endpoint is right-censored that opens up this possibility. An obvious and immediately appealing approach would be to incorporate surrogate information directly into the final endpoint likelihood function.

Suppose a specific parametric survival distribution is known up to a vector parameter β and that there is available for inference about β a single sample of censored failure times on a final endpoint. A subject observed to fail at t contributes a term $f(t|\beta)$ to the likelihood, the probability of failure at t. The contribution from a subject whose survival time is censored at c is $F(c|\beta)$, the probability of survival beyond c. The full likelihood from n independent subjects indexed by i is then

$$L(\beta) = \prod_{\delta i=1} f(t_i \mid \beta) \prod_{\delta i=0} F(c_i \mid \beta) \tag{15.6}$$

The two products are taken over uncensored and censored subjects, respectively, where δ_i is the censoring indicator such that for a uncensored event $t_i = c_i$ if $\delta i = 1$, and for a censored observation $t_i > c_i$ if $\delta_i = 0$.

Suppose the data now includes a surrogate variable S for each subject. Two strategies are apparent:

- Replacing censored observations by their surrogate counterparts
- Augmenting the censored observations with their surrogate counterparts

We discuss each of these strategies below.

Replacing Censored Observations by Their Surrogates

If we use the surrogate S to replace censored subjects, the surrogated adapted likelihood is given by

$$L(\beta) = \prod_{\delta i=1} f(t_i \mid \beta) \prod_{\delta i=0} F(s_i \mid \beta) \tag{15.7}$$

With perfect association[24] between the surrogate and final endpoint this is equivalent to the likelihood based on the true failure time data on all subjects without censoring:

$$L(\beta) = \prod_{i=1}^{n} f(t_i \mid \beta) \tag{15.8}$$

Therefore, in this ideal situation the use of the surrogate variable improves the precision of the parameter estimates without introducing bias. In practice, perfect association is rather unlikely. Where perfect association does not hold, we cannot be certain that the likelihood of Equation 15.7 will be maximized at the same parameter values as the likelihood of Equation 15.8. Thus, there may remain considerable uncertainty as to the appropriate interpretation of parameter estimates from Equation 15.7.

Augmenting the Censored Observations with Their Surrogates

If we use a surrogate S to augment the likelihood for the censored individuals, we face a similar problem. The surrogate augmented likelihood is given by

$$L(\beta) = \prod_{\delta i=1} f(t_i \mid \beta) \prod_{\delta i=0} F(s_i, c_i \mid \beta)$$
$$= \prod_{\delta i=1} f(t_i \mid \beta) \prod_{\delta i=0} F(s_i \mid c_i, \beta) F(c_i \mid \beta) \tag{15.9}$$

If the final endpoint and surrogate variable are independent (so that there is no association), then

$$F(s_i c_i \mid \beta) = F(s_i \mid \beta) F(c_i \mid \beta)$$

so that the surrogate augmented likelihood is given by

$$L(\beta) = \prod_{\delta i=1} f(t_i \mid \beta) \prod_{\delta i=0} F(s_i \mid \beta) F(c_i \mid \beta) \tag{15.10}$$

from which it should be obvious that Equation 15.8 $\neq$ Equation 15.10. Even where the final endpoint and surrogate variable are not independent (as given in Equation 15.9), we cannot be certain that the maximized value of Equation 15.9 will yield parameter estimates close to the parameter estimates of the maximized value of Equation 15.8.

Practical Limitations

A final endpoint and surrogate variable are very unlikely to be perfectly associated. The idea of augmenting or adapting a likelihood function with surrogate information, although appealing, is clearly fraught with danger. It requires the validation of the surrogate variable, specification of specific models, simulation, and extensive empirical testing because even if the correlation between the surrogate endpoint and final endpoint is large, an effect of clinical significance on the surrogate endpoint will not necessarily imply a clinically significant effect on the final endpoint.

A WORD OF CAUTION FROM THE MEDICAL STATISTICS LITERATURE

When the surrogate variable and final endpoint are not perfectly associated, extreme care must be taken. To see why, consider again a medical analogy in which it is quite possible that a treatment is beneficial for the surrogate endpoint but harmful for the final outcome. An example of just such a finding can be seen in a cardiac arrhythmia suppression trial.[25] Asymptomatic ventricular premature depolarisation's are known to be associated with sudden death after myocardial infarction and are often treated with antiarrhythmic drugs.[26] In the Cardiac Arrhythmia Suppression Trial, a multicenter, randomized placebo-controlled study, it was hoped that the suppression of asymptomatic or mildly symptomatic ventricular arrhythmias after myocardial infarction would reduce the death from arrhythmia. Unfortunately, the trial showed that that patients who took antiarrhythmic drugs were more likely to die than those who received the placebo. The authors comment (p. 406):

During an average of 10 months of follow-up, the patients treated with active drug (encainide, flecainide, or moricizine) had a higher rate of death from arrhythmia than the patients assigned to placebo. Encainide and flecainide accounted for the excess of deaths from arrhythmia and non-fatal cardiac arrests (33 of 730 patients taking encainide or flecainide [4.5 percent]; 9 of 725 taking placebo [1.2 percent]; relative risk, 3.6; 95 percent confidence interval 1.7 to 8.5). They also accounted for the higher total mortality (56 of 730 [7.7 percent] and 22 of 725 [3.0 percent], respectively, relative risk, 2.5; 95 percent confidence interval, 1.6 to 4.5). We conclude that neither encainide nor flecainide should be used in the treatment of patients with asymptomatic or minimally symptomatic ventricular arrhythmia after myocardial infarction, even though these drugs may be effective initially in suppressing ventricular arrhythmia.

VALIDATION VIA THE PROPORTION EXPLAINED

Perhaps a more realistic expectation, for the type of surrogate variables encountered in OR practice, is that they will account for a proportion of the treatment or independent variable effect on the final endpoint. Freedman et al.[27] called such surrogate variables *intermediate endpoints*. They suggested that we focus attention on the proportion of the treatment effect explained by the surrogate variable. The authors developed their intermediate end-point procedure within the context of logistic regression for a binary final endpoint T and a binary surrogate variable S.

Let PE stand for the proportion of the treatment effect on the final end-point that can be explained by the surrogate variable. An estimate of this proportion is given by

$$PE = 1 - \frac{\beta_S}{\beta} \tag{15.11}$$

where β and β_S are the estimates of the treatment effect on the final endpoint without and with adjustment for the surrogate variable calculated from the following logistic regressions:

$$P_{T|X} = \frac{\exp(\alpha + \beta X)}{1 + \exp(\alpha + \beta X)} \tag{15.12}$$

and

$$P_{T|XS} = \frac{\exp(\alpha + \beta_S X + \delta S)}{1 + \exp(\alpha + \beta_S X + \delta S)} \tag{15.13}$$

where β, β_S, α, α_S and δ are unknown model parameters and X is the treatment vector.

The proportion explained is large if β_S is small relative to β. The Prentice criterion requires $\beta_S = 0$, or equivalently, PE = 1. In many cases, we suspect that PE < 1, indicating that the surrogate variable only explains a propor-tion of the treatment effect on the final endpoint. Confidence intervals can be calculated around PE using a method based on Fieller's theorem[28] or the delta method.[29]

Lin et al.[30] extend the test procedure of Freedman et al. to failure time endpoints. Let $S(t)$ denote a time-dependent surrogate variable observed at times $t_1, \ldots, t_n$. The PE is calculated as

$$PE = 1 - \frac{\beta_S}{\beta}$$

where β_S and β are calculated from the following Cox proportional hazards models:

$$\lambda(t \mid X) = \lambda_{10}(t) e^{(\beta X)} \tag{15.14}$$

and

$$\lambda(t \mid S, X) = \lambda_{20}(t)e^{(\beta_S X + \overline{\omega}S(t))} \tag{15.15}$$

β_S, β, and φ are unknown model parameters.

The authors show that Equations 15.14 and 15.15 cannot hold simultaneously. If we assume Equation 15.15 holds and that $S(t) = S$, that is, the surrogate is time-invariant, Lin et al. show that

$$\lambda(t \mid X) = \lambda_{20}(t)e^{(\beta X)} \frac{\int e^{\omega s} \exp\{-\tilde{\lambda}(t)e^{\beta X + \omega s}\}d\mathrm{Prob}(s \mid X)}{\int \exp\{-\tilde{\lambda}(t)e^{\beta X + \omega s}\}d\mathrm{Prob}(s \mid X)} \tag{15.16}$$

where $\quad \tilde{\lambda}(t) = \int\limits_0^t \lambda_{20}(u)\,du$

They also argue that for Equation 15.14 to provide a reasonable approximation to Equation 15.16, $\lambda(t)$ or α must be small. However, there is no guarantee that this condition will be satisfied. The authors suggest its appropriateness be validated via empirical analysis.

Practical Limitations of the Proportion Explained

There are a number of concerns about the practical use of PE. First, PE is not well calibrated as a measure of a proportion because when the adjustment for the surrogate variable changes the direction of the treatment effect on the final endpoint, PE does not necessarily lie in the range 0 to 1. How should we interpret PE < 0 or PE > 1? Second, PE is not unique. In Freedman et al.'s model, 2β is a measure of log odds ratio of disease given exposure. We could also use the excess relative odds $\exp(2\beta)-1$ to give an alternative measure:

$$PA = 1 - \left[\frac{\exp(2\beta_S) - 1}{\exp(2\beta) - 1}\right]$$

In Table 15.1 we calculate the difference between these two measures for various values of β_S. The difference between the two measures can be substantial.

Finally, Buyse and Molenberghs[31] outline a third practical problem with PE (p. 194):

> *Even when large numbers of observations are available, however, the denominator of the proportion explained (the effect of treatment on the true endpoint) will be estimated with little precision, for otherwise the need for a surrogate endpoint would no longer exist. Therefore the pro-*

TABLE 15.1 The Difference between the Proportion Explained (PE) and an Alternative Measure of the Proportion Explained (PA), for Various Values of the Log Odds Ratio on the Surrogate Endpoint (β_S) Given the Log Odds Ratio on the Final Endpoint (β)

β_S	1	0.8	0.6	0.4	0.2
β	1	1	1	1	1
PA	0.00%	38.13%	63.69%	80.82%	92.30%
PE	0.00%	20.00%	40.00%	60.00%	80.00%

portion explained will generally be too poorly estimated to be of much practical value.

Buyse and Molenberghs Validation

Buyse and Molenberghs[32] suggest an alternative to the proportion explained that consists of two components:

1. The *relative effect* (RE), which is a measure of the effect of the treatment on the surrogate variable relative to the treatment effect on the final

   endpoint. The relative effect is captured by $RE = \lambda/\beta$, where β, in the binary setting, is estimated from the logistic regression of Equation 15.12, and l is estimated from logistic regression of the surrogate S on the treatment X given by

   $$P_{S|X} = \frac{\exp(\pi + \lambda X)}{1 + \exp(\pi + \lambda X)}$$

2. *The adjusted association* (AA), which is δ in Equation 15.13

PROBLEMS WITH THE BUYSE AND MOLENBERGHS ALTERNATIVE

A key problem with using the pair RE and AA as a complement to the proportion explained is that the interpretation of RE and AA is model-dependent. For example, the authors define a perfect surrogate in the binary setting (where both the final endpoint and surrogate variable are binary) as one for which RE = 1 and AA = ∞. When the surrogate variable and final endpoint are normally distributed, they define a perfect surrogate as AA = 1 and RE = 1. The authors acknowledge this to be a considerable drawback.[33]

If RE = 1, the treatment effects on the surrogate variable and final endpoint are of the same magnitude. Buyse and Molenberghs argue a perfect surrogate, in the binary setting, has RE = 1 and AA = ∞.

Further Problems with the Proportion Explained and the Buyse and Molenberghs Alternative

The above discussion provides some insight into why the notions of the proportion explained and relative effect are fraught with difficulties. It has frequently been reported (and acknowledged by Freedman et al. and Buyse and Molenberghs) that both RE and PE suffer from unacceptably wide confidence intervals. This seriously restricts the practical usefulness of these measures. Notwithstanding this important point and irrespective of the value of the proportion explained, relative effect, and adjusted association estimated in a particular study, it will still be necessary to directly examine the relationship between the final endpoint and the treatment. This is because the relationship between the surrogate variable and the treatment cannot generally convey definitive information concerning the relationship between the final endpoint and the treatment. Thus, we argue the use of surrogate variables in place of the endpoint of principal concern should only be considered with caution. In such circumstances, effort will need to be directed toward extracting as much information about these relationships as possible.

LIMITATIONS OF SURROGATE MODELING IN OPERATIONAL RISK MANAGEMENT

In his article "Surrogate Endpoints in Clinical Trials: Definition and Operational Criteria," Prentice[34] suggested that a surrogate variable is (p. 432):

> A *response variable for which a test of the null hypothesis of no relationship to the treatment groups under comparison is also a valid test of the corresponding null hypothesis based on the true endpoint.*

This idealized view of the nature of the relationship between a surrogate variable and final endpoint has been a persistent one, and the nature of subsequent research seems to have been much influenced by this basic premise. We are led to believe that the identification of such variables can facilitate a more speedy evaluation of competing treatments and thus provide the necessary scientific background against which the development of alternative, more appropriate treatments can be designed. Yet, in the literature there has been surprising little interest in investigating the practical limits inherent in this *idealized* notion of a surrogate variable.

Unfortunately, the nature of the fundamental issues that can be addressed when considering, reasoning, and arguing about the relationship between a treatment regimen, surrogate variable, and final endpoint have largely been ignored. Understanding what issues can be legitimately addressed within any specific surrogate variable framework is important because rigorously controlled experimental research cannot be executed effectively until the fundamental descriptive work has been carried out to establish a context within which meaningful questions and hypotheses about treatment effects on surrogate variables, final endpoints, and their interrelationships can be made and interpreted.

Since a surrogate variable either does or does not satisfy the Prentice criterion, the question of "how good" will remain if the surrogate variable fails the Prentice test. This is because inherent in the question is an underlying scale (for example, perfect, very good, good, poor, and very poor) whose gradations cannot be captured in the two-state "is a surrogate–is not a surrogate" dichotomization of Prentice. Buyse and Molenberghs report an odds ratio between the final endpoint and the treatment, adjusted for the surrogate variable (see Equation 15.3) of 1.44 ($p = 0.34$). Thus, they fail to find any evidence that the full effect of the treatment on the final endpoint is mediated through the surrogate variable, and therefore conclude that the Prentice criterion is not satisfied.

CASE STUDY 15.1: LEGAL EXPERIENCE AS A SURROGATE ENDPOINT FOR LEGAL COSTS FOR A BUSINESS UNIT

The proportion explained of Freedman et al. and the relative effect and adjusted association metrics of Buyse and Molenberghs attempt to measure the deviation from the Prentice criterion. In this sense they seek to quantify the underlying scale inherent in the question, "How good?" Table 15.2 shows the estimate of these measures for an OR example in which the surrogate variable is years of legal experience (dichotomized into a binary variable of high and low) of a business unit and the final endpoint is legal costs. The confidence interval on the PE covers the whole interval 0 to 1, although

TABLE 15.2 Estimates of the PE, RE, and AA with their Respective 95% Confidence Intervals for a Study on Legal Experience as a Surrogate for Legal Costs

	PE	RE	AA
Estimate	0.45	0.94	2.92
Lower 95% CI	−0.30	0.20	8.86
Upper 95% CI	4.35	3.15	38.77

the estimate at 0.45 suggests the surrogate endpoint may have some potential as a surrogate variable for legal costs. The RE and AA are both positive with very wide confidence intervals. Unfortunately, by juggling the two variables of RE and AA, it is difficult to grasp exactly how suitable the surrogate variable is. For example, is a surrogate variable with an RE = 2 and AA = 3 better than a surrogate variable with an RE = 1.5 and AA = 2.0? If so, by how much?

SUMMARY

Surrogate endpoint validation offers a scientific mechanism for replacing OR events that are rare or difficult to measure. Although the validation procedures outlined in this chapter are far from perfect, they do offer OR analysts a rational procedure by which to select potential surrogate endpoints for use in further statistical modeling.

REVIEW QUESTIONS

1. Why is there a potential need for surrogate endpoint modeling in OR?
2. Do you feel it is possible to use such endpoints to yield meaningful insight into future OR events?
3. How would you validate a surrogate endpoint?
4. What do you see as being the practical limitations that would hinder such a validation?
5. How useful are the current surrogate endpoint validation procedures?
6. How can they be improved for OR modeling?

FURTHER READING

Further details can be found in Herson (1989), Prentice (1989), Lin et al. (1997), Buyse and Molenberghs (1998), and Lewis (2003).

CHAPTER 16

Introduction to Extreme Value Theory

Managing the risk of OR events that could lead to catastrophic losses lies at the heart of OR management. What is the maximum amount of loss due to operational risk that can be expected in a specific business unit over a period of one year at a very high confidence level? The answer requires estimation of high percentiles of the aggregate loss distribution. The primary difficulty is that such events are rare by definition and therefore we may have very little information about them. Even though such events occur with very low probability, OR managers may seek to ensure that their financial institutions maintain (or are at least aware of) a minimum level of capital in reserve to adequately cover such events. Extreme value theory (EVT) offers one way by which this can be achieved. It provides a theoretical framework for studying rare events by focusing on the tails of probability distributions. Whereas statisticians have used EVT techniques for a long time, they have only recently been proposed in operational risk management. In this chapter we explore how EVT can be used to assist in the quantification and management of operational risk.

FISHER-TIPPET–GNEDENKO THEOREM

The Fisher-Tippet–Gnedenko theorem states that given a sample of independent identically distributed loss data $\{x_1, x_2, \ldots, x_n\}$, as the number of observations n becomes increasingly large, the maximum of the sequence of observations, under very general conditions, is approximately distributed as the generalized extreme value (GEV) distribution with cumulative probability distribution function

$$
F(x) =
\begin{cases}
\exp\left\{-\left[1 + \xi\left(\dfrac{x-\mu}{\sigma}\right)\right]^{-1/\xi}\right\} & \text{for } \xi \neq 0 \\[4mm]
\exp-\left\{\exp\left[-\left(\dfrac{x-\mu}{\sigma}\right)\right]\right\} & \text{for } \xi = 0
\end{cases}
$$

where μ is the location parameter, $\sigma > 0$ is a scale parameter, $1 + \xi z > 0$, $-\infty \leq \xi \leq \infty$, $\sigma > 0$, and ξ is the tail index parameter.

The GEV distribution has three forms. If $\xi > 0$, then the distribution takes the form of a type II (Frechet) heavy-tailed distribution. For $\xi < 0$, the distribution is the type III (Weibull) distribution. When $\xi = 0$, the distribution is the type I (Gumbel) light-tailed distribution. In fact, the larger the tail index parameter, the fatter is the tail. As we have seen in Chapter 9, operational losses are often fat-tailed.

Parameter Estimation

The parameters μ and σ can be estimated from the sample mean and sample standard deviation, respectively. If we rank the data in order of size so that $x_1 > x_2 > \ldots > x_n$, the tail index parameter ξ can be estimated using the Hill estimator:

$$\textit{Method I:} \quad \hat{\xi}_k = \left(\frac{1}{k-1} \sum_{j=1}^{k-1} \ln (x_j) \right) - \ln (x_k)$$

or

$$\textit{Method II:} \quad \hat{\xi}_k = \left(\frac{1}{k} \sum_{j=1}^{k} \ln (x_j) \right) - \ln (x_k)$$

The problem is how to choose k. Theory gives little advice as to what value to choose. Furthermore, the actual estimate will be sensitive to the value of k chosen. In practice, the average estimator, using either of the following two formulas, often works well:

$$\textit{Method 1:} \quad \hat{\xi} = \frac{1}{n} \sum_{i=1}^{n} \theta_i \quad \text{where } \theta_k = \left(\frac{1}{k-1} \sum_{j=1}^{k-1} \ln (x_j) \right) - \ln (x_k)$$

for k = 1, 2, ..., n

$$\textit{Method 2:} \quad \hat{\xi} = \frac{1}{n} \sum_{i=1}^{n} \theta_i \text{ where } \theta_k = \left(\frac{1}{k} \sum_{j=1}^{k} \ln (x_j) \right) - \ln (x_k) \text{ for k = 1, 2, ..., n}$$

EXAMPLE 16.1: CALCULATION OF GEV PARAMETERS FOR RETAIL BANK FRAUD

To illustrate the calculation of the parameters of the GEV distribution, consider the loss data shown in Table 16.1. The table shows the monthly maximum loss from fraud for a retail bank over a 14-month period, ranked by size. The data has been rounded up to the nearest $1,000. The first and second columns shows the rank and observed losses; the largest value of $195,000 has a rank of 1 and the smallest value of $11,000 has a rank of 14. The third column gives the natural logarithm of the data. The fourth and fifth columns show the value of the tail index parameter for a particular k using

TABLE 16.1 Calculation of Tail Index Parameter Using the Hill Estimator

Rank	Loss $(thousands)	$\ln(x)$	ξ (Method I)	ξ (Method II)
1	195	5.273		
2	185	5.220	0.053	0.026
3	177	5.176	0.071	0.047
4	166	5.112	0.111	0.083
5	161	5.081	0.114	0.091
6	142	4.956	0.217	0.181
7	108	4.682	0.454	0.389
8	89	4.489	0.583	0.510
9	88	4.477	0.520	0.462
10	61	4.111	0.829	0.746
11	36	3.584	1.273	1.157
12	33	3.497	1.244	1.141
13	29	3.367	1.270	1.172
14	11	2.398	2.142	1.989

method I and method II, respectively. The average of columns four and five yields an estimate of the tail index parameter as $\hat{\xi} = 0.684$ and $\hat{\xi} = 0.615$, respectively. The value of $\hat{\mu} = 105.786$ and $\hat{\sigma} = 65.014$.

METHOD OF BLOCK MAXIMA

The method of block maxima (BM) can be used to calculate OpVaR for high percentiles of the loss distribution. In this approach we first divide our loss sample into L non-overlapping subsamples of fixed length of time. The length is usually a month, quarter, or year. The absolute value of the maximum loss in each of the L blocks is then used to estimate the parameters of a suitable probability distribution. The question then becomes, which is the most suitable probability distribution to fit? Fortunately as we have seen, the Fisher-Tippet–Gnedenko theorem tells us exactly what distribution to fit. Indeed, the method of block maxima exploits the fact that the Fisher-Tippet–Gnedenko theorem tells us that limiting distribution of the maximum is from the generalized extreme value distribution, irrespective of the probability distribution that generated the losses. Once we have obtained estimates of the parameters for the K non-overlapping subsamples, we can plug them into the following formula to obtain an estimate of the α percent OpVaR:

$$\text{OpVaR}_\alpha = \begin{cases} \hat{\mu} - \dfrac{\hat{\sigma}}{\hat{\xi}}\left[1 - (-\ln \alpha)^{-\hat{\xi}}\right] & \text{if } \hat{\xi} > 0 \\[2em] \hat{\mu} - \hat{\sigma}\log\left[-\ln(\alpha)\right] & \text{if } \hat{\xi} = 0 \end{cases}$$

EXAMPLE 16.2: CALCULATION OF OPVAR FOR RETAIL BANK FRAUD

From Example 16.1 we found estimated the tail index parameter as $\hat{\xi}$ = 0.684 (method I) with $\hat{\mu}$ = 105.786 and $\hat{\sigma}$ = 65.014. This implies OpVaR at 0.99 percent confidence is approximately equal to \$2.2 million. Alternatively, if we use the tail index estimate $\hat{\xi}$ = 0.615, then OpVaR is approximately \$1.8 million.

PEAKS OVER THRESHOLD MODELING

An alternative EVT approach to calculate OpVaR is to use peaks over threshold modeling (POTM). Although the method of block maxima utilizes the Fisher-Tippet–Gnedenko theorem to inform us what the distribution of the maximum loss is, POTM uses the Picklands-Dalkema-de Hann theorem to inform us what is the probability distribution of all events greater than some large preset threshold. The Picklands-Dalkema-de Hann theorem states that if F_u is the conditional excess distribution function of values of the ordered losses X above some threshold, μ is given by F_u = Prob($X - \mu \leq y \mid X > \mu$), $0 \leq y \leq x_F - \mu$. Then for a suitably high threshold the limiting distribution of F_u is a generalized Pareto distribution (GPD) with cumulative distribution function

$$
F(x) = \begin{cases} 1 - \left(1 + \dfrac{\xi}{\sigma} x\right)^{-\frac{1}{\xi}} & \text{if } \xi \neq 0 \\[4mm] 1 - \exp\left(-x / \sigma\right) & \text{for } \xi = 0 \end{cases}
$$

This is an important result because it tells us the exact distribution of excesses above some threshold. How do we choose a suitably high value of the threshold μ? One tool for choosing a suitable threshold is to use the sample mean excess function, which is a measure of the excess over the threshold divided by the number of data points that exceed the threshold:

$$
e_n(u) = \frac{\displaystyle\sum_{i=1}^{n} \left(x_i - \mu\right)^{+}}{\displaystyle\sum_{i=1}^{n} 1_{\{x_i > \mu\}}}
$$

The sample mean excess function describes the expected overshoot of the threshold given that an exceedance has occurred. If the GPD is a suitable distribution, a plot of the mean excess against the threshold should follow a straight line with slope approximately equal to $\dfrac{\xi}{1-\xi}$. A value for μ can be chosen as the value at which the plotted curve becomes linear. The parameters of the GPD distribution can be estimated using the method of maximum likelihood or L moments.

One advantage of fitting the GPD via POTM is that once we have the parameter estimates, we can easily obtain an estimate of OpVaR:

$$\text{OpVaR}_{\alpha} = \hat{\mu} + \frac{\hat{\sigma}}{\hat{\xi}}\left\{\left[\frac{N}{N_u}(1-\alpha)\right]^{-\hat{\xi}} - 1\right\}$$

Furthermore, we can also easily obtain an estimate of ES:

$$\text{ES}_{\alpha} = \frac{\text{VAR}_{\alpha}}{1-\hat{\xi}} + \frac{\sigma - \hat{\xi}\hat{\mu}}{1-\hat{\xi}}$$

SUMMARY

Due to their rarity, catastrophic losses have very limited data and are therefore likely to give imprecise associated risk estimates. The use of EVT to estimate operational risk at high percentiles has a number of advantages over the more traditional methods discussed in Chapters 7 to 9. This is because methods discussed in these chapters use all the return data and fit the majority of observations that tend to lie near the center of a probability distribution, rather than specifically accommodating the tail observations. Yet it is the tail observations that are important for operational risk management. The key disadvantage of EVT is that model calibration is demanding, requiring a large amount of data.

REVIEW QUESTIONS

1. What are the benefits and limitations of the practical use of EVT?
2. Explain the difference between POTM and BM.
3. Which method do you feel is most appropriate for your practice?

FURTHER READING

Further discussion of applied extreme value theory can be found in Bassi et al. (1997), Danielsson and de Vries (1997), Longin (1997), Embrechts et al. (1998), and Lewis (2003). More theoretical work can be found in Gumbel (1954).

CHAPTER 17

Managing Operational Risk with Bayesian Belief Networks

Bayesian belief networks (BBNs) have attracted much attention as a possible solution to many of the complex issues surrounding operational risk management. By providing a succinct way to encode knowledge about a business environment in terms of simple probabilities, BBNs are increasingly being seen as attractive knowledge representation tools for reasoning about operational risk. They have proven useful in a wide range of practical applications. For example, fraud debt detection,[1] optimization of traffic flow,[2] validation of rocket engines,[3] and providing assistance in formulating diagnoses.[4] In this chapter we explore how BBNs make it possible to base inferences within complex business environments about operational risk events on the sound foundations of probability theory.

WHAT IS A BAYESIAN BELIEF NETWORK?

A BBN is a directed graph, together with an associated set of probability tables. Figure 17.1 shows a simple BBN to predict settlement loss. The figure consists of nodes and directed arcs. It describes the relationship between staff experience, product complexity, and design effort that went into developing the settlement system and settlement loss. The nodes represent random variables that can be discrete or continuous. For example, the node *Staff Experience* is discrete, having two states: *Experienced* and *Novice*. The directed arcs between the nodes represent directed causal relationships between variables. To see this, look at the directed arc between *Design Effort* and *Settlement Loss*; the direction of the arc designates *Design Effort* as a cause and *Settlement Loss* as the effect. The absence of a link between two nodes, for example, between *Staff Experience* and *Product Complexity*, signifies that the corresponding variables do not influence each other directly in a probabilistic sense.

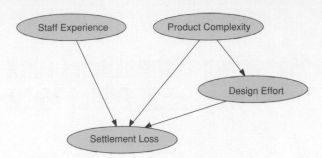

FIGURE 17.1   A simple Bayesian Belief Network to predict settlement loss.

Each node in a BBN is a random variable; as such, it will have an underlying probability distribution. How do we represent this probability distribution? The probability distribution of the node is captured in a node probability table (NPT). To illustrate this, consider the NPT for *Staff Experience* in Figure 17.1 It might consist of two states: *Novice* with 25 percent probability and *Experienced* with 75 percent probability. The node *Product Complexity* might also consist of two states: *High* with probability 40 percent and *Low* with probability 60 percent. Since *Staff Experience* and *Product Complexity* are nodes without parents, their NPTs are known as *prior probabilities*. The node *Design Effort* has two states: *Low* with 50 percent probability and *High* with 50 percent probability. Finally, we shall assume the node *Settlement Loss* has three states: *None* with 51 percent probability, *Low* with 19.5 percent probability, and *High* with 29.5 percent probability. Because *Settlement Loss* has parent nodes (*Staff Experience, Product Complexity, Design Effort*) its NPT captures the conditional probabilities of a particular type of settlement loss given the state of its parent nodes.

EXAMPLE 17.1 SIMPLE EVIDENCE PROPAGATION THROUGH BAYESIAN BELIEF NETWORKS

Suppose we know that the member of the staff who processes an individual transaction is a novice. We might expect the probability of a high settlement loss to be larger than if we know the staff member is experienced. The NPT of *Settlement Loss* might look like that shown in Table 17.1.

The construction of BBN models requires the user to specify the probability distribution for each node. These can be frequency probabilities derived from empirical data or subjective probabilities elicited from domain experts. Given new information about the state of one or more of the random variables, Bayes' theorem is used to update the values of all the other probabilities in the BBN. The process of updating probabilities is known as *evidence propagation*.

TABLE 17.1   Node Probability Table for a Simple Settlement Loss BBN

System design effort	Low				High			
Product complexity	Low		High		Low		High	
Staff experience	Novice (%)	Expert (%)	Novice (%)	Expert (%)	Novice (%)	Expert (%)	Novice (%)	Expert (%)
Settlement loss								
None	50	75	5	10	75	90	10	15
Low	35	20	15	20	20	9	27	25
High	15	5	80	70	5	1	63	60

For example, suppose the probabilities for the settlement loss BBN are those mentioned above, so that the probability of a large settlement loss is 29.5 percent. Suppose the operational risk manager receives information that for the next three hours only trainee members of the staff will be available to process transactions. This information can be entered into the BBN and propagated through the network recursively using Bayes' theorem. Although Bayes' theorem has been around for a long time, the propagation computations required to calculate the probabilities in BBNs become very complex as the number of nodes in the network increases. It is only fairly recently that efficient algorithms and tools to implement them have emerged.[5] These algorithms enable quick evidence propagation even in very large networks. The result of evidence propagation in the above example is that the probability of a high settlement loss rises slightly from 29.5 percent to 34.6 percent. What happens if a complex product needs to be processed? This evidence can also be entered into the BBN; in this case, the probability of a high settlement loss rises to 71.5 percent. Given this information, the operational risk manager may insist that an experienced member of the staff be made available.

COMPONENTS OF A BAYESIAN BELIEF NETWORK

BBN modeling consists of three components:

1. A graph that provides information about the relationships between variables
2. An associated set of probability tables that provide information about the dependencies between variables
3. Bayes' theorem applied recursively to propagate probabilistic information through the network

CASE STUDY 17.1: A BBN MODEL FOR SOFTWARE PRODUCT RISK

Investments in information technology (IT) and information systems (ISs) take place in an environment rife with uncertainty. As a consequence, projects are frequently behind schedule and over budget. The resulting systems may be of poor quality or fit inadequately to user requirements. As the dollar cost of such investments continues to rise, the competitive advantage of IT/IS projects needs to be carefully scrutinized and justified. Senior managers are increasingly seeking the assistance of decision-making tools to improve their ability to reason about the progress and outcome of a particular project. In this section we illustrate how BBNs can be used by operational risk and other managers as a project management tool. We consider a retail bank that is considering releasing a new software product to its customers. The key concern is to identify the number of serious defects in the software prior to release and to investigate the impact of different managerial policies on product quality, cost, and schedule during the development of the software product.

Large and complex commercial software is usually constructed using multiple modules. The initial requirements are analyzed and converted into a design, and the software modules are coded, tested, and debugged. We assume the software development consists of four stages:

1. Requirements analysis
2. Product design
3. Product coding
4. Testing

We discuss each of these stages below.

The first stage covers requirements analysis, a complete validated specification of the required interfaces, functions, and performance of the software product to be developed. The BBN topology is presented in Figure 17.2 The node *Problem Complexity* represents the degree of complexity inherent in the new product to be developed. Problem complexity simultaneously influences the actual effort allocated to the requirements initiative and the number of serious defects introduced in the initial requirements specification. During requirements rework, a number of these serious defects may be discovered and others introduced. The node *Residual Defects after Rework* contains the total number of defects inherent in the product at the end of the requirements analysis. It is directly influenced by the number of defects introduced in the initial requirements specification, defects introduced during any subsequent requirements rework, and defects found during the requirements analysis.

The second stage of the software development process covers product design. The BBN topology is presented in Figure 17.3. The node *Problem*

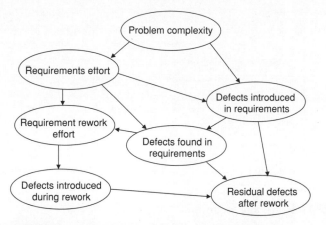

FIGURE 17.2 Requirements fragment.

Complexity influences the node *Design Effort*, which measures actual design effort and the node *Design Complexity*. Design rework plays a significant role in many software development processes, and it is both a means to correct identified defects and a potential source of additional design defects. The node *Residual Defects after Design* represents the total number of defects inherent in the product at the end of the design phase.

The third stage of development covers product coding. It involves the creation of a complete set of program components aimed at satisfying the design produced in the previous phase. The BBN topology is presented in

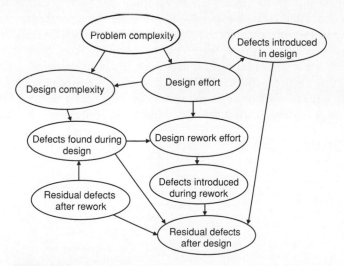

FIGURE 17.3 Design fragment.

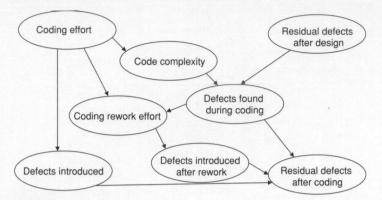

FIGURE 17.4   Coding fragment.

Figure 17.4. The node *Coding Effort* represents the actual resources allocated by management to the coding task. Coding effort influences the number of coding defects introduced into the product and the amount of effort allocated to coding rework. The node *Residual Defects after Coding* represents the total number of defects inherent in the development process at the end of the design phase.

The final stage in our process model covers product testing. The BBN topology is illustrated in Figure 17.5. The amount of resources allocated to testing effort influences the number of defects detected during testing and subsequently the number of defects delivered to the customer.

The full BBN model is illustrated in Figure 17.6. The model provides interim information to ensure the developing product is satisfying cost, schedule, and quality requirements. It provides the operational risk and other managers with an objective basis for assessing risk, predicting outcomes, and tracking progress. We do not make any claims about this model being correct for all situations. Indeed, we freely acknowledge that this model may not reflect what really happens during the product development in many organizations. For other organizations a cyclical model may be more appropriate, or perhaps software development is an iterative, evolutionary

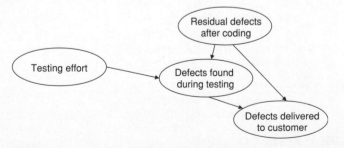

FIGURE 17.5   Testing fragment.

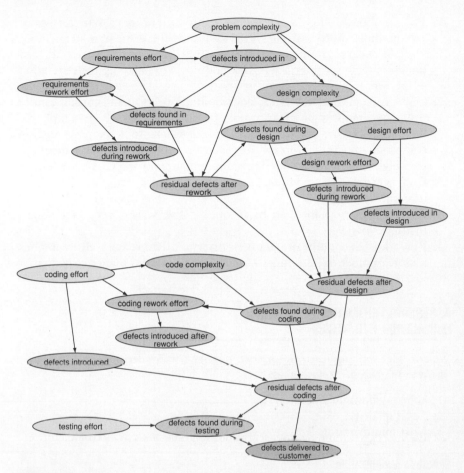

FIGURE 17.6 BBN process model for cost, schedule, and defects.

process where design, coding, etc., are performed in parallel. The reality is that the development of new products is performed in many different ways. What is important is that this activity can be captured in a BBN model. Of course, one may be able to think of many other variables that might also be included in the BBN topology of Figure 17.6. The exact process variables and topology are context-dependent.

CREATING A BBN-BASED SIMULATION

Simulation requires a number of assumptions necessary for exploring the dynamics of the development process. These assumptions should not be seen as irrevocable. They can be relaxed, changed, or added to as necessary. We shall assume the development process is characterized as follows:

1. The retail back office is developing a software product that consists of 100 modules. Forty percent of the system will consist of systems modules. Application modules will make up 30 percent of the system, and the graphical user interface (GUI) modules will make up the remaining 40 percent.
2. High problem complexity modules require more effort and consume more resources than low problem complexity modules. Very high complexity modules cost twice as much and take twice as long to develop as very low complexity modules. Problem complexity is very low for system modules, very high for application modules, and medium for the GUI modules.
3. Each process stage (requirements, design, coding, testing) has five teams of dedicated staff.
4. Each process variable can be in one of five states (very high, high, medium, low, very low).
5. Rework is essentially an iterative activity. A high rework effort implies a large number of iterations, a longer schedule, and higher costs than a low rework effort.

ASSESSING THE IMPACT OF DIFFERENT MANAGERIAL STRATEGIES

We consider the implications for cost, quality (defect density), and schedule of three management strategies:

1. Schedule minimization
2. Total quality
3. Cost minimization

Schedule Minimization

Schedule minimization is a strategy employed by an organization whose priority is to bring the product to the market in the minimum development time possible. Such a strategy involves the organization committing enough resources to support very high requirements and design, coding, and testing efforts while keeping rework to a minimum. Table 17.2 presents the expected

TABLE 17.2 Module Expected Cost and Expected Schedule Implications of a Schedule Minimization Strategy

Managerial strategy: schedule minimization	Module complexity	Cost ($)	Schedule
	Systems modules	5,180	11.66 days
	GUI modules	7,770	17.49 days
	Application modules	10,360	23.32 days

TABLE 17.3   Total Expected Cost and Schedule for Schedule Minimization Strategy

	Schedule minimization
Expected project cost	$4,144,062
Expected project schedule	53.31 weeks

cost and expected schedule per module for this strategy. A full breakdown of costs and schedule for each stage of the development process is given in Table 17.2. The expected total project cost and expected schedule are given in Table 17.3. The project is expected to be completed in just over a year at a cost of $4.1 million. Table 17.4 gives the probability distribution of defects likely to be present in the product after testing and debugging. There is approximately a 96 percent likelihood that the project will be delivered with a medium to very low number of defects. If we assume the number of product defects is positively correlated with maintenance cost, the project manager can reasonably expect the maintenance cost of the developed software to be low.

Total Quality

A strategy of total quality places product quality ahead of schedule or cost. For the software development process in our example, it implies very high requirements, a heavy design, coding, and testing effort, and a large number of rework iterations. Table 17.5 presents the expected cost and expected schedule per module for this strategy. The very high levels of rework increase the cost of each module by around 19 percent over the schedule minimization strategy. Heavy rework also increases schedule. Table 17.6 presents the total cost and schedule figures for the total quality strategy. The overall impact of a total quality strategy is an increase in schedule by 25.7 weeks and an additional cost of approximately $782,000 over a schedule minimization strategy. Table 17.7 shows the probability distribution of defects remaining in the product at the end of the testing and debugging phase. As

TABLE 17.4   Defects Delivered with Schedule Minimization Strategy

Managerial strategy: schedule minimization	Defects delivered	Likelihood (%)
	Very low	69.7
	Low	15.5
	Medium	10.3
	High	3.9
	Very high	0.6

TABLE 17.5   Module Expected Cost and Expected Schedule Implications of a Total
Quality Strategy

Managerial strategy: total quality	Module complexity	Cost ($)	Schedule
	Systems modules	6,157	17.28 days
	GUI modules	9,236	25.93 days
	Application modules	12,314	34.57 days

we might expect, the total quality strategy yields a very high likelihood of
a low number of defects in the developed software product.

Cost Minimization

When product quality or schedule is not at a premium, cost minimization
may prove a more suitable corporate objective. Cost minimization implies
allocating a minimum amount of effort to requirements and design and testing, with very low level of rework at each stage of development. Table 17.8
gives the expected cost and expected schedule per module for this strategy.
The cost minimization strategy results in a 54 percent reduction in module
costs over the schedule minimization strategy and a 65 percent reduction over
the total quality strategy. However, development time tends to be longer and
defects remaining in the product higher. Table 17.9 presents the total expected project cost and schedule. Table 17.10 shows the probability distribution of introduced defects.

PERCEIVED BENEFITS OF BAYESIAN BELIEF NETWORK MODELING

Since a key feature of BBNs is that they allow us to model and reason about
uncertainty surrounding future events, they appear to provide a natural tool
for dealing with two of the central problems that hinder effective operational risk management—uncertainty and complexity. Other important
benefits include:

TABLE 17.6   Total Expected Cost and Schedule
for Total Quality Strategy

	Total quality
Expected project cost	$4,925,763
Expected project schedule	79.01 weeks

TABLE 17.7   Defects Delivered with Total Quality Strategy

Managerial strategy: total quality	Defects delivered	Likelihood (%)
	Very low	95.4
	Low	3.0
	Medium	1.3
	High	0.4
	Very high	0.0

1. *A scientific and rigorous framework:*   Bayesian belief networks combine a rigorous probabilistic framework for representing the relationships among variables with an inherently appealing graphical structure that encourages easy communication between the user and the probabilistic model. In addition, the BBN graphical structure forces the model builder/user to expose all assumptions about the impact of different forms of evidence. In this sense BBNs provide a visible and auditable tool for building consistent and comparable models about risk inherent in differing business lines.

2. *Easy representation and manipulation of evidence from diverse sources:* A key strength of BBNs lies in their ability to take into account evidence from diverse sources. Empirical evidence, judgment, and uncertainty about tools, methods, and procedures can all be incorporated into a BBN model. They can take the plausibility (or prior belief) about the current operational risk processes of a business line. Plausibility is established from the prior knowledge and experience of the management practices, people, and technology involved in the various processes that constitute a particular business line. This can be combined with any available empirical evidence to obtain a probability statement about the likely severity and frequency of losses. Therefore, BBNs give operational risk managers the ability to integrate experiences of people, technology, and management style into a model of the operational process for their

TABLE 17.8   Module Expected Cost and Expected Schedule Implications of a Cost Minimization Strategy

Managerial strategy: cost minimization	Module complexity	Cost ($)	Schedule
	Systems modules	3,352	19.93 days
	GUI modules	4,945	29.61 days
	Application modules	6,584	39.17 days

TABLE 17.9   Total Expected Cost and Schedule for
Cost Minimization Strategy

	Cost minimization
Expected project cost	$2,647,015
Expected project schedule	90.20 weeks

organization. This is particularly important in the business environment because management practices, policies, and operational procedures can differ substantially from organization to organization. Indeed, in practice there are likely to be large variations in the way successful companies organize their people and processes. In such circumstances the use of BBN models provides operational risk managers with a tool that can be tailored to their own individual organization. In this sense, the scope of BBN modeling is not limited to any one specific management approach or to any specific organizational domain, and BBN modeling allows operational risk to be evaluated relative to the methodology and technology of the particular organization.

3. *Ability to quickly integrate new structural knowledge:*   Another important benefit is the ability of BBN models to represent and respond to changing structural knowledge. New knowledge about business lines can be translated easily into a reconfiguration of the network topology. As an example, consider an operational risk manager who after many years of settlement experience realizes that for the settlement process in his organization, staff experience has no impact on the number or severity of settlement losses. To represent this new knowledge, we simply delete from the BBN model of Figure 17.1 all links incident to the node *Staff Experience,* as shown in Figure 17.7. This flexibility enables managers to assess how the probability distribution of target variables

TABLE 17.10   Defects Delivered with Cost Minimization Strategy

Managerial Strategy: cost minimization	Defects delivered	Likelihood (%)
	Very low	54.4
	Low	18.1
	Medium	15.4
	High	13.7
	Very high	8.5

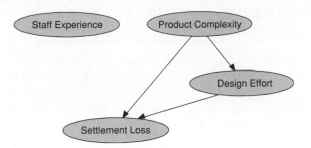

FIGURE 17.7　Impact of new structural knowledge on a BBN.

changes in response to new structural knowledge, thereby providing a basis for systematic planning in the presence of uncertainty. Once the manager knows the identity of the causal mechanism to be altered, the overall effect can be propagated through the network.

4. *Ease of use and interpretation:*　Real-world modeling of operational risk involves complex knowledge structures comprised of large numbers of variables. Traditional statistical techniques involve sophisticated mathematics even for relatively simple knowledge structures. In addition, they frequently impose restrictive assumptions on the variables modeled. The BBN combination of a rigorous probabilistic framework for representing the relationships among variables and an inherently appealing graphical structure that encourages easy communication between the user and the probabilistic model allows complex knowledge structures to be modeled using relatively simple mathematics.

　There are numerous statistical techniques that are useful in modeling operational risk. However, one of the disadvantages with these methods is the high level of quantitative expertise required before they can be used effectively. The consequences are obvious and important. Mastery of the appropriate statistical concepts and techniques requires a level of statistical sophistication not readily available in the general operational risk community. Even where such expertise exists, explaining the details of a statistical model and conveying the implications in a convincing manner to senior management often prove difficult. In contrast, BBNs allow the user to unlock the intricacies of complex business processes using simple mathematics and easily interpretable graphs. Advanced statistical knowledge is not required. BBNs offer an easy to use practical decision-making tool that enables both quantitative specialists and senior managers to communicate, analyze, interpret, and assess the impact of decisions made on their business lines.

COMMON MYTHS ABOUT BBNS—THE TRUTH FOR OPERATIONAL RISK MANAGEMENT

Despite the above advantages of BBN modeling, there remains a high degree of confusion and skepticism about its true value in an operational risk contest. On the one side are commercial vendors often founded by pseudo-academics[6] keen to exploit a cash-rich market niche. On the other side are the practitioners, bemused and skeptical about the ability of BBNs to deliver. Amid this confusion have arisen a number of oft-quoted myths:

Myth 1—Bayesian belief networks are difficult to build: On the contrary, BBNs are extremely easy to build since they require only a domain expert. The real difficulty lies not in specifying and building a BBN, but in determining whether the BBN correctly represents the relationships between the variables that make up the model. At the heart of the problem lies a lack of quantitative data. Without quantitative data, the highly successful tools of classical statistical inference, which have underpinned many scientific, medical, and industrial advances over the past century, are not available to us. We have little choice but to rely almost exclusively on domain experts. This might not be a serious drawback in other applications, but in operational risk management domain experts will inevitably be managers of the business line and their co-workers whose operational risk the OR manager wishes to assess. How can one elicit from self-interested individuals an unbiased and verifiable BBN model?

Myth 2—Operational risk is too complicated to be captured in a Bayesian belief network: This is not necessarily the case. The BBNs of complex processes can be easily and rapidly developed. The real difficulty is two-fold. First, the BBNs themselves might become very large and too complex to be easily understandable. Second, even if we believe that the BBN topology is correct, how can we be certain that the probabilities in the NPTs are well specified? The first point can be dealt with via careful design and the appropriate software tools to hide the complexity of very large BBNs. The second problem is not easily addressed because it revolves around the issue of how to validate a BBN model. One solution is to build the BBN model for a particular OR event and see how it performs through a considerable period of time. Although this approach to validation might be adequate for monitoring software development or a manufacturing processes, it certainly is not a responsible approach for a regulated financial institution.

Myth 3—Bayesian belief networks for operational risk can be easily maintained: In practice, BBNs are subject to domain expert risk, the possibility that key domain experts may leave an organization. To see why this is a serious issue, consider an operational risk BBN for a specific business line. Because the model will have been developed from the experience of the domain experts, its topology and NPTs will reflect the views of these experts. Over time all businesses evolve, and should the key domain experts leave, the operational risk manager may be faced with using a BBN model that does not reflect the operational risk inherent in the specific business line. This may remain the case *even if* experienced staff are hired to replace those leaving, simply because it takes time for new individuals to absorb the culture and peculiarities of a business. Even for very experienced individuals, it takes time to become a domain expert.[7] Traditional statistical models are not subject to this risk. BBN models may therefore have a much shorter life than traditional statistical models.

Myth 4—Bayesian belief networks are not forward-looking: In actual fact, BBNs are used to make predictions and are in this sense forward-looking. However, in this they are no different from standard statistical models, which although built using historical data, have been used successfully for a century to provide a rational basis for decision making in medicine, industry, and science. Related to this myth is the frequent claim by advocates of BBNs that key knowledge about operational risk is contained in the total sum of key individuals' experiences in their current and previous organizations. This knowledge is valuable, and often overlooked, but easily captured in a BBN. Thus, it is claimed by purveyors of BBN systems that they are superior to aggregate loss distribution simulations, scorecards, or other well proven statistical and nonstatistical methods!

Our answer to this claim is essentially pragmatic. The loss distribution approach has served the insurance industry well, and scorecards are widely used in assessing credit risk. If it works use it; if not, discard it. But be aware of the weaknesses and risks. This goes for all modeling approaches, widely accepted or not. In the final analysis operational risk modeling is more of an art than a science. As such BBNs have a role in providing a rigorous framework for incorporating both qualitative and quantitative information into management decision making. However, reliance on an approach based on subjective opinions, which can be manipulated through institutional pressure to get the desired results, is a major weakness. At some point quantitative data must to be collected on all of the important risk indicators and operational risk events. Where this is not (yet) possible, the use of BBNs for incorporating qualitative information into decision making may be an appropriate choice. However, in the end, quantitative information on all key risk indicators and types of OR events will have to be collected. If you do not quantitatively measure operational risk indicators and events, how can you expect to objectively assess, model, and control the operational risk environment?

SUMMARY

Bayesian belief networks enable reasoning under uncertainty and combine the advantages of an intuitive visual representation with a sound mathematical basis in Bayesian probability. They can accommodate both subjective probabilities elicited from domain experts and probabilities obtained from objective data. With BBNs it is possible to capture both expert beliefs and empirically derived rules about the dependencies between the variables. The impact of new evidence on the probabilities can be propagated consistently throughout the model. BBN models for operational risk offer

- A systematic mechanism for incorporating human reasoning and judgement about knowledge, such as the past behavior of a key attribute or other company-specific information
- Rigorous probabilistic information on the likely impact on key product or process attributes of varying risk factors
- A systematic decision-making tool that can provide explicit justifications for management actions

REVIEW QUESTIONS

1. Describe the elements that make up a BBN.
2. What theory of probability is used in evidence propagation?
3. Explain why, despite the claims to the contrary, BBNs do not represent a full solution to the problems faced in operational risk.

FURTHER READING

We have given extensive references in the chapter notes collected at the end of the book. Additional information on BBNs for real-world problems can be found in Lewis (1999). Further applications in operational risk management are given in Alexander (2000, 2001, 2003) and King (2001). There are a number of free software packages for building BBNs. A popular package is MSBN, which is fully compatible with Excel and developed by Microsoft. It can be found at http://research.microsoft.com/adapt/msbnx/. Another freely available Internet-based application called Belief Net can be found at http://www.cs.ubc.ca/labs/lci/CIspace/bayes/. An alternative for commercial use (with a free demonstration version) is Hugin, which can be found at http://www.hugin.com/.

CHAPTER 18

Epilogue

In writing this book my aims purposely have been rather limited. These aims will have been achieved if someone who has read the previous chapters carefully and experimented with the Excel/VBA examples has a fair idea of what can and cannot be achieved using the statistical methods that are most widely suggested as useful for operational risk management. My hope is that the book will help many individuals take the first step in the new and rapidly evolving field of operational risk modeling. For those who wish to develop further their knowledge, experience is best achieved by analyzing different sets of data, creating Excel worksheets and VBA functions, and interpreting the results obtained. Competence in operational risk modeling requires practice.

WINNING THE OPERATIONAL RISK ARGUMENT

Although few senior executives doubt the need to improve operational controls, often they are skeptical about whether operational risk such as fraud or rogue trading can be adequately measured and modeled. In persuading senior management to allocate resources to operational risk management, a number of arguments can be used:

1. The recent changes in the regulatory environment have many important dimensions. The most significant is its role in institutionalizing operational risk as a category for regulatory attention. It is something that must be managed alongside market and credit risk.
2. The statistical analysis of operational risk provides the necessary tools for modeling high-frequency low-impact events as well as low-frequency high-impact extreme events. It allows institutions to identify operational loss events to which they have exposure but have yet to experience.
3. Senior management needs to take into account operational risk alongside credit and market risk if it is to accurately assess capital requirements, profitability, and which business lines to invest in or shut down.

4. Operational risk management is not simply a compliance or back office function because if offers significant value beyond regulatory compliance by contributing to shareholder value. If adequately funded, operational risk management offers significant benefits for an institution.

FINAL TIPS ON APPLIED OPERATIONAL RISK MODELING

The statistical analysis and modeling of operational risk make sound business sense. Institutions that measure and manage operational risk can significantly reduce costs and are likely to be less susceptible to systemic problems. Once the decision has been made to adopt a statistical approach, the key question for the operational risk analyst is: What modeling assumptions are reasonable? In answering this question, it should be remembered that there are often alternative ways of approaching the analysis, none of which is necessarily the best approach. Indeed, as we have emphasized throughout this text, there are many different types of models that can be employed, models that are idiosyncratic to a firm, models that are idiosyncratic to a business line, and models that are idiosyncratic to controls. At the same time, several types of analysis may be carried out to investigate different aspects of the data.

It is important to keep in sight the goal of attaining flexible firm-specific modeling and consistency of treatment across all business lines of an institution. In order to use statistical techniques, it is important to collect appropriate data. The minimum that is required is the total loss amount, line of business causing the loss, risk categorization, and date of occurrence. Of course, the type and extent of data collected will depend on how an institution defines operational risk and their objectives in respect to operational risk management.

One further issue is whether to use qualitative or quantitative modeling. The key issue in selection will center on how the two different aspects of modeling contribute to our understanding of operational risk and help us in assessing controls. Therefore, it is the purpose that drives the technique. If we are interested in pricing operational risk, then a quantitative approach has the advantage of not relying on local management for subjective input.

FURTHER READING

Texts on operational risk are remarkably silent on the question of applied statistical modeling. To some extent, this is because the field of operational risk is rapidly evolving and partly because useful analysis is by no means a straightforward matter. Useful further reading includes, Hussain (2000), Marshall (2000), King (2001), Cruz (2002), Hoffman (2002), and Alexander (2003). For a slightly broader perspective and the application of statistical methods in other areas of risk management see Lewis (2003) and Saunders et al. (2004).

Statistical Tables

This Appendix contains statistical tables of the common sampling distributions of test statistics. Refer to the text for examples of their use.

CUMULATIVE DISTRIBUTION FUNCTION OF THE STANDARD NORMAL DISTRIBUTION

Table A.1 shows the probability, $F(z)$ that a standard normal random variable is less than the value z. For example, the probability is 0.97725 that a standard normal random variable is less than 2.

TABLE A.1 Cumulative Distribution Function of the Standard Normal Distribution

z	$F(z)$	z	$F(z)$	z	$F(z)$	z	$F(z)$
0	0.5	0.17	0.567495	0.34	0.633072	0.51	0.694974
0.01	0.503989	0.18	0.571424	0.35	0.636831	0.52	0.698468
0.02	0.507978	0.19	0.575345	0.36	0.640576	0.53	0.701944
0.03	0.511967	0.2	0.57926	0.37	0.644309	0.54	0.705402
0.04	0.515953	0.21	0.583166	0.38	0.648027	0.55	0.70884
0.05	0.519939	0.22	0.587064	0.39	0.651732	0.56	0.71226
0.06	0.523922	0.23	0.590954	0.4	0.655422	0.57	0.715661
0.07	0.527903	0.24	0.594835	0.41	0.659097	0.58	0.719043
0.08	0.531881	0.25	0.598706	0.42	0.662757	0.59	0.722405
0.09	0.535856	0.26	0.602568	0.43	0.666402	0.6	0.725747
0.1	0.539828	0.27	0.60642	0.44	0.670031	0.61	0.729069
0.11	0.543795	0.28	0.610261	0.45	0.673645	0.62	0.732371
0.12	0.547758	0.29	0.614092	0.46	0.677242	0.63	0.735653
0.13	0.551717	0.3	0.617911	0.47	0.680822	0.64	0.738914
0.14	0.55567	0.31	0.621719	0.48	0.684386	0.65	0.742154
0.15	0.559618	0.32	0.625516	0.49	0.687933	0.66	0.745373
0.16	0.563559	0.33	0.6293	0.5	0.691462	0.67	0.748571

(continued)

TABLE A.1 *(continued)*

z	F(z)	z	F(z)	z	F(z)	z	F(z)
0.68	0.751748	1.1	0.864334	1.52	0.935744	1.94	0.97381
0.69	0.754903	1.11	0.8665	1.53	0.936992	1.95	0.974412
0.7	0.758036	1.12	0.868643	1.54	0.93822	1.96	0.975002
0.71	0.761148	1.13	0.870762	1.55	0.939429	1.97	0.975581
0.72	0.764238	1.14	0.872857	1.56	0.94062	1.98	0.976148
0.73	0.767305	1.15	0.874928	1.57	0.941792	1.99	0.976705
0.74	0.77035	1.16	0.876976	1.58	0.942947	2	0.97725
0.75	0.773373	1.17	0.878999	1.59	0.944083	2.01	0.977784
0.76	0.776373	1.18	0.881	1.6	0.945201	2.02	0.978308
0.77	0.77935	1.19	0.882977	1.61	0.946301	2.03	0.978822
0.78	0.782305	1.2	0.88493	1.62	0.947384	2.04	0.979325
0.79	0.785236	1.21	0.88686	1.63	0.948449	2.05	0.979818
0.8	0.788145	1.22	0.888767	1.64	0.949497	2.06	0.980301
0.81	0.79103	1.23	0.890651	1.65	0.950529	2.07	0.980774
0.82	0.793892	1.24	0.892512	1.66	0.951543	2.08	0.981237
0.83	0.796731	1.25	0.89435	1.67	0.95254	2.09	0.981691
0.84	0.799546	1.26	0.896165	1.68	0.953521	2.1	0.982136
0.85	0.802338	1.27	0.897958	1.69	0.954486	2.11	0.982571
0.86	0.805106	1.28	0.899727	1.7	0.955435	2.12	0.982997
0.87	0.80785	1.29	0.901475	1.71	0.956367	2.13	0.983414
0.88	0.81057	1.3	0.903199	1.72	0.957284	2.14	0.983823
0.89	0.813267	1.31	0.904902	1.73	0.958185	2.15	0.984222
0.9	0.81594	1.32	0.906582	1.74	0.959071	2.16	0.984614
0.91	0.818589	1.33	0.908241	1.75	0.959941	2.17	0.984997
0.92	0.821214	1.34	0.909877	1.76	0.960796	2.18	0.985371
0.93	0.823814	1.35	0.911492	1.77	0.961636	2.19	0.985738
0.94	0.826391	1.36	0.913085	1.78	0.962462	2.2	0.986097
0.95	0.828944	1.37	0.914656	1.79	0.963273	2.21	0.986447
0.96	0.831472	1.38	0.916207	1.8	0.96407	2.22	0.986791
0.97	0.833977	1.39	0.917736	1.81	0.964852	2.23	0.987126
0.98	0.836457	1.4	0.919243	1.82	0.965621	2.24	0.987455
0.99	0.838913	1.41	0.92073	1.83	0.966375	2.25	0.987776
1	0.841345	1.42	0.922196	1.84	0.967116	2.26	0.988089
1.01	0.843752	1.43	0.923641	1.85	0.967843	2.27	0.988396
1.02	0.846136	1.44	0.925066	1.86	0.968557	2.28	0.988696
1.03	0.848495	1.45	0.926471	1.87	0.969258	2.29	0.988989
1.04	0.85083	1.46	0.927855	1.88	0.969946	2.3	0.989276
1.05	0.853141	1.47	0.929219	1.89	0.970621	2.31	0.989556
1.06	0.855428	1.48	0.930563	1.9	0.971284	2.32	0.98983
1.07	0.85769	1.49	0.931888	1.91	0.971933	2.33	0.990097
1.08	0.859929	1.5	0.933193	1.92	0.972571	2.34	0.990358
1.09	0.862143	1.51	0.934478	1.93	0.973197	2.35	0.990613

TABLE A.1 *(continued)*

z	F(z)	z	F(z)	z	F(z)	z	F(z)
2.36	0.990863	2.78	0.997282	3.19	0.999289	3.6	0.999841
2.37	0.991106	2.79	0.997365	3.2	0.999313	3.61	0.999847
2.38	0.991344	2.8	0.997445	3.21	0.999336	3.62	0.999853
2.39	0.991576	2.81	0.997523	3.22	0.999359	3.63	0.999858
2.4	0.991802	2.82	0.997599	3.23	0.999381	3.64	0.999864
2.41	0.992024	2.83	0.997673	3.24	0.999402	3.65	0.999869
2.42	0.99224	2.84	0.997744	3.25	0.999423	3.66	0.999874
2.43	0.992451	2.85	0.997814	3.26	0.999443	3.67	0.999879
2.44	0.992656	2.86	0.997882	3.27	0.999462	3.68	0.999883
2.45	0.992857	2.87	0.997948	3.28	0.999481	3.69	0.999888
2.46	0.993053	2.88	0.998012	3.29	0.999499	3.7	0.999892
2.47	0.993244	2.89	0.998074	3.3	0.999517	3.71	0.999896
2.48	0.993431	2.9	0.998134	3.31	0.999533	3.72	0.9999
2.49	0.993613	2.91	0.998193	3.32	0.99955	3.73	0.999904
2.5	0.99379	2.92	0.99825	3.33	0.999566	3.74	0.999908
2.51	0.993963	2.93	0.998305	3.34	0.999581	3.75	0.999912
2.52	0.994132	2.94	0.998359	3.35	0.999596	3.76	0.999915
2.53	0.994297	2.95	0.998411	3.36	0.99961	3.77	0.999918
2.54	0.994457	2.96	0.998462	3.37	0.999624	3.78	0.999922
2.55	0.994614	2.97	0.998511	3.38	0.999638	3.79	0.999925
2.56	0.994766	2.98	0.998559	3.39	0.99965	3.8	0.999928
2.57	0.994915	2.99	0.998605	3.4	0.999663	3.81	0.99993
2.58	0.99506	3	0.99865	3.41	0.999675	3.82	0.999933
2.59	0.995201	3.01	0.998694	3.42	0.999687	3.83	0.999936
2.6	0.995339	3.02	0.998736	3.43	0.999698	3.84	0.999938
2.61	0.995473	3.03	0.998777	3.44	0.999709	3.85	0.999941
2.62	0.995603	3.04	0.998817	3.45	0.99972	3.86	0.999943
2.63	0.995731	3.05	0.998856	3.46	0.99973	3.87	0.999946
2.64	0.995855	3.06	0.998893	3.47	0.99974	3.88	0.999948
2.65	0.995975	3.07	0.99893	3.48	0.999749	3.89	0.99995
2.66	0.996093	3.08	0.998965	3.49	0.999758	3.9	0.999952
2.67	0.996207	3.09	0.998999	3.5	0.999767	3.91	0.999954
2.68	0.996319	3.1	0.999032	3.51	0.999776	3.92	0.999956
2.69	0.996427	3.11	0.999064	3.52	0.999784	3.93	0.999958
2.7	0.996533	3.12	0.999096	3.53	0.999792	3.94	0.999959
2.71	0.996636	3.13	0.999126	3.54	0.9998	3.95	0.999961
2.72	0.996736	3.14	0.999155	3.55	0.999807	3.96	0.999963
2.73	0.996833	3.15	0.999184	3.56	0.999815	3.97	0.999964
2.74	0.996928	3.16	0.999211	3.57	0.999821	3.98	0.999966
2.75	0.99702	3.17	0.999238	3.58	0.999828	3.99	0.999967
2.76	0.99711	3.18	0.999264	3.59	0.999835	4	0.999968
2.77	0.997197						

CHI-SQUARED DISTRIBUTION

For a given probabily α, Table A.2 shows the values of the chi-squared distribution. For example, the probability is 0.05 that a chi-squared random variable with 10 degrees of freedom is greater than 18.31.

TABLE A.2 Cut-off Points for the Chi-squared Distribution

			α		
Degrees of freedom	0.005	0.01	0.025	0.05	0.1
1	7.88	6.63	5.02	3.84	2.71
2	10.60	9.21	7.38	5.99	4.61
3	12.84	11.34	9.35	7.81	6.25
4	14.86	13.28	11.14	9.49	7.78
5	16.75	15.09	12.83	11.07	9.24
6	18.55	16.81	14.45	12.59	10.64
7	20.28	18.48	16.01	14.07	12.02
8	21.95	20.09	17.53	15.51	13.36
9	23.59	21.67	19.02	16.92	14.68
10	25.19	23.21	20.48	18.31	15.99
11	26.76	24.73	21.92	19.68	17.28
12	28.30	26.22	23.34	21.03	18.55
13	29.82	27.69	24.74	22.36	19.81
14	31.32	29.14	26.12	23.68	21.06
15	32.80	30.58	27.49	25.00	22.31
16	34.27	32.00	28.85	26.30	23.54
17	35.72	33.41	30.19	27.59	24.77
18	37.16	34.81	31.53	28.87	25.99
19	38.58	36.19	32.85	30.14	27.20
20	40.00	37.57	34.17	31.41	28.41
21	41.40	38.93	35.48	32.67	29.62
22	42.80	40.29	36.78	33.92	30.81
23	44.18	41.64	38.08	35.17	32.01
24	45.56	42.98	39.36	36.42	33.20
25	46.93	44.31	40.65	37.65	34.38
26	48.29	45.64	41.92	38.89	35.56
27	49.65	46.96	43.19	40.11	36.74
28	50.99	48.28	44.46	41.34	37.92
29	52.34	49.59	45.72	42.56	39.09
30	53.67	50.89	46.98	43.77	40.26

TABLE A.2   *(continued)*

Degrees of freedom	α				
	0.005	0.01	0.025	0.05	0.1
31	55.00	52.19	48.23	44.99	41.42
32	56.33	53.49	49.48	46.19	42.58
33	57.65	54.78	50.73	47.40	43.75
34	58.96	56.06	51.97	48.60	44.90
35	60.27	57.34	53.20	49.80	46.06
36	61.58	58.62	54.44	51.00	47.21
37	62.88	59.89	55.67	52.19	48.36
38	64.18	61.16	56.90	53.38	49.51
39	65.48	62.43	58.12	54.57	50.66
40	66.77	63.69	59.34	55.76	51.81
41	68.05	64.95	60.56	56.94	52.95
42	69.34	66.21	61.78	58.12	54.09
43	70.62	67.46	62.99	59.30	55.23
44	71.89	68.71	64.20	60.48	56.37
45	73.17	69.96	65.41	61.66	57.51
46	74.44	71.20	66.62	62.83	58.64
47	75.70	72.44	67.82	64.00	59.77
48	76.97	73.68	69.02	65.17	60.91
49	78.23	74.92	70.22	66.34	62.04
50	79.49	76.15	71.42	67.50	63.17
51	80.75	77.39	72.62	68.67	64.30
52	82.00	78.62	73.81	69.83	65.42
53	83.25	79.84	75.00	70.99	66.55
54	84.50	81.07	76.19	72.15	67.67
55	85.75	82.29	77.38	73.31	68.80
56	86.99	83.51	78.57	74.47	69.92
57	88.24	84.73	79.75	75.62	71.04
58	89.48	85.95	80.94	76.78	72.16
59	90.72	87.17	82.12	77.93	73.28
60	91.95	88.38	83.30	79.08	74.40
61	93.19	89.59	84.48	80.23	75.51
62	94.42	90.80	85.65	81.38	76.63
63	95.65	92.01	86.83	82.53	77.75
64	96.88	93.22	88.00	83.68	78.86
65	98.10	94.42	89.18	84.82	79.97
66	99.33	95.63	90.35	85.96	81.09
67	100.55	96.83	91.52	87.11	82.20
68	101.78	98.03	92.69	88.25	83.31

(continued)

TABLE A.2   *(continued)*

| | | | α | | |
Degrees of freedom	0.005	0.01	0.025	0.05	0.1
69	103.00	99.23	93.86	89.39	84.42
70	104.21	100.43	95.02	90.53	85.53
71	105.43	101.62	96.19	91.67	86.64
72	106.65	102.82	97.35	92.81	87.74
73	107.86	104.01	98.52	93.95	88.85
74	109.07	105.20	99.68	95.08	89.96
75	110.29	106.39	100.84	96.22	91.06
76	111.50	107.58	102.00	97.35	92.17
77	112.70	108.77	103.16	98.48	93.27
78	113.91	109.96	104.32	99.62	94.37
79	115.12	111.14	105.47	100.75	95.48
80	116.32	112.33	106.63	101.88	96.58
81	117.52	113.51	107.78	103.01	97.68
82	118.73	114.69	108.94	104.14	98.78
83	119.93	115.88	110.09	105.27	99.88
84	121.13	117.06	111.24	106.39	100.98
85	122.32	118.24	112.39	107.52	102.08
86	123.52	119.41	113.54	108.65	103.18
87	124.72	120.59	114.69	109.77	104.28
88	125.91	121.77	115.84	110.90	105.37
89	127.11	122.94	116.99	112.02	106.47
90	128.30	124.12	118.14	113.15	107.57
91	129.49	125.29	119.28	114.27	108.66
92	130.68	126.46	120.43	115.39	109.76
93	131.87	127.63	121.57	116.51	110.85
94	133.06	128.80	122.72	117.63	111.94
95	134.25	129.97	123.86	118.75	113.04
96	135.43	131.14	125.00	119.87	114.13
97	136.62	132.31	126.14	120.99	115.22
98	137.80	133.48	127.28	122.11	116.32
99	138.99	134.64	128.42	123.23	117.41
100	140.17	135.81	129.56	124.34	118.50

STUDENT'S *t* DISTRIBUTION

For a given probability α, Table A.3 shows the values of the Student's t distribution. For example, the probability is 0.05 that a Student's t random variable with 10 degrees of freedom is greater than 1.812.

TABLE A.3 Cut-off Points for the Student's t Distribution

Degrees of freedom	α				
	0.005	0.01	0.025	0.05	0.1
1	63.656	31.821	12.706	6.314	3.078
2	9.925	6.965	4.303	2.920	1.886
3	5.841	4.541	3.182	2.353	1.638
4	4.604	3.747	2.776	2.132	1.533
5	4.032	3.365	2.571	2.015	1.476
6	3.707	3.143	2.447	1.943	1.440
7	3.499	2.998	2.365	1.895	1.415
8	3.355	2.896	2.306	1.860	1.397
9	3.250	2.821	2.262	1.833	1.383
10	3.169	2.764	2.228	1.812	1.372
11	3.106	2.718	2.201	1.796	1.363
12	3.055	2.681	2.179	1.782	1.356
13	3.012	2.650	2.160	1.771	1.350
14	2.977	2.624	2.145	1.761	1.345
15	2.947	2.602	2.131	1.753	1.341
16	2.921	2.583	2.120	1.746	1.337
17	2.898	2.567	2.110	1.740	1.333
18	2.878	2.552	2.101	1.734	1.330
19	2.861	2.539	2.093	1.729	1.328
20	2.845	2.528	2.086	1.725	1.325
21	2.831	2.518	2.080	1.721	1.323
22	2.819	2.508	2.074	1.717	1.321
23	2.807	2.500	2.069	1.714	1.319
24	2.797	2.492	2.064	1.711	1.318
25	2.787	2.485	2.060	1.708	1.316
26	2.779	2.479	2.056	1.706	1.315
27	2.771	2.473	2.052	1.703	1.314
28	2.763	2.467	2.048	1.701	1.313
29	2.756	2.462	2.045	1.699	1.311
30	2.750	2.457	2.042	1.697	1.310
40	2.704	2.423	2.021	1.684	1.303
60	2.660	2.390	2.000	1.671	1.296
100	2.626	2.364	1.984	1.660	1.290
500	2.586	2.334	1.965	1.648	1.283
1000	2.581	2.330	1.962	1.646	1.282
∞	2.576	2.327	1.960	1.645	1.282

F DISTRIBUTION

Tables A.4, A.5, and A.6 show, for a given probability α, the values of the F distribution. For example, the probability is 0.05 that an $F_{v,k}$ distributed random variable, with $v = 8$ and $k = 10$, is greater than 6.0.

TABLE A.4 Cut-off Points for the *F* Distribution, where $\alpha = 0.01$

Denominator degrees of freedom = k	Numerator Degrees of Freedom = v									
	1	4	8	10	20	50	100	500	1000	∞
1	4052.2	5624.3	5981.0	6055.9	6208.7	6302.3	6333.9	6359.5	6362.8	6365.6
4	21.2	16.0	14.8	14.5	14.0	13.7	13.6	13.5	13.5	13.5
8	11.3	7.0	6.0	5.8	5.4	5.1	5.0	4.9	4.9	4.9
10	10.0	6.0	5.1	4.8	4.4	4.1	4.0	3.9	3.9	3.9
20	8.1	4.4	3.6	3.4	2.9	2.6	2.5	2.4	2.4	2.4
50	7.2	3.7	2.9	2.7	2.3	1.9	1.8	1.7	1.7	1.7
100	6.9	3.5	2.7	2.5	2.1	1.7	1.6	1.5	1.4	1.4
500	6.7	3.4	2.5	2.4	1.9	1.6	1.4	1.2	1.2	1.2
1000	6.7	3.3	2.5	2.3	1.9	1.5	1.4	1.2	1.2	1.1
∞	6.6	3.3	2.5	2.3	1.9	1.5	1.4	1.2	1.1	1.0

TABLE A.5 Cut-off Points for the F Distribution, where $\alpha = 0.05$

Denominator degrees of freedom	Numerator Degrees of Freedom									
	1	4	8	10	20	50	100	500	1000	∞
1	161.4	224.6	238.9	241.9	248.0	251.8	253.0	254.1	254.2	254.3
4	7.7	6.4	6.0	6.0	5.8	5.7	5.7	5.6	5.6	5.6
8	5.3	3.8	3.4	3.3	3.2	3.0	3.0	2.9	2.9	2.9
10	5.0	3.5	3.1	3.0	2.8	2.6	2.6	2.5	2.5	2.5
20	4.4	2.9	2.4	2.3	2.1	2.0	1.9	1.9	1.8	1.8
50	4.0	2.6	2.1	2.0	1.8	1.6	1.5	1.5	1.4	1.4
100	3.9	2.5	2.0	1.9	1.7	1.5	1.4	1.3	1.3	1.3
500	3.9	2.4	2.0	1.8	1.6	1.4	1.3	1.2	1.1	1.1
1000	3.9	2.4	1.9	1.8	1.6	1.4	1.3	1.1	1.1	1.1
∞	3.8	2.4	1.9	1.8	1.6	1.4	1.2	1.1	1.1	1.0

TABLE A.6 Cut-off Points for the F Distribution, where $\alpha = 0.1$

Denominator degrees of freedom	Numerator Degrees of Freedom									
	1	4	8	10	20	50	100	500	1000	∞
1	39.9	55.8	59.4	60.2	61.7	62.7	63.0	63.3	63.3	63.3
4	4.5	4.1	4.0	3.9	3.8	3.8	3.8	3.8	3.8	3.8
8	3.5	2.8	2.6	2.5	2.4	2.3	2.3	2.3	2.3	2.3
1	3.3	2.6	2.4	2.3	2.2	2.1	2.1	2.1	2.1	2.
20	3.0	2.2	2.0	1.9	1.8	1.7	1.7	1.6	1.6	1.6
5	2.8	2.1	1.8	1.7	1.6	1.4	1.4	1.3	1.3	1.3
100	2.8	2.0	1.7	1.7	1.5	1.4	1.3	1.2	1.2	1.2
500	2.7	2.0	1.7	1.6	1.4	1.3	1.2	1.1	1.1	1.1
1000	2.7	2.0	1.7	1.6	1.4	1.3	1.2	1.1	1.1	1.1
∞	2.7	1.9	1.7	1.6	1.4	1.3	1.2	1.1	1.1	1.0

Notes

CHAPTER 7 SEVERITY OF LOSS PROBABILITY MODELS

1. Throughout this and the following sections we refer to the sample mean with the symbol $\bar{X}$.

2. There is an argument that profits from OR events should also be modeled, in which case the loss distribution will no longer be bounded by 0 and our choice of potential probability distributions is much greater.

CHAPTER 8 FREQUENCY OF LOSS PROBABILITY MODELS

1. On occasion in the literature you will also see the notation $q = (1 - p)$.

CHAPTER 11 CORRELATION AND DEPENDENCE

1. Camp, B.H. (1934). *The Mathematical Part of Elementary Statistics*. D.C. Heath. New York; Castellan, N.J. (1966). On the estimation of the tetrachoric correlation coefficient. *Psychometrika*, 31, 67–73.

2. Several approximations have been reviewed by Castellan (1966). The most accurate of these is the one given by Camp (1934), but it is restricted to $|\rho| < 0.8$ and cannot be expressed in analytical form.

3. Fisher, R.A. (1915). Frequency distribution of the values of the correlation coefficient in samples from an indefinitely large population. *Biometrika*, 10, 507; Fisher, R.A. (1921). On the "probable error" of a coefficient of correlation deduced from a small sample. *Merton*, 1, 309; Fisher, R.A. (1941). *Statistical Methods for Research Workers*. London.

4. Cramér, H. (1946). *Mathematical Methods of Statistics*. Princeton University Press. Princeton, NJ.

5. Joe, H. (1997). *Multivariate Models and Dependence Concepts*. Chapman & Hall. London.

6. See Note 5.

7. See Note 5.

8. See Note 5.

9. See Note 5.

CHAPTER 12 LINEAR REGRESSION IN OPERATIONAL RISK MANAGEMENT

1. See Esa Ollila et al. (2002) for an overview. These authors also introduce a new approach to estimates of regression coefficients based on the sign covariance matrix. Their approach appears to be highly efficient and may perform better than other methods, especially where the multivariate data is fat-tailed.

2. See, for example, Diebold et al. (1994), Durland and McCurdy (1994), Elliot et al. (1995), Engel (1994), Engel and Hamilton (1990), Gable et al. (1995), Goldfeld and Quandt (1973), Hamilton (1989, 1992, 1994, 1996), Hansen (1992), Hartley (1978), and Kim (1994).

CHAPTER 13 LOGISTIC REGRESSION IN OPERATIONAL RISK MANAGEMENT

1. Chow, G.C. (1988). *Econometrics*. McGraw-Hill. New York.

2. Ashford, J.R., and R.R. Sowden (1970). Multivariate probit analysis. (Biometrics), 26, 535–546.

3. Le Cessie, S., and J.C. Van Houweligen (1994). Logistic regression for correlated binary data. *Applied Statistician*, 43, 95–108.

4. Pearson, K. (1901). Mathematical contribution to the theory of evolution: VII, On the correlation of characters not quantitatively measurable. *Philosophical Transactions of the Royal Society of London*, Series A, 200, 1–66.

5. See Note 1.

6. See Note 1.

7. See Note 1.

8. Gumbel, E.J. (1961). Bivariate logistic distributions. *Journal of the American Statistical Association*, 56, 335–349.

9. Grizzle, J. (1971). Multivariate logit analysis. *Biometrics*, 27, 1057–1062.

10. Nerlove, M., and J. Press (1973). "Univariate and Multivariate Log-Linear and Logistic Models." RAND report R-1306-EDA/NIH.

11. Morimune, K. (1979). Comparisons of the normal and logistic models in the bivariate dichotomous analysis. *Econometrica*. 47, 957–75.

12. Maddala, G.S. (1983). *Limited Dependent and Qualitative Variables in Econometrics*. Cambridge University Press. Cambridge, UK.

13. Plackett, R.L. (1965). A class of bivariate distributions. *Journal of the American Statistical Association*, 60, 516–522.

14. Dale, J.R. (1986). Global cross-ratio models for bivariate, discrete, ordered responses. *Biometrics*, 42, 909–917.

15. See Note 3.

16. See Note 14.

17. See Note 3.

CHAPTER 14 MIXED DEPENDENT VARIABLE MODELING

1. Catalano, P.J. (1997). Bivariate modelling of clustered continuous and ordered categorical outcomes. *Statistics in Medicine*, 16, 883–900.

2. Catalano, P.J., and L.M. Ryan (1992). Bivariate latent variable models for clustered discrete and continuous outcomes. *Journal of the American Statistical Association*, 87, 651–658.

3. Olkin, L., and R.F. Tate. (1961). Multivariate correlation models with mixed discrete and continuous outcome variables. *Annals of Mathematical Statistics*, 32, 448–465.

4. Fitzmaurice, G.M., and N.M. Laird (1995). Regression models for bivariate discrete and continuous outcomes. *Journal of the American Statistical Association*, 90, 845–852.

5. O'Brien, P. (1984). Procedures for comparing samples with multiple endpoints. *Biometrics*, 40, 1079–1087.

6. Pocock, S.J., N.L. Geller, and A.A. Tsiatis (1987). The analysis of multiple endpoints in clinical trials. *Biometrics*, 43, 487–498.

7. Lefkopoulou, M., D. Moore, and L. Ryan (1989). The analysis of multiple correlated binary outcomes: application to rodent teratology experiments. *Journal of the American Statistical Association*, 84, 810–815.

8. Molenberghs, G., H. Geys, and M. Buyse (1998). Validation of surrogate endpoints in randomized experiments with mixed discrete and continuous outcomes. Unpublished manuscript. Limburgs Universitair Centrum, Belgium.

9. See, for example, Lewis (2003).

10. Ziegler, A., C. Kastner, and M. Blettner (1998). The generalised estimating equations: an annotated bibliography. *Biometrical Journal*, 40, 115–139.

11. Huster, W.J., R. Brookmeyer, and S.G. Self (1989). Modelling paired survival data with covariates. *Biometrics*, 45,145–156.

12. Wei, L.J., D.Y. Lin, and L. Weissfeld (1989). Regression analysis of multivariate incomplete failure time by modelling marginal distributions. *Journal of the American Statistical Association*, 84, 1064–1073.

13. Cox, D.R., and D.V. Hinkley (1974). *Theoretical Statistics*. Chapman and Hall. London.

14. See Note 13.

15. Royall, R.M. (1986). Model robust confidence intervals using maximum likelihood estimators. *International Statistics Review*, 54, 221–226.

16. Zeger, S.L., and K.Y. Liang (1986). Longitudinal data analysis for discrete and continuous outcomes. *Biometrics*, 42, 1019–1031.

17. Johnson, M.E., H.D. Tolley, M.C. Bryson, and A.S. Goldman (1982). Covariate analysis of survival data: a small sample study of Cox's model. *Biometrics*, 48, 685–698; Loughin, T.M. (1995). A residual bootstrap for regression parameters in proportional hazards models. *Journal of Statistical Computation and Simulation*, 52, 367–384.

18. Loughin, T.M., and K.J. Koehler (1997). Bootstrapping regression parameters in multivariate survival analysis. *Lifetime Data Analysis*, 3, 157–177.

CHAPTER 15 VALIDATING OPERATIONAL RISK PROXIES USING SURROGATE ENDPOINTS

1. Herson, J. 1989. The use of surrogate endpoints in clinical trails (an introduction to a series of four papers). *Statistics in Medicine*, 8, 403–404; Ellenberg, S.S, and J. Michael Hamilton (1989). Surrogate endpoints in clinical trails: cancer. *Statistics in Medicine*, 8, 405–413; Burke, H.B. (1994). Increasing the power of surrogate endpoint biomarkers: the aggregation of predictive factors. *Journal of Cellular Biochemistry*, Supplement 19, 278–282; Lipkin, M., M. Bhandari, M. Hakissian, W. Croll, and G. Wong (1994). Surrogate endpoint biomarker assays in phase II chemoprevention clinical trials. *Journal of Cellular Biochemistry*, Supplement 19, 46–54; Kellof, G.J., C.W. Boone, J.A. Crowell, V.E. Steele, R. Lubert, and L.A. Doody (1994).

Surrogate endpoint biomarkers for phase II cancer chemoprevention trials. *Journal of Cellular Biochemistry*, Supplement 19, 1–9; Karlan, B.Y. (1995). Screening for ovarian cancer: what are the optimal surrogate endpoints for clinical trials? *Journal of Cellular Biochemistry*, Supplement 23, 227–232; Ruffin, M.T., M.P.H. Mohammed, S. Ogaily, C.M. Johnston, L. Gregoire, W.D. Lancaster, and D.E. Brenner. Surrogate endpoint biomarkers for cervical cancer chemoprevention trials. *Journal of Cellular Biochemistry*, Supplement 23, 113–124; Dhingra., K. (1995). A phase II chemoprevention trial design to identify surrogate endpoint biomarkers in breast cancer. *Journal of Cellular Biochemistry*, Supplement 23, 19–24.

2. Prentice, R.L. (1989). Surrogate endpoints in clinical trials: definition and operational criteria. *Statistics in Medicine*, 8, 431–440; Kellof, G.J., C.W. Boone, J.A. Crowell, V.E. Steele, R. Lubert, and L.A. Doody (1994). Surrogate endpoint biomarkers for phase II cancer chemoprevention trials. *Journal of Cellular Biochemistry*, Supplement 19, 1–9.

3. Piantadosi, S. (1997). *Clinical Trials: A Methodologic Perspective*. John Wiley & Sons. New York.

4. Stone, R. (1993). The assumptions on which causal inferences rest. *Journal of the Royal Statistical Society*, B, 55, 455–466.

5. Ellenberg, S.S., and J. Michael Hamilton (1989). Surrogate endpoints in clinical trials: cancer. *Statistics in Medicine*, 8, 405–413.

6. Hillis, A., and D. Siegel (1989). Surrogate endpoints in clinical trials: ophthalmologic disorders. *Statistics in Medicine*, 8, 427–430.

7. Prentice, R.L. (1989). Surrogate endpoints in clinical trials: definition and operational criteria. *Statistics in Medicine*, 8, 431–440.

8. There is also another condition that direct tests of Equation 15.2 require restricting the class of alternative distributions to those for which the treatment effects on the surrogate response distribution have some impact on the final endpoint failure such that $E[\lambda_T(t|S(t)|x, F(t))] \neq E(\lambda_T(t|S(t))| F(t)]$, although in practical terms it is Equation 15.2 that provides the basis for empirical testing.

9. Kalbfleusch, J.D., and R.L. Prentice (1980). *The Statistical Analysis of Failure Time Data*. John Wiley & Sons. New York.

10. See Note 9.

11. Freedman, L.S., B.I. Graubard, and A. Schatzkin (1992). Statistical validation of intermediate endpoints for chronic diseases. *Statistics in Medicine*, 11, 167–178.

12. Notice the clear distinction between a *surrogate variable* and a *surrogate endpoint* introduced by Prentice. Surrogate endpoints are that subset of surrogate variables that satisfy the Prentice criterion.

13. Begg, C.B., and D.H.Y. Leung (2000). On the use of surrogate endpoints in randomised trials. *Journal of the Royal Statistical Society*, A,163, 15–28.

14. Buyse, M., and G. Molenberghs (1998). Criteria for the validation of surrogate endpoints in randomized experiments. *Biometrics*, 54, 186–201.

15. See Notes 11 and 14; Lin, D.Y., T.R. Flemming, and V. De Gruttola (1997). Estimating the propotion of treatment effect explained by a surrogate marker. *Statistics in Medicine*, 16, 1515–1527.

16. See Note 13.

17. See Note 13.

18. Prentice, R.L. (1989). Surrogate endpoints in clinical trials: definition and operational criteria. *Statistics in Medicine*, 8, 431–440.

19. See Notes 11 and 14.

20. See Note 13.

21. Cox., D.R. (1993). A remark on censoring and surrogate response variables. *Journal of the Royal Statistical Society*, B, 45, 391–393.

22. Flemming, T.R., R.L. Prentice, M.S. Pepe, and D. Glidden (1994). Surrogate and auxiliary endpoints in clinical trails, with potential applications in cancer and AIDS research. *Statistics in Medicine*, 13, 955–968.

23. Taylor, J.M.G., A. Munoz, S.M. Bass, A.J. Saah, J.S. Chimiel, and L.A. Kingsley (1990). Estimating the distribution of times from HIV sero-conversion to AIDS using multiple imputation. *Statistics in Medicine*, 9, 505–514; see Note 22.

24. A surrogate variable is perfectly associated if it is a perfect substitute for the final endpoint, that is, given a treatment it always reacts in exactly the same direction and degree as the final endpoint.

25. The Cardiac Arrhythmia Suppression Trial Investigators. 1989. Effect of encainide and flecainide on mortality in a randomized trial of arrhythmia suppression after myocardial infarction. *New England Journal of Medicine*, 321, 406–412.

26. See Note 25.

27. See Note 11.

28. Fieller, E.C. (1940). The biological standardization of insulin. *Journal of the Royal Statistical Society, 7, Supplement, 1–15.*

29. Lin, D.Y., T.R. Flemming, and V. De Gruttola (1997). Estimating the proportion of treatment effect explained by a surrogate marker. *Statistics in Medicine,* 16, 1515–1527.

30. See Note 29.

31. See Note 14.

32. See Note 14.

33. See Note 11.

34. See Note 2.

Bibliography

Aitchison, J., and J. A. C. Brown (1957). *The Log-Normal Distribution,* Cambridge University Press, New York.

Alexander, C. (2000). Bayesian methods for measuring operational risks. *Derivatives, Use Trading and Regulation,* ISMA Centre Discussion Paper in Finance, University of Reading. 6(2), 166–186.

Alexander, C. (2001). *Mastering Risk.* Vol. 2. Financial Times Prentice Hall. London.

Alexander, C. (2003). *Operational Risk.* Financial Times Prentice Hall. London.

Arbous, A.G., and J. E. Kerrich (1951). Accident statistics and the concept of accident-proneness. Part I: a critical valuation. Part II: The mathematical background. *Biometrics,* 341–433.

Artzner, P., F. Delbaen, J.M. Eber, and D. Heath (1997). Thinking coherently. *Risk,* 10, 68–71.

Artzner, P., F. Delbaen, J. M. Eber, and D. Heath (1999). Coherent measures of risk, *Mathematical Finance,* 9, 203–228.

Ascher, H. (1981), Weibull distribution vs Weibull process, *Proceedings Annual Reliability and Maintainability Symposium,* pp. 426–431.

Ashford, J.R., and, R.R. Sowden (1970). Multivariate probit analysis. *Biometrics,* 26, 535–546.

Bahar, R., M.Gold, T. Kitto, and C. Polizu (1997). Making the best of the worst. *Risk,* 10, 100–103.

Basle Committee on Banking Supervision (1999). "A New Capital Adequacy Framework."

Basel Committee on Banking Supervision (2001a). "Consultative Document: The New Basel Capital Accord."

Basel Committee on Banking Supervision (2001b). "Consultative Document: Operational Risk."

Basel Committee on Banking Supervision (2001c). "Working Paper on the Regulatory Treatment of Operational Risk."

Basel Committee on Banking Supervision (2003). "Sound Practices for the Management and Supervision of Operational Risk."

Becker, A., and D. Geiger (1994). Approximation algorithms for the loop cutset problem. In: *Proceedings of the Tenth Conference on Uncertainty in Artificial Intelligence*. Morgan Kauffman. San Francisco. pp. 60–68.

Begg, C.B., and D.H.Y. Leung (2000). On the use of surrogate endpoints in randomised trials. *Journal of the Royal Statistical Society*, A, 163, 15–28.

Bickmore, T. W. (1994). "Real-Time Sensor Data Validation." NASA Contractor Report 195295, National Aeronatics and Space Administration.

BIS Committee on the Global Financial System (2000). "Stress Testing by Large Financial Institutions: Current Practice and Aggregation Issues."

British Bankers' Association. (1997). "Operational Risk Management Survey."

Burke, H.B. (1994). Increasing the power of surrogate endpoint biomarkers: the aggregation of predictive factors. *Journal of Cellular Biochemistry*, Supplement 19, 278–282.

Butler, C. (1999). Mastering value at risk. *Financial Times*. London.

Buyse, M., and G. Molenberghs (1998). Criteria for the validation of surrogate endpoints in randomized experiments. *Biometrics*, 54, 186–201.

Camp, B.H. (1934). *The mathematical part of elementary statistics*. D.C. Heath. New York.

Carver, R. P. (1993). The case against statistical significance testing, revisited. *Journal of Experimental Education*, 61, 287–292.

Castellan, N.J. (1966). On the estimation of the tetrachoric correlation coefficient. *Psychometrika*, 31, 67–73.

Catalano, P.J. (1997). Bivariate modelling of clustered continuous and ordered categorical outcomes. *Statistics in Medicine*, 16, 883–900.

Catalano, P.J., and L.M. Ryan (1992). Bivariate latent variable models for clustered discrete and continuous outcomes. *Journal of the American Statistical Association*, 87, 651–658.

Chatfield, C. (1985). The initial examination of data (with discussion). *Journal of the Royal Statistical Society*, Series A, 148, 214–253.

Chow, G.C. (1988). *Econometrics*. McGraw-Hill. New York.

Clark, C. A. (1963). Hypothesis testing in relation to statistical methodology. *Review of Educational Research*, 33, 455–473.

Cox, D.R. (1993). A remark on censoring and surrogate response variables. *Journal of the Royal Statistical Society*, B, 45, 391–393.

Cox, D.R. and D.V. Hinkley (1974). *Theoretical Statistics*. Chapman and Hall. London.

Cramér, H. (1946). *Mathematical Methods of Statistics*. Princeton University Press. Princeton, NJ.

Cruz, M.G. (2002). *Modeling, Measuring and Hedging Operational Risk*. John Wiley. New York.

Dale, J.R. (1986). Global cross-ratio models for bivariate, discrete, ordered responses. *Biometrics*, 42, 909–917.

Darwiche, A. (1995). Conditioning methods for exact approximate inference in causal networks. *Proceedings of the Eleventh Annual Conference on Uncertainty in Artificial Intelligence*. Morgan Kauffmann. San Francisco.

De Pril, N. (1986). On the exact computaton of the aggregate clalms distribution in the individual life model. *ASTIN Bulletin*, 16, 109–112.

Dhingra, K. (1995). A phase II chemoprevention trial design to identify surrogate endpoint biomarkers in breast cancer. *Journal of Cellular Biochemistry*. Supplement 23, 19–24.

Diebold, F.X., J.H. Lee, and G.C. Weinbach (1994). Regime switching with time varying transition probabilities. In: Hargreaves, C., *Nonstationary Time Series Analysis and Cointegration*. Oxford University Press, Oxford, UK.

Duffie, D., and J. Pan (1997). An overview of value at risk. *Journal of Derivatives*, 4, pp. 7–49.

Durland, J. M. and T. H. McCurdy (1994). Duration dependent transition in a Markov model of U.S. GNP growth. *Journal of Business & Economic Statistics*, 3, 279–288.

Ellenberg, S.S., and J. Michael Hamilton (1989). Surrogate endpoints in clinical trails: cancer. *Statistics in Medicine*, 8, 405–413.

Elliot, R. J., A. Lakhdar, and J. B. Moore (1995). *Hidden Markov Models Estimation and Control*. Springer Verlag. New York.

Engel, C. (1994). Can the Markov switching model forecast exchange rates? *Journal of International Economics*, 36, 151–165.

Engel, C. and J. D. Hamilton (1990). Long swings in the dollar: are they in the data and do markets know it? *American Economic Review*, 4, 689–713.

Ezawa, K. J., and T. Schuermann (1995). Fraud/uncollectible debt detection using a Bayesian network based learning system: a rare binary outcome with mixed data structures. Computer bottleneck detection with belief nets. *Proceedings of the Conference on Uncertainty in Artificial Intelligence*. Morgan Kaufmann, San Francisco. pp. 157–166.

Fieller, E.C. (1940). The biological standardization of insulin. *Journal of the Royal Statistical Society*, 7, Supplement 1–15.

Fisher, R.A. (1915). Frequency distribution of the values of the correlation coefficient in samples from an indefinitely large population. *Biometrika*, 10, 507.

Fisher, R.A. (1921). On the "probable error" of a coefficient of correlation deduced from a small sample. *Merton* 1, 309.

Fisher, R.A. (1941). *Statistical Methods for Research Workers*. Oliver and Boyd. London.

Fitzmaurice, G.M., and N.M. Laird (1995). Regression models for bivariate discrete and continuous outcomes. *Journal of the American Statistical Association*, 90, 845–852.

Flemming, T.R., R.L. Prentice, M.S. Pepe, and D. Glidden (1994). Surrogate and auxiliary endpoints in clinical trails, with potential applications in cancer and AIDS research. *Statistics in Medicine*, 13, 955–968.

Freedman, L.S., B.I. Graubard, and A. Schatzkin (1992). Statistical validation of intermediate endpoints for chronic diseases. *Statistics in Medicine* 11, 167–178.

Gable, J., S. van Norden, and R. Vigfusson (1995). "Analytical Derivatives for Markov-Switching Models." Bank of Canada Working Paper, pp. 95–97.

Goldfeld, S.M., and R.E. Quandt (1973). A Markov model for switching regressions. *Journal of Econometrics*, 1, 3–16.

Gumbel, E. J. (1954). "Statistical Theory of Extreme Values and Some Practical Applications," National Bureau of Standards Applied Mathematics Series 33, U.S. Government Printing Office, Washington, D.C.

Gumbel, E.J. (1961). Bivariate logistic distributions. *Journal of the American Statistical Association*, 56, 335–349.

Grizzle, J. (1971). Multivariate logit Analysis. *Biometrics*, 27, 1057–1062.

Groeneveld, R.A. (1998). A class of quartile measures for kurtosis. *American Statistician*, 51, 325–329.

Hahn, G.J., and S.S. Shapiro (1967). *Statistical Models in Engineering*. John Wiley & Sons. New York.

Hamilton, J.D. (1989). A new approach to the economic analysis of nonstationary time series and the business cycle. *Econometrica*, 57, 357–384.

Hamilton, J.D. (1992). Estimation, inference, and forecasting of time series subject to changes in regime. In: Rao, C. R. and G.S. Maddala, *Handbook of Statistics*. Vol. 10. North Holand, Amsterdam.

Hamilton, J.D. (1994). *Time Series Analysis*. Princeton University Press. Princeton, NJ.

Hamilton, J.D. (1996). Specification testing in Markov-switching time-series models. *Journal of Econometrics*, 1, 127–157.

Hansen, B. E. (1992). The likelihood ratio test under nonstandard conditions: testing the Markov-switching model of GNP. *Journal of Applied Econometrics*, 7, Supplement.

Herson, J. (1989). The use of surrogate endpoints in clinical trails (an introduction to a series of four papers). *Statistics in Medicine*, 8, 403–404.

Hartley, M.J. (1978). Comment on Quandt and Ramsey. *Journal of the American Statistical Association*, 12, 12–25.

Hill, T.P. (1995). The first digit phenomenon. *American Mathematical Monthly*, 192, 322.

Hill, T.P. (1998a). A statistical derivation of the significant-digit law. *Statistical Science*, 10, 354–363.

Hill, T.P. (1998b). The first digit phenomenon. *American Scientist*, 86, 358.

Hillis, A., and D. Siegel (1989). Surrogate endpoints in clinical trials: ophthalmologic disorders. *Statistics in Medicine*, 8, 427–430.

Hoffman, D.G. (2002). *Managing Operational Risk: 20 Firmwide Best Practice Strategies*. John Wiley. New York.

Holton, G.A., (1997). Subjective value at risk. *Financial Engineering News*, 1, 8-9, 11.

Huang, T., D. Koller, J. Malik, G. Ogasawara, B. Rao, S. Russell, and J. Weber (1994). Automatic symbolic traffic scene analysis using belief networks. *Proceedings of National Conference on Artificial Intelligence*. Morgan Kaufmann. San Francisco.

Hussain, A. (2000). Managing Operational Risk in Financial Markets. Butterworth Heineman, London.

Huster, W.J., R. Brookmeyer, and S.G. Self (1989). Modeling paired survival data with covariates. *Biometrics*, 45, 145–156.

Jameson, R., (1998). Playing the name game. *Risk*, 11, 38–42.

Joe, H. (1997). *Multivariate Models and Dependence Concepts*. Chapman & Hall. London.

Johnson, M.E., H.D. Tolley, M.C. Bryson, and A.S. Goldman (1982). Covariate analysis of survival data: a small sample study of Cox's model. *Biometrics*, 48, 685–698.

Johnson, N.L., S. Kotz, and N. Balakrishnan (1994). *Continuous Univariate Distributions*. Vol. 1, 2nd ed. John Wiley & Sons. New York.

Johnson, N.L., S. Kotz, and N. Balakrishnan (1995). *Continuous Univariate Distributions* Vol. 2, 2nd ed. John Wiley & Sons. New York.

Jorion, P. (1997). *Value at Risk: The New Benchmark for Controlling Market Risk*. McGraw-Hill, Chicago.

Kahn, C.E. Jr, L. M. Roberts, K. Wang, D. Jenks, and P. Haddawy (1995). Preliminary investigation of a Bayesian network for mammographic diagnosis of b breast cancer. *Proceedings of the 19th Annual Symposium on Computer Applications in Medical Care*. Hanley & Belfus. Philadelphia. pp. 208–212.

Kalbfleusch, J.D., and R.L. Prentice (1980). *The Statistical Analysis of Failure Time Data*. John Wiley & Sons. New York.

Karlan, B.Y. (1995). Screening for ovarian cancer: what are the optimal surrogate endpoints for clinical trials? *Journal of Cellular Biochemistry*, Supplement 23, 227–232.

Kellof, G.J., C.W. Boone, J.A. Crowell, V.E. Steele, R. Lubert, and L.A. Doody (1994). Surrogate endpoint biomarkers for phase II cancer chemoprevention trials. *Journal of Cellular Biochemistry*, Supplement 19, 1–9.

Kim, C. J. (1994). Dynamic linear models with Markov-switching. *Journal of Econometrics*, 60, 1–22.

Kim, H., and J. Pearl (1992). A computational model for combined causal and diagnostic reasoning in inference systems. In: *Proceedings of the Eighth International Joint Conference on Artificial Intelligence*. Los Angeles pp. 190–193.

King, J. (2001). *Operational Risk: Measurement and Modeling*. Wiley. Chichester, UK.

Kornya, P.S. (1983). Distribution of aggregate claims the individual risk theory. *Society of Actuaries Transactions*, 35, 823–858.

Le Cessie, S., and J.C. Van Houwelingen (1994). Logistic regression for correlated binary data. *Applied Statistician*, 43, 95–108.

Lefkopoulou, M., D. Moore, and L. Ryan (1989). The analysis of multiple correlated binary outcomes: application to rodent teratology experiments. *Journal of the American Statistical Association*, 84, 810–815.

Levin, J. R. (1993). Statistical significance testing from three perspectives. *Journal of Experimental Education*, 61, 378–382.

Lewis, N.D. (1999). Continuous process improvement using Bayesian belief networks. The lessons to be learnt. *Journal of Computers and Industrial Engineering*, 37, 449–452.

Lewis, N.D. (2003). *Market Risk Modeling: Applied Statistical Methods for Practitioners*. Risk Books. London.

Ley, E. (1996). On the peculiar distributon of the U.S. stock indices digits. *American Statistician*, Vol. 50, p. 311–313.

Lin, D.Y., T.R. Flemming, and V. De Gruttola (1997). Estimating the proportion of treatment effect explained by a surrogate marker. *Statistics in Medicine*, 16, 1515–1527.

Lipkin, M., M. Bhandari, M. Hakissian, W. Croll, and G. Wong (1994). Surrogate endpoint biomarker assays in phase II chemoprevention clinical trials. *Journal of Cellular Biochemistry*. Supplement 19, 46–54.

Loughin, T.M., (1995). A residual bootstrap for regression parameters in proportional hazards models. *Journal of Statistical Computation and Simulation*, 52, 367–384.

Loughin, T.M., and K.J. Koehler (1997). Bootstrapping regression parameters in multivariate survival analysis. *Lifetime Data Analysis*, 3, 157–177.

Maddala, G.S. (1983). *Limited Dependent and Qualitative Variables in Econometrics*. Cambridge University Press. Cambridge, UK.

Mari, D.D. and S. Kotz (2001). *Correlation and Dependence*. Imperial College Press. London.

Marshall, C.L. (2000). Measuring and Managing Operational Risks in Financial Institutions : Tools, Techniques, and other Resources. Wiley, New York.

McCullagh, P. and J.A. Nelder (1992). *Generalized Linear Models*. Chapman & Hall. London.

Molenberghs, G., H. Geys, and M. Buyse (1998). Validation of surrogate endpoints in randomized experiments with mixed discrete and continuous outcomes. Unpublished manuscript. Limburgs Universitair Centrum, Belgium.

Montgomery, D.C., and E. A. Peck (1982). *Introduction to Linear Regression Analysis*. John Wiley & Sons. New York.

Moors, J.J.A. (1988). A quantile alternative for kurtosis. *Statistician*, 37, 25–32.

Morimune, K. (1979). Comparisons of the normal and logistic models in the bivariate dichotomous analysis. *Econometrica, 47*, 957–975.

Nerlove, M., and J. Press (1973). "Univariate and Multivariate Log-Linear and Logistic Models." RAND report R-1306-EDA/NIH.

Nigrini, M.J. (1999). I've got your number. *Journal of Accountancy*, 5, 79–83.

Nigrini, M.J., and L.J. Mittermaier (1997). The use of Benford's law as an aid in analytical procedures. *Auditing: A Journal of Practice and Theory*, 16, 52–67.

O'Brien, P. (1984). Procedures for comparing samples with multiple endpoints. *Biometrics*, 40, 1079–1087.

Olkin, L., and R.F. Tate (1961). Multivariate correlation models with mixed discrete and continuous outcome variables. *Annals of Mathematical Statistics*, 32, 448–465.

Ollila, E., H. Oja, and T. Hettmansperger (2002). Estimates of regression coefficients based on the sign covariance matrix. *Journal of the Royal Statistical Society*, Series B, 3, 447.

Panjer, H.H. (1980). The aggregate claims distribution and stop-loss reinsurance. *Transactions of the Society of Actuaries*, 32, 523–545.

Panjer, H.H. (1981). Recursive evaluation of a family of compound distributions. *ASTIN Bulletin*, 12, 22–26.

Pearson, K. (1901). Mathematical contribution to the theory of evolution: VII, On the correlation of characters not quantitatively measurable. *Philosophical Transactions of the Royal Society of London*, Series A. 200, 1–66.

Peot, M.A., and R.D. Shacther (1991). Fusion and propagation with multiple observations in belief networks. *Artificial Intelligence* , 48, 299–318.

Piantadosi, S. (1997). *Clinical Trials: A Methodologic Perspective*. John Wiley & Sons. New York.

Plackett, R.L., (1965). A class of bivariate distributions. *Journal of the American Statistical Association*, 60, 516–522.

Pocock, S.J., N.L. Geller, and A.A. Tsiatis (1987). The analysis of multiple endpoints in clinical trials. *Biometrics*, 43, 487–498.

Prentice, R.L. (1989). Surrogate endpoints in clinical trials: definition and operational criteria. *Statistics in Medicine*, 8, 431–440.

Press, W.H., S. Teukolsky, W. Vetterling, and B. Flannery (1995). *Numerical Recipes in C*: The Art of Scientific Computing. Cambridge University Press. Cambridge, UK.

Royall, R.M. (1986). Model robust confidence intervals using maximum likelihood estimators. *International Statistics Review*, 54, 221–226.

Ruffin, M.T., M.P.H. Mohammed, S. Ogaily, C.M. Johnston, L. Gregoire, W.D.Lancaster, and D.E. Brenner, Surrogate endpoint biomarkers for cervical cancer chemoprevention trials. *Journal of Cellular Biochemistry.* Supplement 23, 113–124.

Saunders, A., J. Boudoukh, L. Allen, and A. Boudoukh (2004). *Understanding Market, Credit, and Operational Risk: The Value at Risk Approach.* Blackwell Publishers. London.

Sharma, H. L. (1988). Estimating the parameters of a Polya-Aeppli distribution. *Rural Demography*, 15, 1–6.

Stone, R. (1993). The assumptions on which causal inferences rest. *Journal of the Royal Statistical Society*, B, 55, 455–466.

Taylor, J.M.G., A. Munoz, S.M. Bass, A.J. Saah, J.S. Chimiel, and L.A. Kingslsey (1990). Estimating the distribution of times from HIV seroconversion to AIDS using multiple imputation. *Statistics in Medicine*, 9, 505–514.

The Cardiac Arrhythmia Suppression Trial Investigators (1989). Effect of encainide and flecainide on mortality in a randomized trial of arrhythmia suppression after myocardial infarction. *New England Journal of Medicine*, 321, 406–412.

Wei, L.J, D.Y. Lin, and L. Weissfeld (1989). Regression analysis of multivariate incomplete failure time by modelling marginal distributions. *Journal of the American Statistical Association*, 84, 1064–1073.

Wilcox, R.R. (1998). How many discoveries have been lost by ignoring modern statistical methods? *American Psychologist* 53, 300–314.

Zeger, S.L., and K.Y. Liang (1986). Longitudinal data analysis for discrete and continuous outcomes. *Biometrics.* 42, 1019–1031.

Zhang, N.L, and D. Poole (1992). Side-stepping the triangulation problem in Bayesian net computations. *Uncertainty in Artificial Intelligence: Proceeding of the Eighth Conference.* Morgan Kaufmann. San Francisco. pp. 360–367.

Ziegler, A., C. Kastner, and M. Blettner (1998). The generalised estimating equations: an annotated bibliography. *Biometrical Journal*, 40, 115–139.

About the CD-ROM

INTRODUCTION

This CD-ROM contains the VBA functions, code and spreadsheets used in the text. In addition it also contains answers to many of the review questions, which appear at the end of most chapters.

CD-ROM Table of Contents

MINIMUM SYSTEM REQUIREMENTS

Make sure that your computer meets the minimum system requirements listed in this section. If your computer doesn't match up to most of these requirements, you may have a problem using the contents of the CD.

For Windows 9x, Windows 2000, Windows NT4 (with SP 4 or later), Windows Me, or Windows XP:

- PC with a Pentium processor running at 120 Mhz or faster
- At least 32 MB of total RAM installed on your computer; for best performance, we recommend at least 64 MB
- A CD-ROM drive

For Macintosh:

- Mac OS computer with a PowerPC 300MHz or faster processor running OS 9.0 or later
- At least 32 MB of total RAM installed on your computer; for best performance, we recommend at least 64 MB

USING THE CD WITH WINDOWS

To install the items from the CD to your hard drive, follow these steps:

1. Insert the CD into your computer's CD-ROM drive.
2. A window appears with the following options:
    Install: Gives you the option to install the supplied software and/or the author-created samples on the CD-ROM.
    Explore: Enables you to view the contents of the CD-ROM in its directory structure.
    Exit: Closes the autorun window.

If you do not have autorun enabled, or if the autorun window does not appear, follow these steps to access the CD:

1. Click Start @> Run.
2. In the dialog box that appears, type *d:*\setup.exe, where *d* is the letter of your CD-ROM drive. This brings up the autorun window described in the preceding set of steps.
3. Choose the desired option from the menu. (See Step 2 in the preceding list for a description of these options.)

USING THE CD WITH THE MAC OS

To install the items from the CD to your hard drive, follow these steps:

1. Insert the CD into your CD-ROM drive.
2. Double-click the icon for the CD after it appears on the desktop.
3. Most programs come with installers; for those, simply open the program's folder on the CD and double-click the Install or Installer icon. *Note:* To install some programs, just drag the program's folder from the CD window and drop it on your hard drive icon.

TROUBLESHOOTING

If you have difficulty installing or using any of the materials on the companion CD, try the following solutions:

- **Turn off any anti-virus software that you may have running.** Installers sometimes mimic virus activity and can make your computer incorrectly believe that it is being infected by a virus. (Be sure to turn the anti-virus software back on later.)
- **Close all running programs.** The more programs you're running, the less memory is available to other programs. Installers also typically update files and programs; if you keep other programs running, installation may not work properly.
- **Reference the ReadMe:** Please refer to the ReadMe file located at the root of the CD-ROM for the latest product information at the time of publication.
- Before the spreadsheets are loaded, the user will need to load the Excel Add-in "Analysis ToolPak." This add-in can be loaded via the Excel toolbar by clicking on "Tools," "Add-Ins," and then "Analysis Toolpak." If you are using Excel 2000 or 1997, you will be asked and prompted to "Enable Macros" and should click "Yes." If you are using Excel 2003, you should also "Enable Macros" or set the macro protection setting to "Low" by hitting the <F1> key or "Macros" and following the software instructions.

If you still have trouble with the CD-ROM, please call the Wiley Product Technical Support phone number: (800) 762-2974. Outside the United States, call 1(317) 572-3994. You can also contact Wiley Product Technical Support at www.wiley.com/techsupport. Wiley Publishing will provide technical support only for installation and other general quality control items; for technical support on the applications themselves, consult the program's vendor or author.

To place additional orders or to request information about other Wiley products, please call (800) 225-5945.

Index

For information about the CD-ROM see the
About the CD-ROM section on page 255.